Phonological Development in Specific Contexts

CHILD LANGUAGE AND CHILD DEVELOPMENT
Series Editor: Professor Li Wei, *University of Newcastle-upon-Tyne, UK*
Editorial Advisors: Professor Gina Conti-Ramsden, *University of Manchester, UK*
Professor Kevin Durkin, *The University of Western Australia*
Professor Susan Ervin-Tripp, *University of California, Berkeley, USA*
Professor Jean Berko Gleason, *Boston University, USA*
Professor Brian MacWhinney, *Carnegie Mellon University, USA*

Children are brought up in diverse yet specific cultural environments; they are engaged from birth in socially meaningful and appropriate activities; their development is affected by an array of social forces. This book series is a response to the need for a comprehensive and interdisciplinary documentation of up-to-date research on child language and child development from a multilingual and multicultural perspective. Publications from the series will cover language development of bilingual and multilingual children, acquisition of languages other than English, cultural variations in child rearing practices, cognitive development of children in multicultural environments, speech and language disorders in bilingual children and children speaking languages other than English, and education and healthcare for children speaking non-standard or non-native varieties of English. The series will be of particular interests to linguists, psychologists, speech and language therapists, and teachers, as well as to other practitioners and professionals working with children of multilingual and multicultural backgrounds.

Other Books in the Series
Culture-Specific Language Styles: The Development of Oral Narrative and Literacy
    Masahiko Minami
Language and Literacy in Bilingual Children
    D. Kimbrough Oller and Rebecca E. Eilers (eds)

Other Books of Interest
The Care and Education of a Deaf Child: A Book for Parents
    Pamela Knight and Ruth Swanwick
The Care and Education of Young Bilinguals: An Introduction to Professionals
    Colin Baker
Child-Rearing in Ethnic Minorities
    J.S. Dosanjh and Paul A.S. Ghuman
Cross-linguistic Influence in Third Language Acquisition
    J. Cenoz, B. Hufeisen and U. Jessner (eds)
Dyslexia: A Parents' and Teachers' Guide
    Trevor Payne and Elizabeth Turner
Foundations of Bilingual Education and Bilingualism
    Colin Baker
Encyclopedia of Bilingualism and Bilingual Education
    Colin Baker and Sylvia Prys Jones
Multicultural Children in the Early Years
    P. Woods, M. Boyle and N. Hubbard
Young Bilingual Children in Nursery School
    Linda Thompson

Please contact us for the latest book information:
Multilingual Matters, Frankfurt Lodge, Clevedon Hall,
Victoria Road, Clevedon, BS21 7HH, England
http://www.multilingual-matters.com

CHILD LANGUAGE AND CHILD DEVELOPMENT 3
Series Editor: Li Wei, University of Newcastle

Phonological Development in Specific Contexts

Studies of Chinese-speaking Children

Zhu Hua

MULTILINGUAL MATTERS LTD
Clevedon • Buffalo • Toronto • Sydney

Library of Congress Cataloging in Publication Data
A catalog record for this book is available from the Library of Congress.

British Library Cataloguing in Publication Data
A catalogue entry for this book is available from the British Library.

ISBN 1-85359-588-8 (hbk)
ISBN 1-85359-587-X (pbk)

Multilingual Matters Ltd
UK: Frankfurt Lodge, Clevedon Hall, Victoria Road, Clevedon BS21 7HH.
USA: UTP, 2250 Military Road, Tonawanda, NY 14150, USA.
Canada: UTP, 5201 Dufferin Street, North York, Ontario M3H 5T8, Canada.
Australia: Footprint Books, PO Box 418, Church Point, NSW 2103, Australia.

Typeset by Wayside Book, Clevedon.
Printed and bound in Great Britain by the Cromwell Press Ltd.

Contents

Preface

This book contains a series of studies of phonological acquisition and development of children in specific contexts. The specific contexts refer to (1) linguistic context – Putonghua or Modern Standard Chinese, the language variety promoted by the Mainland Chinese government since the 1950s; (2) developmental contexts – normally developing children, children with speech disorders, children with hearing impairment and twins.

By any account, Chinese is a major world language. Its native-speaking population is over 1.3 billion, that is, approximately a quarter of the world's population. Its speakers are found in every continent of the world. Among those oft-cited typological characteristics associated with Chinese are:

- Morphology: low structural complexity of words. It is an 'isolating' language in the sense that it has very limited grammatical morphological markers such as case, number and tense markers.
- Syntax: topic-prominent in the sense that the topic, not the subject, always comes first in a Chinese sentence.
- Writing system: largely logographic, i.e. because each symbol, or character, is, or originates from a logograph.
- Phonology: a lexical tonal language with a highly constrained syllable structure. Few varieties of Chinese allow consonant clusters and only a restricted set of consonants are permitted at syllable-final position.

As such, Chinese provides an excellent, perhaps unique, opportunity for the evaluation and expansion of theories of language and language acquisition. Nevertheless, acquisitional studies of Chinese, i.e. studies of how native Chinese-speaking Chinese children acquire the language, remain under-developed. Within the existing studies of Chinese language acquisition, the acquisition of phonology is perhaps the least explored. Erbaugh's (1992) detailed review of the acquisition of Mandarin, for example, did not describe aspects of phonology, except for noting error-free tonal acquisition. Lee's (1996) survey cited only a few case studies that described the phoneme acquisition of Mandarin-speaking children in Taiwan. This is ironic, to say the least, as the phonological system of

Chinese contains perhaps some of the most prominent characteristics that distinguish it from other languages in the world.

As far as language acquisition is concerned, a good theory needs to be able to account for at least two aspects:

- *cross-linguistic* similarities and differences in acquisitional patterns; and
- *cross-populational* similarities and differences in acquisitional patterns.

In other words, a good theory must be able to explain acquisitional patterns of children speaking Arabic, English, Chinese, Spanish, Tamil, etc., as well as those of children from the same language background but in different and specific developmental contexts, e.g. normally developing children, speech disordered children, children with hearing impairment, twins, etc.

The aims of this book are twofold:

- to account for the phonological acquisition of Putonghua-speaking children, providing the first normative data on this population;
- to investigate phonological acquisition of Putonghua-speaking children in specific contexts, i.e. normally developing children, children with speech disorders, children with hearing impairment, and twins.

The structure of the book is as follows:

Chapter 1 reviews the existing cross-linguistic studies of language acquisition from a cross-populational perspective and proposes factual and theoretical questions to be addressed in this book. Chapter 2 describes the phonological structure of Putonghua, focusing on the aspects that are relevant to the subsequent discussion of phonological acquisition in various conditions. Chapter 3 reports a normative, cross-sectional study of 129 normally developing Putonghua-speaking children aged 1;6–4;0, followed by a longitudinal study of four children at their early stage of phonological acquisition in Chapter 4. Chapter 4 complements the previous chapter by providing information on the sequential development of suprasegmental and segmental features which are acquired either in an early stage or within a short period of time.

Chapters 5–8 focus on the phonological systems of Putonghua-speaking children in atypical developmental circumstances. Chapter 5 examines the characteristics of the phonological systems of 33 Putonghua-speaking children with speech disorders. Chapter 6, as a follow-up study to Chapter 5, documents the development and change in the phonology of seven Putonghua-speaking children with speech difficulties. Chapter 7 investigates the phonological systems of a set of identical Putonghua-speaking twins, who are in a different language learning situation from singletons.

Chapter 8 presents a longitudinal case study of the phonological development of a Putonghua-speaking child with prelingual hearing impairment.
The findings of the studies are summarised in Chapter 9 in response
to the factual and theoretical research questions proposed in Chapter
1. In addition, the developmental patterns identified in monolingual
Putonghua-speaking children who are either developing normally or
atypically, are discussed in the framework of 'developmental universals'
and 'particulars'.

Zhu Hua
Newcastle upon Tyne

Acknowledgements

I am grateful to many people whose expertise and support have made the book possible. My special thanks go to Barbara Dodd, whose insights have ever been so important throughout the process of project design, data collection, analysis and interpretation. Jiang Tao and Zhu Xun of Beijing Normal University assisted me in the data collection process. I have also benefited from formal and informal discussions with many people. They include, in alphabetic order, Gerry Docherty, Alison Holm Dodd, David Howard, Siew-Yue Killingley, and Neil Smith. Personal communications with Bao Zhiming, Duanmu San, Tao Hongyin, and Moria Yip contributed to my understanding of tonal acquisition. The studies reported in this book were financially supported by a University Research Committee grant from the University of Newcastle upon Tyne.

Li Wei has acted as one of the key consultants for the project as a whole and provided a great deal of input throughout the writing of the book. His comments and critique, sometimes brutally honest, have always been stimulating and constructive. It is his understanding, trust, care and love that have enabled me to be committed to the project from the beginning to the end. I'd like to dedicate this book to him and our baby Andrew An-Zhu whose arrival has brought tremendous happiness to our lives. A big thank you to my parents who have always encouraged and supported me in many, many ways.

Parts of the research findings reported in this book have been presented as conference papers at *the 6th International Conference on Chinese Linguistics*, 19–21 June 1997, Leiden, the Netherlands; *the Child Language Seminar*, 4–6 September, 1998, Sheffield, UK; *Advanced Studies Institute on Cognitive Processing of Chinese*, the University of Hong Kong, 26–30 November, 1998, Hong Kong; *the Child Language Seminar*, 4–6 September, 1999, City University, UK; *ICPLA 2000 Conference*, September, 2000, Edinburgh, UK. Other versions of parts of the research findings have appeared in the papers that I have published (with Barbara Dodd) in *Journal of Child Language, Clinical Linguistics & Phonetics, International Journal of Language and Communication Disorders*, and *Asia Pacific Journal of Speech Language and Hearing*.

Conventions on Transcriptions

Phonetic examples are transcribed in the International Phonetic Alphabets (IPA). Apart from IPA, some Chinese examples are also given in *Hanyu Pinyin* or *Pinyin*, i.e. Chinese romanisation system, especially when there is no equivalent counterpart in English. Examples in *Pinyin* are italicised when cited in text, but not in tables.

The tones in Putonghua are indicated by numbers 1, 2, 3 & 4, representing high level, rising, falling–rising and high falling tones respectively. The tone of weakly stressed syllable is marked by the number 0. Where the information on tones or weakly stressed syllable is not relevant, tonal markers are omitted.

Adult / target forms are given in slashes (e.g. /pA/); children's realisations (sometimes erroneous forms) are given in square brackets (e.g. [pA]).

Chapter 1

Language Universals and Cross-linguistic Studies of Phonological Acquisition

1.1 Introduction

One of the aims of this book is to add to the fast expanding body of literature on cross-linguistic studies of language acquisition with a study of the phonological acquisition of Putonghua-speaking children. Cross-linguistic research, as exemplified in Slobin (1985, 1992, 1995, 1997), not only explores and suggests new and neglected areas for investigation, but also evaluates and challenges claims about language acquisition, particularly, the claims concerning universality of language acquisition patterns. The first section of this chapter is to clarify what is meant by 'universals' by reviewing three streams of research on 'universality' (i.e. typological *universals*, the *universal* grammar, and developmental *universals*) and their influence and input on the study of language acquisition. The second and third sections will review in detail the developmental universals which have emerged from the previous cross-linguistic studies in different populations. The factual and theoretical research questions to be addressed in this book are presented in 1.4.

1.1.1 Typological universals

Studies on typological universals began in the 1960s and were primarily aimed to identify language or linguistic universals by comparing a representative sample of natural languages (for a review, see Greenberg, 1978; Croft, 1990). According to Ferguson (1978), the term 'language universals', which was introduced by Aginsky and Aginsky (1948), only became widely used in the early 1960s. The term 'linguistic universals', which first appeared in Katz and Postal (1964) and subsequently in Chomsky (1965), is sometimes used interchangeably with 'language universals'. Typological universals are mostly concerned with the typological relatedness and similarities between languages. They have the following characteristics:

1

- Typological universals can be unrestricted and absolute in the sense that features are shared by all languages; for example, all languages have nouns and verbs, and vowels and consonants.
- Typological universals can be tendencies occurring in a large number of, but not all, languages.
- Typological universals can be implicational and hierarchical in the sense that the presence of one feature implies the presence of another.

One research question relating typological universals to language acquisition is whether the order of acquisition or developmental sequence of linguistic features may be influenced by typological universals, i.e. features shared by languages or unique to a language. In other words, could similarities and differences in the developmental patterns of children speaking different languages be accounted for in terms of typological similarities and differences?

Another contribution of typological universals to language acquisition study is that it provides a principled basis for determining the degree of markedness of a particular linguistic feature. In the context of typological universals, markedness is regarded as relative and existing on a continuum (Greenberg, 1966). As reviewed in Croft (1990), the three basic principles for judging the degree of markedness of a feature are:

- structural simplicity – a structurally simple feature would be considered unmarked compared to a structurally complicated feature;
- functional flexibility – a feature which can occur more in different structures and serves different functions would be considered unmarked compared to a feature with less flexibility; and
- frequency of occurrence in world languages.

The concept of markedness has often been resorted to in the studies of language acquisition as an explanatory theory for the ease or difficulty associated with the learning of some features (for its role in phonological acquisition, see Jakobson, 1941/1968, Eckman, 1977; for syntax, see Rutherford, 1983). The role of markedness in interpreting phonological acquisition patterns, particularly the order of phoneme acquisition, will be discussed in 1.2.1.2.

1.1.2 Universal grammar and the universal language learning mechanism

The second stream of study on 'universals' takes the form of Universal Grammar – the abstract knowledge of language or the subconscious mental representation of language which underlines all language varieties (for a review, see Mitchell & Myles, 1998: 43). The Universal Grammar

(UG) claims that all human beings inherit a set of principles and parameters. Principles govern the form grammatical rules can take in all languages and make human languages similar to one another. In contrast, parameters vary in certain restricted ways from one language to another and characterise differences between languages. According to UG theory, each child is born with such an innate linguistic knowledge that constrains the shape of the particular language system being acquired. This explains why similarities exist among children speaking different languages during their process of language acquisition.

UG's underlying assumption about language acquisition is, in essence, in line with nativist theories which purport that it is an innate biological endowment that enables children to acquire their target languages with remarkable speed. The innateness can either take the form of 'innate knowledge of general linguistic principles' (Chomsky, 1965), or consist of general cognitive notions and mechanism such as dependency, adjacency, precedence, continuity, etc. whereby a child learns the rules and conventions of the language being learned (O'Grady, 1987).

Against the nativist theory, 'environmentalists' play down the role of innateness in language development. They propose that one's nurture, or experience, is of more importance to development than the nature or innate contributions (Larsen-Freeman & Long, 1991). The 'environmentalist' approach, originated in Skinner's (1957) behaviourism, considers children's learning as a stimulus-response process. Although Skinner's view on the cause-and-effect relationship between acquisition and environment takes the risk of being too strong and is therefore criticised by nativists, he succeeds in drawing attention to the role of the environment, for example, language input, in acquisition. Since the 1970s many empirical studies have investigated the characteristics of child-directed speech or motherese and their functions and necessity to language acquisition (see Snow & Ferguson, 1977; Waterson & Snow, 1978; Snow, 1996). These studies showed that child-directed speech (CDS) is characterised by adjustments made by adults at various levels. For example, Sachs (1977) found that mothers tuned pitch, intonation and rhythm to some extent to suit their children. Little is known about how fine-tuned CDS facilitates language learning process; yet evidence suggests that it is important for children's language development (Snow, 1996).

The recent advances in connectionism are another attempt to explain the role of the environment in language acquisition in terms of cognitive processes. McClelland *et al.* (1986) put forward a 'Parallel Distributed Processing' hypothesis which holds that acquisition is a process of strengthening and weakening connections in complex neural networks as a result of the frequency of stimuli in the input. They believe that learners are sensitive to regularities in the language input (i.e. the regular co-occurrence of particular language forms), and are able to extract probabilistic patterns on the basis of these regularities. However, at present, the models in connectionism have been mainly built upon and tested on the acquisition of very simple, often artificial data. It remains to see whether the models would apply to the learning of rich and complex natural languages.

While both nativists and environmentalists are working in different directions, it is now generally accepted that language development is the result of interaction between innate and environmental factors. The innate mechanism, termed as the Language Acquisition Device (LAD) by Chomsky (1965) or Language-Making Capacity by Slobin (1985), is the mental equipment responsible for language development and should be universal for

- children from different language backgrounds;
- children from the same language background but belonging to different groups due to differences in gender, social backgrounds, etc.; and
- children whose language are developing normally or atypically.

Environmental factors refer to, among other things, language input, interactional patterns, and individual preference. These factors may vary for children speaking different languages and *different* populations of children speaking the *same* language (for example, normally developing population and atypically developing population such as children with functional speech disorders (i.e. speech disorders with no known organic cause) or children with hearing impairment). It may also vary from one child to another even if the children appear to share a similar language learning environment (for example, twins).

1.1.3 Developmental universals

Though it is accepted that both innate and environmental factors are essential for language development, it is unclear to what extent, and in what aspects, language acquisition is affected by these innate and environmental factors. One solution is to compare patterns of language development across children acquiring different languages and different populations of children acquiring the same language. The common and general patterns in child language development are termed 'developmental universals' (Slobin, 1985). Language-specific patterns or 'particulars', as opposed to developmental universals, are those unique to children acquiring one language or a particular group of children. According to Slobin,

> By combining attention to universals and particulars, we are beginning to discern a more differentiated picture of child language – one in which we can see why patterns of acquisition of specific properties VARY from language to language, while they are determined by common principles of a higher order.
>
> (Slobin, 1985: 5, emphasis original)

Strictly speaking, developmental universals are those commonalities shared by

- children acquiring different languages in monolingual or bilingual conditions;
- different groups of children acquiring the same target language;
- both normally developing children and children in exceptional circumstances.

The developmental universals can be identified by examining comparable data from children acquiring different languages, different groups of children acquiring the same language and children in normally or atypically developing conditions. Before comparison can be made between different languages, however, it is essential to identify typical developmental patterns of children speaking a particular language. Therefore, this book is not aimed to test a particular model or phonological theory, although it is believed that the studies have implications for theorisation. Instead, it is aimed to contribute to the knowledge of developmental universals by examining developmental patterns, specifically those of phonological acquisition, in monolingual Putonghua-speaking children. The developmental patterns are to be panned out not only from the phonological development of normally developing children, but also from that of children in atypically developing conditions. The latter includes children with functional speech disorders, children with hearing impairment, and twins.

For the purpose of this book, the book adopts phoneme as the main unit of analysis in its description. Most of the previous cross-linguistic normative studies on phonological development presented their findings in terms of phonemes (e.g. English data, Templin, 1957; Prather *et al.*, 1975; Stoel-Gammon & Dunn, 1985; Arabic, Amayreh & Dyson, 1998; Cantonese, So & Dodd, 1995; German, Fox & Dodd, 1999; Italian, Battacchi *et al.*, 1964; Maltese, Grech, 1998; Portuguese, Yavas, 1988; Quiche, Pye *et al.*, 1987; Spanish, Mann & Hodson, 1994; Swedish, Magnusson, 1983; Turkish, Topbas, 1997; Xhosa, Mowrer & Burger, 1991). Features, a more detailed unit of analysis, though used occasionally in data description and interpretation in these studies, do not seem to be able to highlight the commonality shared by a population as explicitly or economically as phonemes. Therefore, for the convenience of comparison, developmental patterns would be charted in this book using phoneme as the main unit of analysis while features would be used in the analysis where necessary. However, although the concept of phoneme is very often associated with segmental phonology, in adopting phonemes as the unit of description it is not assumed that children are learning a phonological system via phonemes – an 'arbitrary' unit of description in itself. Neither is it assumed that learning a lexical item is equivalent to learning of a sequence of speech sounds. Since the purpose of the book is to chart developmental patterns of children speaking a particular language and then to compare these patterns across languages, issues which are not of direct relevance to the data analysis and interpretation (e.g. the unit of acquisition, the relationships between units during acquisition) are beyond the scope of this book.

The rest of this chapter will review previous cross-linguistic studies on normally developing children, children with speech disorders, children with hearing impairment and twins, with the purpose of highlighting comparable findings on developmental universals and particulars.

1.2 Phonological Acquisition in Normally Developing Circumstances

1.2.1 Cross-linguistic studies of normal phonological development and phonological acquisition theories

Previous cross-linguistic phonological acquisition research has focused on either descriptive comparisons of acquisition data, or theoretical interpretations of cross-linguistic similarities and differences.

1.2.1.1 Cross-linguistic comparisons of phonological acquisition

A number of studies have examined the similarities and differences in the developmental patterns of children from various language backgrounds by investigating the order and rate of acquisition of phonemes and developmental error patterns.[1] Not surprisingly, English has received most attention. Some norms of phonological acquisition of English-speaking children, including the developmental age of phonemes (or distinctive features) and error patterns, have been established (for example, Wellman *et al.*, 1931; Poole, 1934; Templin, 1957; Prather *et al.*, 1975; Irwin & Wong, 1983; Stoel-Gammon & Dunn, 1985; Grunwell, 1987). Almost all the studies showed that stops, nasals and glides tend to be mastered earlier than liquids, fricatives and affricates during the acquisition of English-speaking children. However, there is controversy on the age of acquisition of phonemes among these studies. For example, Prather *et al.* (1975) reported that phonemes /ð, ʒ/ were acquired around the age of 4;0–4;6 by 75% of the subjects, while Stoel-Gammon & Dunn (1985) found these two sounds would not be mastered until 7;0 by 75% of the subjects. Such disagreement was largely the result of differences in the criteria used in defining when a sound would be considered 'acquired' (i.e. phonetic and phonological accuracy), what percentage of subjects is a minimal level of requirement in judging whether a sound is acquired by an age group, whether syllable or word positions are taken into account, or types of data collected (e.g. spontaneous speech vs. imitation, single word vs. connected speech), etc. Table 1.1 summarises the age of phoneme acquisition by English-speaking children reported in Prather *et al.*'s study (1975), whose methodology was comparable to the studies carried out in this book.

Table 1.1 Age of phoneme acquisition by English-speaking children*

	Phonemes
2;0–2;6	n, p, m, h
2;6–3;0	t, j, w, ŋ, k, d, b, f
3;0–3;6	g, s, r, l
3;6–4;0	ʃ, tʃ
4;0–4;6	ð, ʒ
>4;6	dʒ, θ, v, z

*Note: The information is based on Prather *et al.* (1975).

Weiner (1979), Shriberg and Kwiatkowski (1980), Hodson (1980), Ingram (1981), Grunwell (1987) and Dean *et al.* (1990), among other studies, identified developmental error patterns in the speech of English-speaking children (for a comparison of differences in the terminology in referring to various error patterns, see Grunwell, 1995). The main error patterns are:

- Weak syllable deletion: the deletion of an unstressed syllable, e.g. /bə'nana/→ [nana].
- Final consonant deletion: the deletion of a syllable-final consonant, e.g. /præm/→ [præ].
- Reduplication: the repetition of a syllable, e.g. /dʌ/→ [dʌdʌ].
- Assimilation/consonant harmony: a sound becomes similar to or is influenced by its preceding or succeeding sound, e.g. /dʌk/→ [gʌk].

- Initial cluster reduction: the deletion of part of initial consonant cluster: e.g. /trein/→ [tein].
- Stopping of fricatives: the replacement of fricatives with stops: e.g. /ʃɪp/→ [tɪp].
- Stopping of affricates/deaffrication: the replacement of affricates with stops: e.g. /tʃɪps/→ [tɪps].
- Velar fronting: the replacement of velar sounds /k, g/ with alveolar stops: e.g. /kʌp/→ [tʌp].
- Fronting palato-alveolar as alveolar: the replacement of palato-alveolars with alveolars, e.g. /ʃɪp/→ [sɪp].
- Fronting alveolar as dental: the replacement of alveolars with dental sounds, e.g. /siː/→ [θiː].
- Fronting dental as labiodental: the replacement of dentals with labiodentals, e.g. /θæŋkjəʊ/→ [fæŋkəʊ].
- Gliding: the replacement of liquids /l, r/ with glides /j, w/, e.g. /leg/→ [weg].
- Voicing: the voicing of a voiceless consonant before a vowel or the devoicing of a voiced consonant after a vowel, e.g. /tɪp/→ [dɪp] or /dɒg/→ [dɒk].

Table 1.2 lists the previous cross-linguistic studies on phonological acquisition and summarises similarities and differences between English-speaking children and children speaking other languages where information is available. Each study is commented in detail as follows.

Table 1.2 Cross-linguistic studies on phonological acquisition

			In comparison with English		
Language	*Sample size*	*Age range*	*Phoneme acquisition rate*	*Phoneme acquisition order*	*Language-specific error patterns*
Arabic (Amayreh & Dyson, 1998)	180	2;0–6;4	/f, t, l/ earlier; /h, dʒ,ð,j/ later	Similar	------
Cantonese (So & Dodd, 1995)	268	2;0–6;0	More rapid	Similar	Affrication of /s/→ [ts]
German (Fox & Dodd, 1999)	177	1;6–5;11	More rapid; /d, v, s, z/ earlier	------	No preference for 1st or 2nd phoneme in cluster reduction of /kv/ and /kn/

| Language | Sample size | Age range | In comparison with English | | |
			Phoneme acquisition rate	Phoneme acquisition order	Language-specific error patterns
Italian (Battacchi *et al.*, 1964)	20	3;1–4;8	------	Similar	Higher frequency of occurrence of weak syllable deletion and metathesis
(Bortolini & Leonard, 1991)	9	2;3–2;11	------	Similar	/r/→ [l] or [n]; /l/ → [r] or [n]
Maltese (Grech, 1998)	21	2;0–3;6	More rapid	Similar	Late suppression of stopping & fronting processes
Portuguese (Yavas, 1988)	90	1;6–5;2	------	------	Early suppression of stopping
Quiche (Pye *et al.*, 1987)	5	1;7–3;0	/ʔ, tʃ, x, l/ earlier	Different	/r/→ [l]; /s/→ [ʃ]
Spanish (Mann & Hodson, 1994)	------	------	Similar; /j/ later	Similar	Different frequency of occurrence
Swedish (Magnusson, 1983; Nettelbladt, 1983)	32	3;9–6;6	------	Similar	/r/→ [h]; /l/→ [j]
Turkish (Topbas, 1997)	22	1;0–3;0	More rapid; completed by 3;0	Similar	Similar substitution patterns; Consonant deletion process occurs to syllable-initial and-final consonants; Cluster reduction is limited to word-final sonorant +plosives; /ɾ/ → [l, j]; Affrication of /t/ to [ts]
Xhosa (Mowrer & Burger, 1991)	71	2;6–6;0	More rapid; fewer stop and fricative errors	Similar	Similar substitution patterns

Note: ------ information not available.

Arabic

Amayreh and Dyson (1998) collected speech samples from 180 normally developing children aged 2;0–6;4. They found that medial consonants were significantly more accurate than initial and final consonants, but no difference was found between the initial and final positions. The age of acquisition of most Arabic consonants was similar to that of English with a few exceptions: the consonants /f, t, l/ were acquired earlier in Arabic than in English, while /h, dʒ, ð, j/ were later in Arabic than in English.

Cantonese

So and Dodd (1995) found that although Cantonese-speaking children's order of consonant acquisition was similar to that of English-speaking children, Cantonese children's acquisition was more rapid. Specific error patterns used by Cantonese children were also identified. For example, while some Cantonese two-year-olds deaffricated /ts/ (e.g. [siw] for /tsiw/), affrication of /s/ was much more common (e.g. [pa tsi] for /pa si/; [tsoej] for /soej/). This pattern would be unusual in English-speaking children who acquire affricates later than fricatives. The more common developmental error pattern for English-speaking children involves stopping of affricates (e.g. [tip] for /tʃip/).

German

Fox and Dodd (1999) examined the phonological development of 177 German-speaking children aged 1;6–5;11. By 4;0, 75% of the German-speaking children were able to produce all the phonemes correctly, while 75% of the English-speaking children aged 4;0–4;6 still had errors with the sounds /dʒ, θ, v, z/. Some language-specific error patterns were observed. For example, when cluster reduction occurred to the clusters /kv/ and /kn/, German-speaking children did not show any preference for the first or second phoneme in the clusters. However, the second consonant deletion rule (i.e. the phonemes /l, r, w, j/ will be deleted at post-consonant position), which normally developing English-speaking children abide by, applied to other clusters in German phonology.

Italian

Battacchi *et al.* (1964) examined the word-initial and – medial consonant production of 20 Italian-speaking children aged 3;1–4;8. Accuracy ratings showed that plosives and nasals were acquired earlier than fricatives, though liquids and affricates did not demonstrate clear patterns. Bortolini and Leonard (1991) identified the error patterns which occurred in the speech of nine normally developing Italian-speaking children aged 2;2–2;11 and found that the prevalence of some error types might be related to characteristics of the Italian lexicon. For example, weak syllable deletion occurred frequently in the speech of Italian children, perhaps as the result of the high percentage of polysyllabic words in Italian. Similarly, they argued that the fact that Italian children were found to frequently transpose two segments within a syllable (resulting in the error pattern 'metathesis') might be an outcome of children's attempts at words with 'challenging complexity'.

Maltese

Grech (1998) analysed the phonological development of 21 Maltese-speaking children aged 2;0–3;6. Differences were evident between Maltese-speaking and English-speaking children in terms of chronology of error patterns. For example, while the error patterns of final consonant deletion, initial cluster reduction and fronting began to disappear in the speech of English-speaking children aged 3;0–3;6, these errors were identified in above 85.7% of Maltese-speaking children of the same age in the study. Maltese-speaking children seemed to have a faster rate of acquisition of phonemes than English-speaking children – by 3;6, 75% of the subjects were able to use all the phonemes correctly in syllable-initial position.

Portuguese

Yavas (1988, cited in Yavas & Lamprecht, 1988) described the chrono-logy of error patterns identified in 90 Portuguese-speaking children aged 1;6–5;2. Compared to English-speaking children, the most striking differ-ence was that the error pattern of stopping was suppressed quite early in the speech of Portuguese-speaking children (around the age of 2;6) whereas the stopping of /θ, ð/ persisted in the speech of English-speaking children aged above 4;6 (Grunwell, 1987). The difference may be due to the fact that /θ/ and /ð/, which are usually acquired late, do not exist in Portuguese phonology. Apart from this difference, the error patterns in Portuguese-speaking children were similar to English-speaking children: assimilation, consonant harmony and context-sensitive voicing disappeared early with the error pattern of initial cluster reduction persisting until five years of age.

Quiche

Pye *et al.* (1987) studied five children learning Quiche, a Mayan lan-guage spoken by half a million people in the western highland region of Guatemala. They found that Quiche-speaking children had a pattern of phonological development that was substantially different from that of children learning English. Quiche-speaking children's early phonetic inventories included sounds (e.g. /tʃ, l/) which were not acquired until later by native English-speaking children. Apart from this, Quiche children also used substitution patterns that were very different from those observed in English-speaking children. They frequently replaced /r/ with [l] while /l/ → [j] and /r/ → [w] would be common in the speech of English-speaking children.

Spanish

Mann & Hodson (1994) reviewed a number of studies on the phono-logical development of Spanish speakers from different parts of Mexico, the United States, and Venezuela. The majority of Spanish phonemes were acquired by the age of four years. Among those phonemes last mastered were /r, r, s, l, tʃ/. The common error patterns that occurred between one and four years of age were initial cluster reduction, syllable deletion, stopping, and fronting. Substitutions frequently affected the phonemes /l, r/ and affricates.

Swedish

Magnusson (1983, cited in Locke, 1983) analysed the percentage of children whose consonants were phonemically correct among 32 Swedish-speaking children aged 3;9–6;6. While nasals had the highest accuracy rating, liquids were produced with the lowest accuracy. Stops, glides and fricative (with the exception of /h/) were in-between. Nettelbladt (1983) also noted that Swedish-speaking children used a number of language-specific error patterns during their phonological acquisition (e.g. /ɹ/→ [h] and /l/→ [j]). In contrast, the common error patterns in English-speaking children were /ɹ/→ [w] and /l/→ [w] or [j]. Leonard (1995) attributed the replacement of /ɹ/ with [h] in Swedish-speaking children to the similar phonetic value of these two sounds in Swedish – /ɹ/ is in fact a uvular in Southern Swedish dialect.

Turkish

Topbas (1997) analysed the speech sample of 22 Turkish-speaking children aged 1;0–3;0. The results showed that Turkish children tended to master most sounds (except for the flap /ɾ/ and its allophonic variations, the velar fricative /ɣ/ and a few clusters) by the age of three. Although the rate of acquisition was more rapid compared to English-speaking children, the order of phoneme acquisition was similar to English-speaking children in that plosives and nasals stops were acquired earlier than affricates, fricatives and liquids. Most error patterns were sup-pressed by the age of three. The influence of the ambient language was evident in the realisation of error patterns. For example, consonants at syllable-initial or syllable-final position, occurring in -C,C- structures, were frequently deleted in the speech of Turkish-speaking children. However, only syllable-final consonants were subject to the deletion process in English (Ingram, 1989b).

Xhosa

Mowrer & Burger (1991) carried out a comparative study of Xhosa- and English-speaking children aged 2;6–6;0. They found that Xhosa-speaking children mastered 20 phonemes shared by Xhosa and English earlier than English-speaking children. The Xhosa-speaking children were able to produce 31 out of the total 41 consonants by 3;0, including some affricates (e.g. /ts, tʃ/) and clicks. The Xhosa-speaking children also made fewer errors on stops and fricatives than the English-speaking group. However, the two groups were shown to use similar error patterns for fricatives, affricates and liquids. The sounds acquired last and most frequently misarticulated by Xhosa-speaking children (e.g. /s, ʃ, r/) were the same phonemes English-, German- and Swedish-speaking children found difficult.

The similarities and differences highlighted in these cross-linguistic studies of phonological acquisition need theoretical interpretation, which is to be elaborated in the next section.

1.2.1.2 Theoretical interpretations of cross-linguistic similarities and differences

Theories of phonological acquisition need to account for evidence from cross-linguistic studies. Two major issues need to be addressed. One is the universal tendencies in children's phonological acquisition; the other the role language-specific features play in influencing the phonological development of the children of a given language.

Jakobson's 'laws of irreversible solidarity'

Jakobson (1941/1968), appealing to typological universals, suggested that whether a sound would be acquired early could be explained in terms of the distribution of the sound among the world's languages. According to his 'laws of irreversible solidarity', nasals, front consonants and stops (found in virtually all the languages) would be acquired earlier than their oppositions, i.e. orals, back consonants and fricatives respectively. He proposed that there were certain sounds which were more basic and central to all human languages and these sounds would therefore be acquired earlier than other sounds. Jakobson's view of phonological acquisition in terms of oppositions or contrasts set the agenda for the subsequent studies of child phonology.

Markedness

As mentioned in Section 1.1.1, the notion of 'markedness' has been used to interpret the similarities and differences in the order of phoneme acquisition (Eckman, 1977; Anderson, 1983). It was hypothesised that those sounds which appeared early in a child's inventory were maximally unmarked, while those occurring late were marked.[2] Therefore, children would use unmarked sounds as substitutions for marked sounds. Edwards' (1974) study of English-speaking children aged 1;8–3;11 found that children usually substituted the unmarked member for those marked contrasts (e.g. [s] for /ʃ/), but details varied from one child to another and from one developmental stage to another.

Some researchers found that the traditional labels in the taxonomy of oppositions such as voice, place and manner of articulation were not adequate when explaining the order of acquisition of phonemes. A more specific descriptive unit was therefore adopted: the feature. The feature system focused on the articulatory differences between phonemes (see Chomsky & Halle, 1968). Among the most important features were those distinguishing between vowels and consonants (sonorant, vocalic, consonantal); those distinguishing the sounds in terms of place of articulation (anterior, coronal, high, low, back and rounded); and those distinguishing the sounds in terms of manner of articulation (nasal, lateral, continuant, delayed release and stridency). Each phoneme was a combination of several features. It was hypothesised that unmarked features would be acquired first because unmarked features were considered more phonetically natural. Therefore, children would tend to replace marked features with unmarked features. A number of studies (e.g. Irwin & Wong, 1983; Yavaş, 1997) have applied the concept of feature to the analysis of children's speech.

Dinnsen (1992) proposed that there might be a universal hierarchical structure with a highly limited set of ordered features applicable to the phonetic inventories of all languages. Each feature in the hierarchy had a number of default specifications (i.e. unmarked values). Children's acquisition would therefore be a process of replacing a default value with a language-specific value. The order of phoneme acquisition of a particular language would correspond with the hierarchical relationships and default values: features ranked highly in the hierarchy would be acquired early; default features would be acquired before non-default features. Dinnsen's model offers an alternative account for cross-linguistic similarities and differences in the order of phoneme acquisition. However, the explanatory power of his model has so far rarely been tested with the phonological acquisition of children other than English- and

Spanish-speaking children. Determining the set of default and non-default values common to all languages is a continuing goal of phonological research.

The biological model

'Laws of irreversible solidarity' and 'markedness' theory sought to explain children's acquisition of sounds in the structure of the language they learned and emphasised the innate nature of acquisition. In contrast, other researchers (e.g. Locke, 1980, 1983; Kent, 1992) emphasised the role of articulatory and perceptual constraints on children's acquisition of phonology. Locke (1980: 207) argued that far from simply being a physical process, 'perception is very much constrained by one's sense of phonological structure and lexical expectation'. Developmental phonological patterns could, therefore, be accounted for by the perceptual similarity between sounds that occur frequently in children's babbling and sounds that occur infrequently. According to Locke, there are three universal mechanisms of development: maintenance, learning, and loss (1983: 85–92). When children have passed the babbling stage and started to acquire a target phonological system, certain sounds are *maintained* from their babbling repertoire. Sounds not present in the babbling repertoire are then developed through interactions in the linguistic environment (a *learning* process). Children must also relinquish and *lose* the 'extrasystemic sounds', sounds existing in the babbling repertoire but not in the target phonological system. The interaction of these three mechanisms would result in the acquisition of the target phonology.

Pye *et al.*'s (1987) study of Quiche-speaking children challenged Locke's theory (for the summary of their study, see section 1.2.1.1). They attributed discrepancies between the phonological acquisition of Quiche and English to the differences existing between the two phonological systems. Pye *et al.* (1987) argued that articulatory and perceptual constraints could not account for the earlier acquisition of /l/ and /tʃ/ by Quiche-speaking children than English-speaking children. They explained the differences by introducing the concept of 'functional load' which was first proposed by the Prague School. Functional load refers to the relative importance of each phoneme within a specific phonological system. However, how to calculate it is a matter of controversy. Pye *et al.* determined the functional load of a phoneme by its frequency of occurrence in oppositions or minimal pairs. For example, they argued that /l/ and /tʃ/ have more minimal pairs in Quiche than in English and therefore these two sounds carry a greater functional load in the phonological system of Quiche than in English, which results in their early acquisition.

Functional load is difficult to measure across languages (Catford, 1988). Pye *et al.* (1987) admitted that phonemes with high frequency of occurrence might not always carry a high functional load. For example, /ð/ occurs in a small class of frequent words (such as *the*, *this*, etc.) and is thus the second most frequent fricative in English. However, the functional load of /ð/ is quite small, since 'we could change all English /ð/ into [d]s and still communicate' (Ingram, 1989a: 218). Despite this, Pye *et al.* measured the functional load of syllable-initial consonants in Quiche by counting the frequency of syllable-initial consonants occurring in the 500 most commonly used words of five- and six-year-old children. There are two problems with this method of determining functional load:

- There is no guarantee that sounds frequently used by children are significant for a phonological system.
- The rank-order of frequencies for syllable-initial consonants common to Quiche and English does not support the similarities and differences found in the children's order of acquisition. For example, the sound /w/ was ranked as the second most frequently used in Quiche and seventh in English, indicating that /w/ should be acquired earlier in Quiche than in English. In fact, it was acquired at the same age in both languages.

So & Dodd (1995) were also critical of Pye *et al.*'s (1987) measurement of functional load: other aspects of phonology that may contribute to the functional load of consonants, such as vowels, syllable structure, and tones had not been considered. Despite these weaknesses, the notion of functional load does explore the relationship between the order of phoneme acquisition and the role of these phonemes in a given language environment.

Children's phonological acquisition is a highly complex process and influenced by a variety of sources. It is conceivable that none of the theories discussed so far account for both universal tendencies and language-specific patterns that have been found. Further cross-linguistic research on phonological acquisition is needed, focusing on both the identification of universal tendencies and the influence of the ambient language.

1.3 Phonological Development in Atypical Circumstances

Apart from the normally developing children, theories of language acquisition should also account for the patterns identified in the language and speech development of children growing up in atypical circumstances (i.e. children whose physical or environmental conditions vary from that of the majority of children). The unusual circumstances may lead to variations in the language and speech development of the children involved. The study of the relationship between the observed variations and unusual conditions can provide important answers to some major theoretical questions about language acquisition. Three questions are specifically related to the aim of the book:

- What characterise the phonology of children with atypical phono-logical development? Any similarities and differences between the phonology of children who are developing normally and who are developing atypically?
- What path of development would children with atypical phono-logical development follow? Longitudinal studies on children with functional speech disorders or hearing impairment may provide another opportunity to examine the influential factors in language development.
- What results in impairment or variations in phonological develop-ment? It is known that most children referred for speech assessment do not have an apparent organic or environmental aetiology (Shriberg *et al.*, 1986). Identifying the underlying deficits is essential both for clinical intervention and to the understanding of language development in general.

The following sections will review the literature on general issues related to speech disorder, development and change in the phonology of children with speech disorders, phonological development of twins and phonological development of children with hearing impairment.

1.3.1 The nature of disordered phonology

The prevalence figures for developmental speech disorders range from 3% to 10% of the pre-school population in English-speaking children (Kirkpatrick & Ward, 1984; Enderby & Philipp, 1986). However, children with speech disorders are not a homogeneous group (Gierut, 1998). They differ in severity, aetiology, symptomatology, and response to treatment (Shriberg *et al.*, 1986; Dodd, 1993). Therefore, categorisation of subgroups of speech disorder is useful for understanding the nature of phonological impairment, differential diagnosis and clinical management.

There are two major approaches to describing and categorising speech disordered children. One is the 'etiologic' approach by which subgroups of speech disordered children are classified according to a range of causal factors of their phonological impairment. Within the etiologic approach there is a dichotomy between organic and non-organic causal factors (Sommers, 1984). Shriberg and Kwiatkowski (1994) used the terms 'speech-hearing mechanism' and 'psychosocial factors' to reflect the dichotomy. Organic causes of speech disorder identified include hearing impairment (Dodd & So, 1994; Meline, 1997); speech mechanism impairment (Winitz & Darley, 1980); genetic transmission (i.e. familial speech disorder history, Lewis & Freebairn, 1997); and motor abilities (Cermak *et al.*, 1986; Sommers, 1988; Bradford & Dodd, 1994). Non-organic factors include 'faulty learning' (Bahr, 1998) and inadequate exposure to language (Savic, 1980; Shriberg & Kwiatkowski, 1994).

Classifying phonological impairment from the etiologic perspective is difficult. It is not always possible to identify a single causal factor, either due to the lack of clear evidence associating developmental speech disorder with specific etiologic antecedents (Shriberg & Kwiatkowski, 1994), or due to the interaction of several causal factors (Dodd, 1995). The etiologic approach to classifying phonological impairment is inadequate for children who present with normal hearing, intelligence, social, emotional and behavioural skills (McReynolds, 1988; Gierut, 1998). Most children referred for speech assessment do not have an apparent organic or environmental aetiology (Shriberg *et al.*, 1986).

An alternative approach to classifying speech disorder is the 'linguistic' approach: the linguistic characteristics of the child's speech are described. The common typological classification systems in the literature include

(a) *phonetic vs. phonological disorders* – differentiating the ability to articulate sounds from that of using sounds (Winitz, 1969; Ingram, 1989b; Fey, 1992; Bernthal & Bankson, 1998; Gierut, 1998; cf. three-way distinction – phonological, phonetic and articulatory disorders, Hewlett, 1985).

(b) *delay vs. disorder* – differentiating children whose speech resembles that of younger children from those whose speech deviates from the normal development course (Leonard, 1985; Ingram, 1989b; Fletcher, 1990). The term 'disorder' is used here in its narrow sense, referring to the subgroup of children whose phonological development is deviant from normal children in nature. Its broad sense, as used in the term 'speech disorder', is a general label for children who mispronounce words.

Although these two classification systems are widely used in the literature, they do not adequately account for all speech disordered children. A major criticism of the taxonomies of phonetic vs. phonological disorders and delay vs. disorder is that such classification tends to focus on speech sounds rather than error patterns (Dodd, 1993). Error patterns are important because they indicate the restricted resources (motor-oral skills, cognitive capacity, perceptual ability, etc.) available to children at a particular stage of development. The role of error patterns is crucial for understanding disordered phonology.

Dodd (1993) identified three subgroups of phonological disorder in addition to phonetic disorder (articulation disorder):

- *delayed development* – use of consistent error patterns that are inappropriate for the child's chronological age but appropriate for a younger child (e.g. cluster reduction: [bu] for blue; [pun] for spoon);
- *consistent disorder* – use of consistent error patterns that are atypical of normal phonological development (e.g. deleting all syllable-initial consonants, marking consonant clusters with a bilabial fricative);
- *inconsistent disorder* – variable pronunciations of the same words or phonological features (e.g. vacuum cleaner pronounced [dɹʌkum kinʌ], [fɒkum timʌ], [bwɒkjum kinʌ], Bradford & Dodd, 1994). Variation due to alternation between a normal developmental error and a correct production is not counted as inconsistent production.

Children's inconsistency or variability in production has been observed by a number of researchers (Ingram, 1979; Leonard, 1985; Dodd & Leahy, 1989; Grunwell, 1992). The speech of these children is often characterised by multiple mismatches between the realisation and the target (Grunwell, 1992). Ingram (1979) described intra- and inter-word variability: intra-word variability takes place when a child produces a given word in different ways in the same context while inter-word variability refers to the situation when a child produces a target segment in different ways across words and contexts. It is intra-word variability that Dodd's classification system exclusively focuses on.

Researchers often group children with consistent and inconsistent speech patterns together (e.g. Ingram, 1989), primarily because standard phonological assessment procedures fail to investigate consistency of production. There is an assumption that inconsistency reflects severity of impairment rather than a different type of disorder. McCormack and Dodd (1998) compared the consistency of production and speech severity measures of normally developing children and children with delayed development, consistent disorder, inconsistent disorder and developmental verbal dyspraxia. The results showed that while the subgroups with the lowest speech severity scores were more consistent, the groups with the highest severity scores varied markedly in their consistency

ratings. The finding indicated that severity could not explain inconsistency and that inconsistent disorder should be regarded as a separate
subgroup.

The characteristic patterns of surface speech errors made by the
subgroups of speech disorder identified seem to reflect the nature of the
subgroups' underlying deficits. Psycholinguistic experiments revealed
that the consistent disorder subgroup performed poorly on phonological
awareness tasks (e.g. detection of phonological legality, awareness of
alliteration and rhyme: Dodd & McCormack, 1995; and standard measures
of literacy: Leitao *et al.*, 1997). These findings suggested that consistent
non-developmental errors might be due to children's impaired ability to
derive the constraints of the phonological system.

In contrast, children who make inconsistent errors appear to have
intact phonological awareness but perform poorly on tasks assessing the
planning of complex motor verbal and non-verbal sequences (Bradford &
Dodd, 1994; 1996) and lexical tasks (Dodd & McCormack, 1995). One
hypothesis about the nature of the deficit underlying inconsistent errors
is that it is a phonological assembly problem: their ability to generate
'blueprints' for word production may be impaired. The subgroups with
articulation disorder or delayed development do not appear to have any
specific deficit, performing similarly to normally speaking controls on all
experimental tasks. Children with an articulation disorder have a peri-
pheral problem in that they have learned the wrong articulatory motor
programme for the production of specific speech sounds. Children with
delayed development are following the normal course of development,
albeit slowly. The factors underlying their delayed development may be
more general (e.g. impoverished language learning environment, slower
neurological maturation, or mild cognitive delay, Powers, 1971).

Dodd's (1993) classification system, proposed on the basis of English-
speaking children's data, has been evaluated cross-linguistically by a
number of studies investigating developmental speech disorder in languages other than English. So and Dodd (1994) described the phonological systems of 17 speech disordered Cantonese-speaking children.
The four subgroups of speech disorder were evident: two children were
identified with an articulation disorder; eight with delayed development;
three with consistent disorder; two with both articulation and consistent
disorders; and two with inconsistent disorder. Goldstein (1996) applied
the classification system in his description of 20 Spanish-speaking children with speech disorders. He identified children with articulation
disorder, delayed development and consistent disorder No children
making inconsistent errors were found. However, the children did not

produce any lexical item on more than one occasion, minimising the opportunity for observing inconsistency. Evidence for Dodd's classification system also came from Tobpas's study (1997) of a Turkish-speaking child and Fox's study (1997) of German-speaking children. Studies of phonologically disordered bilingual children (Cantonese–English, Dodd *et al.*, 1997; Punjabi–English, Holm *et al.*, 1999; Italian–English, Holm & Dodd, 1999) also supported the existence of the four subgroups. These studies on bilingual children reported that despite the influence of the ambient phonology of the language, the bilingual children had similar surface error characteristics in both their languages.

1.3.2 Development and change in the phonology of children with speech difficulties

Both longitudinal and cross-sectional studies of normal phonological acquisition provide evidence of immense changes in the number and type of phonological errors made between the age of 2;0 and 5;0 (Grunwell, 1981; Dodd, 1995). However, little is known about the developmental changes occurring in children with speech disorders, especially those with phonological disorders, in this chronological age range. The two questions which are of both theoretical and practical significance are:

- when phonological disorder emerges; and
- whether phonological disorder in young children spontaneously resolves.

There is disagreement as to when developmental phonological disorder emerges. Some researchers argue that children with phonological disorders initially follow a normal path of development from which they later deviate (Compton, 1976; McReynolds, 1988; Ingram, 1989; Fletcher, 1990), while some studies suggest that the deficits in the speech processing systems of phonologically disordered children operate from speech onset and persist if no intervention is provided (Leahy & Dodd, 1987). McReynolds (1988) claimed that children with an 'articulation problem' were those who failed to make appropriate corrections at a time in development when such corrections were expected. Fletcher (1990) reviewed the existing literature and asserted that phonological disorder took place when development of pronunciation skills was delayed or 'frozen' relative to other aspects of language development, particularly vocabulary size. Ingram (1989b) argued that children with phonological disorder were those whose normal developmental error patterns failed to be eliminated, resulting in early error patterns co-existing with later ones. Similarly, Compton (1976) suggested that children with defective speech retained and accumulated phonological error patterns which would otherwise be dropped or replaced by others. Despite the diversity of points of view, all these arguments seem to agree that it is when normal phonological acquisition is interrupted that phonological disorder occurs.

One case study (Leahy & Dodd, 1987), however, provided evidence that phonological disorder was apparent from speech onset. They documented the phonological changes made by a girl (AJ) between the age of 24 and 44 months in terms of phonetic repertoire, error patterns and number of errors. Although AJ's vocabulary size and phonetic repertoire developed during that time, there were few changes in the use of atypical error patterns. This study suggested that deficits in the speech processing mechanism can operate from speech onset and persist if no treatment is provided.

From a practical point of view, limited speech and language therapy resources call for better differentiation of those children whose speech difficulties will spontaneously resolve from those whose difficulties will persist. Paradoxically, however, the provision of speech and language therapy services in Britain and other European language-speaking countries means that data about spontaneous resolution of phonological disorder are rather difficult to obtain, as most children, once they are suspected of having speech and language problem, are referred for assessment and treatment in the pre-school years (e.g. Dodd & Iacano, 1989; Shriberg *et al.*, 1997; Gierut, 1998). Weiner and Wacker (1982) charted the changes in number and types of errors made by children aged 3;0–5;0 who were either normally developing or had been diagnosed as having a severe phonological disorder. While the normally developing children made considerable gains, children with disordered speech experienced little change in their speech. However, it is not clear whether these children had received any intervention targeting their speech. Children with speech disorders living in countries where no speech and language therapy service is available, as in China, present a unique opportunity for investigating development and change in disordered phonology.

1.3.3 The phonological development of twins

Most studies of multiple-birth children (MBC) agree that their communication development is delayed or atypical compared to that of singletons (for a review, see Johnston *et al.*, 1984; McEvoy & Dodd, 1992). The aspects of delayed or atypical development of twins' communication include late speech onset (Zazzo, 1960; Mittler, 1970), non-age-appropriate mean length of utterance (Day, 1932; Davis, 1937), delayed semantic development (Day, 1932; Hay *et al.*, 1984), poor syntactic ability (Conway *et al.*, 1980), unintelligible speech (Matheny & Bruggemann, 1972; Dodd & McEvoy, 1994), and literacy problems (Johnston *et al.*, 1984; McMahon *et al.*, 1998).

Phonological difficulties have been reported to be the feature of their communication profiles that are most likely to interfere with functional communication. Using a number of measures, McEvoy and Dodd (1992) investigated the syntactic, semantic, pragmatic, and phonological abilities of 19 sets of twins. The results indicated that they performed more poorly than the singleton controls on two measures – syntax and phonology. However, although the twins had a shorter mean length of utterance (MLU) than their singleton controls, most performed within the normal range. In contrast, there was a high incidence of atypical phonological errors. All but four of the twins used at least one unusual error patterns (i.e. error patterns seldom used by normally developing children) as well as delayed error patterns (i.e. error patterns inappropriate for chronological age). This suggested that twins' phonological development is the aspect of communication most at risk of delay or disorder.

Earlier studies of twins' communication abilities characterised the unintelligible speech as 'twin language' (Luria & Yudovich, 1959), 'cryptophasia' (Zazzo, 1978) or 'idioglossia' (Morley, 1972). These terms imply that the observed differences between the speech and language development of twins and that of singletons reflect a private language shared by individual sets of twins. This conclusion was driven by the observation that twins appeared to understand each other's speech, while adults did not. There is, however, limited empirical evidence in support of such an argument. Dodd and McEvoy's (1994) study on phonological abilities of 19 sets of twins found that the phonologies of siblings were not identical. Although there were some similarities, the pronunciation of many words was different, providing evidence against 'twin language'. Dodd and McEvoy's (1994) study also showed that twin children could recognise single words better than singleton controls, when these words were edited from the spontaneous speech of their co-twins and presented in isolation in a picture pointing task. None of the twins had difficulty recognising the same pictures when the stimulus were given in the adult form.

One explanation for this finding is that a listener's ability to match variant input with a stored form is indicative of an ability to recognise the same word despite phonetic differences associated with age, gender and accent of the speaker. If this were so, however, there would be no reason to suppose that twins would perform better than singleton controls on the task requiring them to recognise their co-twins' mispronunciations. Alternatively, the results might indicate that although twins did not use an autonomous language, they did lexically store at least some of their co-twins' word pronunciations for recognition. That is, it would seem that twin children might store more than one phonological representation for recognition of some lexical items.

That it is possible to store more than one phonological representation for recognition of the same lexical items is demonstrated by the ease of recognition of variants in pronunciation for words. For example, in Greek, [andrə] and [andrəs] differ phonologically, but both allow retrieval of the same vocabulary item *'man'*. Similarly parents learn to recognise their young children's pronunciation of words, e.g. [pʊsi tæt] for *pussy cat*, [mætmɛt] for *Vegamite*, [lɛlitɒt] for *helicopter*. This does *not* imply that there needs to be a separate phonological store that is specific for the recognition of any individual speaker. Rather it implies that there can be more than one phonological representation laid down for a single lexical item in a single recognition lexicon. While having more than one phonological representation for a single lexical item is unlikely to disrupt the output of those who have already established their phonological systems, it may affect a developing phonological system.

Planning production of those words with competing phonological representations, as in the case of, for example, the emerging phonology of twins, would be likely to be impaired. If a large number of words had competing phonological representations, the acquisition of knowledge about the constraints and contrasts of the phonology being learned would be affected or even disrupted. In support of this hypothesis there is evidence that twins' phonological awareness abilities (one's implicit knowledge about the contrasts and constraints of the phonology) are impaired even after their speech disorder has been successfully remedied (Johnston *et al.*, 1984, McMahon *et al.*, 1998). However, it should be noted that dual phonological representation is not a necessary condition for speech disorder in children. An impaired understanding of the contrasts and constraints of a phonological system could arise from a variety of deficits (e.g. hearing impairment).

Data from bilingual children seem to lend support to the hypothesis that having competing phonological representations at the lexical level is associated with atypical phonological development. Children learning language in a bilingual environment are consistently exposed to two phonological forms for many vocabulary items. Recent research on their phonological development indicated that exposure to a second language in the pre-school years gives rise to the use of atypical phonological error patterns in both languages (Dodd *et al.*, 1997; Holm & Dodd, 1999).

The suggestion that twins' unintelligible speech may be accounted for in terms of the language learning situation (where twins within sets are each other's primary communication partner leading to dual phonological representations of many of their lexical items) raises the issue of whether children in higher multiple birth sets (triplets, quadruplets and quintuplets) might also have competing sets of lexical items. Studies of children in higher multiple birth sets indicated that while their phonological systems might experience delay, they showed no signs of atypical developmental patterns (McMahon & Dodd, 1997, McMahon *et al.*, 1998). A plausible explanation for this finding is that since there is more than one sibling in a set in such a case, each sibling has no primary communicative partner and the diversity of pronunciations heard might focus attention on the stable adult realisation.

However, almost all of the existing twin studies are based on English-speaking children (cf. the three Serbo-Croatian twin pairs in Savic, 1980). The above-discussed arguments, such as whether the phonological development of twins would follow the same path as normally developing singletons, and whether twins have dual phonological representations for some lexical items, have not been tested on twins speaking languages other than English.

1.3.4 Phonological development of children with hearing impairment

One in every 1000 children is born with severe or profound hearing impairment (NIH, 1993). Studies of this population will not only facilitate the diagnosis and treatment for hearing impaired children, but also provide answers to general questions about language acquisition concerning the role of auditory input in language acquisition and whether oral language can be acquired through the visual medium (Dodd & Hermelin, 1977; Dodd, 1987; cf. Abberton *et al.*, 1990).

Among all the aspects of spoken language, phonological or speech skills are most often susceptible to disruption as a result of hearing loss (Elfenbein *et al.*, 1994), though children with hearing impairment have also been reported to have associated unusual developmental patterns in syntax (Presnell, 1973; Davis, 1977; Geers & Moog, 1978), morphology (Brown, 1984; Elfenbein *et al.*, 1994), semantics (Davis, 1974; Skarakis & Prutting, 1977) and pragmatics (Schirmer, 1985, cf. Curtiss *et al.*, 1979). In terms of phonetic description, the speech of the children with hearing impairment is often characterised by distorted articulation, breathy phonation, narrow pitch range, wrong airstream mechanism and excessive use of nasality in the production of both vowels and consonants (Hudgins & Numbers, 1942; Abberton *et al.*, 1990). Nevertheless, the phonological systems of the children with hearing loss are consistent and rule-governed.

Dodd (1976) analysed the speech production of 10 profoundly congenitally deaf English-speaking children and found that about 35 phonological rules were used consistently both individually and as a group. Similar findings were also reported by Oller and Kelly (1974) and Abraham (1989). Among those error patterns occurring very frequently in the speech of children with hearing impairment were final consonant deletion, cluster reduction, liquid simplification, deaffrication, and stridency deletion (Dodd, 1976; Stoel-Gammon, 1982; Levitt & Stromberg, 1983; Abraham, 1989). Some of the error patterns (e.g. voicing, devoicing or stopping) were typical of young hearing children (West & Weber, 1973; Oller & Kelly, 1974; Dodd, 1976; Abraham, 1989). The use of some unusual error patterns characteristic of disordered phonology (e.g. replacing final stops, fricatives and affricates with a glottal stop) was also reported in Stoel-Gammon's study (1982) on children with hearing impairment.

Several studies have been carried out on hearing impaired children speaking languages other than English (cf. Dodd & So, 1994; Vasanta, 1997). In Dodd and So's study (1994) on the phonological abilities of Cantonese-speaking children with moderate-to-profound hearing loss, the phonology of all the children with hearing loss was shown to primarily resemble that of young hearing Cantonese children. Some unusual error patterns, i.e. friction and initial consonant deletion, were also identified. Unlike English-speaking children with hearing impairment, none of the Cantonese children used the error pattern of syllable-final consonant deletion. These findings not only highlighted similarities in the phonological abilities of children with hearing loss acquiring English and Cantonese, but also reflected the influence of the ambient language on the acquisition of the children with hearing impairment. For example, the relative ease in the mastery of syllable-final consonants by Cantonese-speaking children with hearing impairment may be related to the fewer number of syllable-final segments and the absence of word-final syntactic markers in Cantonese.

Compared to the studies on the phonological abilities of hearing impaired children at a given time during their acquisition, relatively little research has been carried out addressing the development and change in the phonological systems of hearing impaired children over time (Carney & Moeller, 1998). It is generally accepted that the phonological development of children with hearing impairment will be slow and difficult. Abraham (1989) observed that some error patterns in the speech of hearing impaired children appeared to persist for a long time and resistant to change. Some children may not develop intelligible spoken language even if they do receive early diagnosis and hearing aid provision (Abberton *et al.*, 1990). Longitudinal studies of the developmental patterns in the phonological systems of the children with hearing impairment would provide information concerning the learning mechanisms of these children and data for planning intervention strategies.

1.4 Aims and Objectives of the Current Book

As reviewed in the previous section, studies of phonological development of children in atypical circumstances not only provide evidence for developmental universals but also raise a number of theoretical issues which need to be accounted for by theories of language acquisition. Most of the existing studies of phonological disorders, however, focus on English-speaking children, partly because normative data, by which delayed and disordered development can be identified, is readily available for English. Cross-linguistic research is needed if the explanations hitherto put forward are to be verified and generally applicable theories and models are to be developed.

The primary aim of this book is to describe developmental patterns of phonological acquisition of Putonghua by normally developing children and those in exceptional circumstances.

The factual research questions to be addressed in this book include:

On normally developing Putonghua-speaking children:
- Order of acquisition of syllable components.
- Age of acquisition of vowels.
- Age of acquisition of syllable-final consonants.
- Age of acquisition of syllable-initial consonants.
- Chronology of error patterns.
- Age of tonal acquisition.
- Patterns of tonal acquisition.
- Age of acquisition of tone sandhi.
- Patterns of acquisition of tone sandhi.
- Age of acquisition of weak stress.
- Patterns of acquisition of weak stress.
- Group variations – the effect of gender or second language exposure on phonological development.

On Putonghua-speaking children in exceptional circumstances:
- Characteristics of the disordered phonology of Putonghua-speaking children.
- Patterns of spontaneous changes in the disordered phonology of children with functional phonological disorders.
- Characteristics of phonology of twins.
- Characteristics and developmental patterns in the phonology of children with hearing impairment.

The theoretical research questions to be addressed in this book include:
- Evaluating existing theories of phonological acquisition accounting for universal and language-specific patterns:
  - (i) Jakobson's law of irreversible solidarity (Jakobson, 1941/1968);
  - (ii) the notion of markedness (e.g. Menyuk, 1968; Eckman, 1977; Anderson, 1983);
  - (iii) Biological model (Locke, 1980, 1983; Kent, 1992); and
  - (iv) Functional load (Pye *et al.*, 1987).
- Evaluating the differential diagnosis system for phonologically disordered children (Dodd, 1995).
- Contributing to the understanding of the natural history (i.e. emergence, persistence or recovery) of phonological disorders.
- Contributing to the understanding of causal factors (e.g. dual phonological representation) for impaired phonology – the most salient characteristic of communication profiles of twins.
- Contributing to the understanding of the nature of phonology of children with hearing impairment and the role of auditory input in phonological acquisition.

Notes

1. Error patterns, rather than phonological processes, are used here to refer to consistent differences between adult targets and children's erroneous realisations. Originated in Natural Phonology (Stampe, 1969), phonological processes are defined as a set of mental operations that change or delete phonological units as the result of the natural limitations and capacities of human vocal production and perception. The innate processes correspond to the phonological regularities found in the languages of the world. The child's task therefore is to suppress those processes which do not occur in the particular target language to which he or she is exposed. Despite criticisms from some researchers that the 'phonological processes' proposed by Stampe lacked psychological reality or explanatory power, the general consensus is that phonological process does provide the most economical way of describing the relationship between the adult targets and the children's erroneous realisation of them.

2. Lindblom (1998) criticises this approach as being circular in that the cause-and-effect relationship seems to be used arbitrarily – a feature is acquired early because it is unmarked and a feature is considered as unmarked because it is acquired early.

Chapter 2
Putonghua Phonology

2.1 Introduction

The Chinese language is manifested in a range of varieties. As far as spoken Chinese is concerned, traditional Chinese linguists distinguish eight major varieties, known as *Fangyan* (loosely translated as 'dialects', but more accurately 'regional speech'). The eight Fangyan are:

(1)   *Beifang* (literally means 'northern'), the native speech of about 70% of the Chinese population in mainland China. It is often referred to as Mandarin in the English-speaking world;

(2)   *Yue*, the majority of its speakers are in Guangdong province of mainland China, with the capital city of Guangzhou (Canton) as its centre. Large numbers of Yue speakers can also be found among the overseas diaspora;

(3)   *Kejia* (also known as Hakka), whose speakers originally came from small agricultural areas and are now scattered throughout south eastern China;

(4)   *Min Bei* (Northern Min), spoken in the northern part of Fujian (Hokkien) province on the western side of the Taiwan Strait;

(5)   *Min Nan* (Southern Min), spoken in the southern part of Fujian, as well as in Taiwan and Hainan islands;

(6)   *Wu*, spoken in the lower Changjiang (the Yangtze River) region, including urban, metropolitan centres such as Shanghai;

(7)   *Xiang*, mainly spoken in south central region of mainland China;

(8)   *Gan*, spoken chiefly in the south eastern inland provinces.

The major linguistic features and historical development of the eight Fangyan groups are discussed in Li and Thompson (1987), Ramsey (1987), and Norman (1988). Within each Fangyan, there are sub-varieties with their own distinctive features. For example, Cantonese as it is known in the West is a sub-variety within the Yue Fangyan group and Hokkien in Min Nan. It is in this sense, i.e. being a sub-variety of a Fangyan group, that the Chinese linguists talk about Cantonese and Hokkien as 'dialects', an important point often misunderstood and misrepresented in the linguistic literature in the West.

A hybrid variety of spoken Chinese is Putonghua, literally 'common speech'. It is the language variety which has been promoted by the Mainland Chinese government since the 1950s. Putonghua is a standardised language variety, based on the phonological and grammatical system of *Beifang* varieties. It is widely used in the mass media and taught in schools in China. Surveys suggest that 90% of the whole population in China understand Putonghua and about 50% can communicate in Putonghua (e.g. Wu & Yin, 1984). This chapter describes the phonological structure of Putonghua, focusing on those aspects that are relevant to the subsequent discussions of phonological acquisition and disorder in children. Comprehensive description and theoretical discussions of Putonghua phonology can be found in Li and Thompson (1981), Norman (1988) and Chen (1999).

2.2 Syllable

A syllable in Putonghua has the following structure (Figure 2.1):

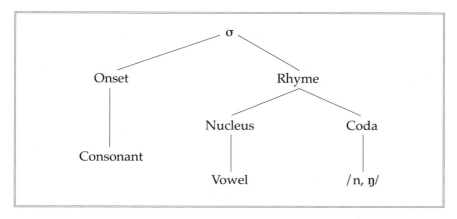

Figure 2.1 Putonghua syllable structure

In a Putonghua syllable, the onset and coda are optional and the vowel in the nucleus is compulsory. The onset can be one of 21 consonants and the coda can only be one of two consonants, /n/ and /ŋ/. Among the 22 consonants in Putonghua, 21 can serve as an onset with the exception of /ŋ/, which can only occur in the coda. There are 22 vowels.

The traditional conceptual framework which is still widely used in the description of Chinese phonology (Li & Thompson, 1981; Norman, 1988;

Chen, 1999) posits that a Putonghua syllable consists of three parts: initials, finals and tones (cf. terms such as onset and rhyme which are used in the modern phonology in the west). It differs from what is presented in Figure 2.1 mainly in that tone is regarded as part of the syllable. The structure of a Putonghua syllable in the traditional conceptual framework is represented in the following way (Table 2.1).

Table 2.1 The traditional representation of a Putonghua syllable

Tone			
Initial	*Final*		
Initial consonants	*Medial*	*Main vowels*	*Syllabic terminal*
(C)	(i)	V	(i)
	(u)		(u)
	(y)		(n)
			(ŋ)

Note: The phonemes in parentheses are optional in the syllable.

While the initial and final are segmental parts of the syllable, tone is a suprasegmental feature associated with the segments that bear tone. Tones and main vowels are compulsory while initial consonants, medials and syllabic terminals are optional in a syllable. Altogether there are about 420 feasible combinations of initials and finals in Putonghua, and 1300 syllables if tonal variations are taken into account (Xiandai Hanyu Cidian, 1979). Consequently, the occurrence of homophones in Putonghua is much more common than in most other languages.

Putonghua has often been described as 'monosyllabic', giving the false impression that Putonghua words are one syllable long. However, most words (with the exception of most particles, determiners, classifiers and prepositions) in Putonghua are disyllabic or more than two syllables long. DeFrancis (1984) suggested that the term 'morphosyllabic' is more suitable in describing the Putonghua syllable, since most morphemes in Putonghua consist of one syllable and vice-versa. Putonghua is regarded as 'stress-timed' rather than 'syllable-timed', since the individual syllables in connected speech are normally produced with unequal stress (i.e. produced with variations in syllable length, amplitude, and amount of time separating the syllables) (Packard, 1993).

2.3 Consonants

The place and manner of articulation of Putonghua consonants are described in Table 2.2.

Table 2.2 The place and manner of Putonghua consonants

	Bilabial	Labio-dental	Alveolar	Retroflex	Alveolo-palatal	Velar
Stop	p pʰ		t tʰ			k kʰ
Nasal	m		n			ŋ
Affricate			ts tsʰ	tʂ tʂʰ	tɕ tɕʰ	
Fricative		f	s	ʂ	ɕ	x
Approximant			ɹ			
Lateral approximant			l			

Examples are: (the numbers 1, 2, 3 and 4 are tonal indicators, representing high level, rising, falling–rising and high falling tones).

Consonant	Example	English translation
p	pʌ1	'eight'
ph	phʌ1	'lean over'
m	mv1	'mother'
f	fʌ1	'distribute'
t	tʌ1	'build'
th	thʌ1	'he'
n	nʌ2	'hold'
ts	tsʌ1	'bind'
tsh	tshʌ1	'rub'
s	sʌ1	'let go'
l	lʌ1	'pull'
tʂ	tʂʌ1	'prick'
tʂh	tʂhʌ1	'fork'
ʂ	ʂʌ1	'kill'
ɹ	ɹaŋ1	'yell'

Consonant	Example	English translation
tɕ	tɕi1	'chicken'
tɕh	tɕhi1	'wife'
ɕ	ɕi1	'west'
k	kan1	'dry'
kh	khan1	'watch'
ŋ	paŋ1	'help'
x	xA1	'breathe out'

Aspiration serves as a distinctive feature of Putonghua consonants. There are six pairs of aspirated and unaspirated consonants and all of them are voiceless.

2.4 Vowels

Simple vowels (9 in total; see Figure 2.2)

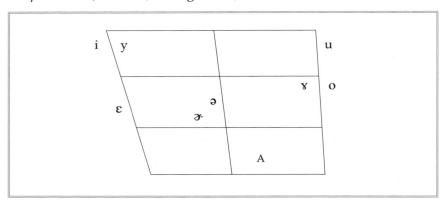

Figure 2.2 Putonghua simple vowel chart

Examples are:

Vowel	Example	English translation
i	ni3	'you'
y	ny3	'woman'
u	su1	'crispy'
ɤ	sɤ4	'colour'
o	po1	'wave'
A	sA1	'let go'
ɚ	ɚ3	'ear'

/ɚ/ is a retroflexed central vowel. It occurs either in isolation or in rhota-cisation and thus has very restricted combination with onset consonants. Apart from the seven vowels listed above, there are two other simple vowels in Putonghua, /ɛ/ and /ə/. They both have very restricted occurrence: /ɛ/, as a simple vowel, is used only in conversational particles expressing a speaker's emotions, such as surprise, agreement; /ə/, as a simple vowel, occurs only in weakly stressed syllables. /i/ has three allophones (Norman, 1988; termed as 'fricative vowels' in Ladefoged & Maddieson, 1996):

- occurring after /ts/, /tsʰ/ and /s/, it represents a weak syllabic pro-longation of the preceding consonants (usually referred to as /ɿ/ in the traditional Chinese phonetic transcription);
- occurring after retroflexes /tʂ/, /tʂʰ/, /ʂ/ and /ɹ/, it represents a weak syllabic retroflex continuant (usually referred to as /ʅ/ in the traditional Chinese phonetic transcription);
- occurring after all other consonants, it represents a high front unrounded /i/.

Diphthongs (9 in total)

Vowel	Example	English translation
ae	sae1	'cheek'
ɑo	sɑo1	'foul smell'
ei	pei1	'cup'
oʊ	soʊ1	'search'
ia	ia1	'duck'
iɛ	piɛ1	'suppress'
ua	xua1	'flower'
uo	suo1	'shrink'
yɛ	yɛ1	'appointment'

The nine diphthongs can be classified into two groups, offgliding and ongliding diphthongs. /ae/, /ɑo/, /ei/ and /oʊ/ are offgliding, in which the first sound is pronounced longer and with more intensity than the other. /ia/, /iɛ/, /ua/, /uo/ and /yɛ/ are ongliding ones with the second element being sonorous.

Triphthongs (4 in total)

Vowel	Example	English translation
iɑo	piɑo1	'mark'
ioʊ	tɕʰioʊ1	'autumn'
uae	uae1	'slanting'
uei	uei1	'danger'

In all the triphthongs, the middle vowels are pronounced longer and with more intensity than the other two vowels.

2.5 Tones

There are four tones in Putonghua. A tone is primarily characterised by voice pitch while other features such as length and intensity may also play a role in its perception. It is believed that the majority of the world's languages are tonal languages in which pitch variations contrast word meanings or mark grammatical properties or both (Fromkin & Rodman, 1993). The four tones in Putonghua are lexical tones. Differences in tones can change the meaning of a word in Putonghua.

There are different description systems of Putonghua tones. The oldest one is called Chao letters (Chao, 1930), in which a speaker's pitch level is divided into five scales. A vertical bar is used to indicate the pitch range and the contour line adjacent to the bar represents the pitch movement within the pitch range. This description system is later adopted by the International Phonetic Association. Out of convenience for transcription, Chao also invented a numeric system (called Chao digits) mirroring the five scales, in which '5' represents highest pitch, and '1' lowest. Therefore, tone '55' starts at the highest pitch level and remains at the same level, while tone '214' starts fairly low, drops to the lowest level and increases to a fairly high level. *Hanyu Pinyin* (known as 'Chinese phonetic writing system'), which was endorsed by the National People's Congress in 1958 in an effort to standardise pronunciation throughout China and to facilitate teaching and learning of Putonghua, uses diacritics to represent high level, rising, falling–rising and falling tones. Finally, numbers 1, 2, 3 and 4, which are convenient typographically, are often used to refer to high level, rising, falling–rising and falling tones in the literature. The equivalent terms in the various systems are compared in Table 2.3, in which a syllable /ma/ occurs with different tones:

Table 2.3 The description systems of Putonghua tones

	Tone description systems				
Tone	*Chao letters/IPA*	*Chao digits*	*Pinyin*	*Numbers*	*Translation*
High level	ma˥	ma55	mā	ma1	mother
Rising	ma˧˥	ma35	má	ma2	hemp
Falling–rising	ma˨˩˦	ma214	mǎ	ma3	horse
High falling	ma˥˩	ma51	mà	ma4	scold

In this book, tones will be referred to as high level, rising, falling–rising or high falling. Numbers 1, 2, 3 and 4 will be used in transcription.

Tones can be classified as either register or contour tone according to whether there is fluctuation in pitch level (Katamba, 1989). In Putonghua there is one register tone (high level) and three contour tones (rising, falling–rising and high falling). The contour tones are a combination of two or more than two basic tones, such as a rising tone made up of a low level tone and a high level tone, or a falling–rising tone made up of a high level tone, a low level tone, and a high level tone.

2.6 Tone Sandhi

Tone sandhi, the alternations of tones, in Putonghua is a phonological process closely associated with the morphological structure of Chinese words (and sometimes with grammatical structures). It falls into the following four categories:

- Tone 3 sandhi rule 1: A falling–rising tone will become a rising tone before another falling–rising tone, if the two syllables involved are in one meaning group (e.g. disyllabic words or phrases);
- Tone 3 sandhi rule 2: A falling–rising tone will only retain the falling part of its contour before high level, rising and high falling tones, if the two syllables involved are in one meaning group. In effect, it is only in isolation or before a pause (usually at word or phrase boundaries) that a falling–rising tone completes its full contour (for a detailed discussion of tone 3 sandhi rule, see Dow, 1972);
- Tone 4 sandhi rule: A high falling tone, followed by another high falling tone, will become a low falling tone;
- Morphologically conditioned sandhi rule: There are four lexical items which follow their own rules. They are /pu4/ ('no'), /i1/ ('one'), /tɕi1/ ('seven') and /pA1/ ('eight'). The citation tones will become rising tones before a high falling tone. Additionally, /i1/ will become a high falling tone before all the tones except a high falling tone.

2.7 Weak Stress

Weak stress, which is often referred to as the neutral tone or weak syllable (see Norman, 1988), is an essential prosodic feature of Putonghua. It is phonologically and morphologically conditioned. Weakly stressed syllables have a very short duration and a much reduced pitch range. Unlike the four basic tones, weakly stressed syllables cannot be pronounced in isolation; when an element which normally has weak stress is cited in isolation, ... it must be supplied with a tone.' (Norman, 1988: 148).

Apart from the changes in duration, weakly stressed syllables are also characterised by other feature changes:

- The original tone of the syllable is dropped. The pitch of a weakly stressed syllable is primarily determined by the preceding tone: it is half-low after a high level tone; mid after a rising tone; half-high after a falling–rising tone; and low after a high falling tone (for a detailed discussion, see Norman, 1988: 148–9).
- The vowel in the syllable may change. The low vowel tends to become a central vowel while an offgliding diphthong tends to become a simple vowel. e.g. /fa/→ /fə/; /lae/→ /lɛ/.
- Some initials may become voiced, especially those unaspirated stops and affricates /p, t, k, tɕ, ts, tʂ/, e.g. /pa/→ /ba/.

There are two categories of weak stress: regular weak stress vs. irregular weak stress (Lu, 1995). 'Regular weak stress' is rule-governed. It is restricted in number and most of the words belong to 'closed class'. The typical examples of this category are:

- 'affix' type in which weak stress occurs to the affix of nouns. For example, /tsi/ '*zi*' in /pitsi/ ('*nose*').
- 'reduplication' type in which the reduplicated second syllables in nouns, verbs and adjectives are weakly stressed; for example, /ɕiŋɕiŋ/ ('*star*') and /ɕiɛɕiɛ/ ('*thank you*').
- 'grammatical particle' type in which particles such as /lɤ/ '*le*', /pɐ/ '*ba*' are weakly stressed.

'Irregular weak stress' is not rule-governed and whether one syllable is weakly stressed is decided on a lexical basis. It is referred to as 'lexeme' type:

- 'lexeme' type in which two lexemes, especially nouns, are combined together and the second lexeme is weakly stressed, for example, /ɚtuo/ ('*ear*'), /tʰowfA/ ('*hair*').

2.8 Rhotacisation

Rhotacisation, originated in Beijing dialect, is a very special feature of the spoken form of Putonghua. With regard to semantics, rhotacisation often indicates that the referent is something common, familiar or small. In some cases, it may carry either a diminutive or a slightly pejorative implication. Though morphemically the rhotacisation is a feature attached to a syllable at syllable-final position (e.g. /xuaɹ/, '*flower*'), the rhotacisation process affects both the vowels and consonants in the coda, depending on which rhyme it is integrated into. In most cases, it leads to changing of vowels and dropping of nasals in the coda:

- the main vowel will turn into a retroflexed vowel, e.g. /xae/ will become /xaˇ/; /tsi/ will become /tsɚˇ/;
- if there is an /n/ in the coda, /n/ will be dropped while the main vowel turns into a retroflexed vowel, e.g. /tɕi/ and /tɕin/ will both become /tɕiɚˇ/;
- if there is an /ŋ/ in the coda, /ŋ/ will be dropped and the vowel in the rhyme becomes a nasalised retroflexed vowel. e.g. /kaŋ/ will become /kãˇ/.

Though theoretically all syllables can be rhotacised, whether and in what context a syllable is rhotacised in speech is determined lexically. Some words are always rhotacised and not using the rhotacised form of the word would be unusual, e.g. /nyxae/ (*'girl'*), /yantɕʰyan/ (*'circle'*). Some are optionally rhotacised, e.g. /mən/ (*'gate'*), /tɕʰitʂʰɤ/ (*'car'*).

2.9 Intonation

Apart from pitch variation within the domain of a morpheme (i.e. tone), Putonghua also has pitch variation within an entire utterance, i.e. intonation. The main intonational patterns include falling (which is typically used to express confirmation, exclamation, etc.), rising (used in questions, calling for attention, etc.), flat (used in statements, description and ordinary conversation) and curve (expressing complicated emotion, exaggeration, surprise, etc.). Intonation is realised mainly on the tail, not on the head or the nucleus of an utterance.

The relationship between tone and intonation is complex and difficult to describe. Intonation is directly related to change in pitch, and so is tone. In Putonghua, the pitch value of a tone overlaps with the pitch value of intonation for the whole utterance. However, intonation does not obliterate tones, even though it may modify the pitch value of tones. Chao (1968) compared the interaction between tone and utterance intonation as 'small ripples riding on large waves (though occasionally the ripples may be 'larger' than the waves)'. Examples:

/tA1 ɕiɛ3 ʂi1/↗ (*'Does he write a poem?'*)
/san1ɕiao3 ʂi2/↗ (*'Three hours?'*)
/kaŋ1 kʰae1 ʂi3/↗ (*'Just began?'*)
/ni2 iou4 ʂi4/↗ (*'Are you busy?'*)

Lin and Wang (1991) argued that in the above four utterances, although the four utterances share a rising intonation, the different pitch value of the last syllable in each utterance is maintained. This may be due to the fact that a tone is not defined in terms of absolute value – the relative difference between pitch value within a syllable constitutes the tone of a syllable. In contrast, the relative difference between pitch value of one or several phonological phrases constitutes the intonation of an utterance.

Chao (1968) argued that (1) intonation exists only in the interaction between intonation and tone in Chinese; (2) the addition of tone and intonation results in the expansion or reduction of pitch range in tone; (3) the addition of tone and intonation takes place in two ways: simultaneous addition and successive addition. As the result of such an interaction, tones change their phonetic shape in connected speech. The changes involve variation in length, amplitude and fundamental frequency (F_0) value.

2.10 Relationship between Tones and Segments

Prior to autosegmental phonology, tones were regarded as a feature of vowels by most early generative theories (e.g. Halle & Stevens, 1971). However, this claim is contradicted by several facts. Firstly, tones can shift, spread and be deleted without affecting the quality of the vowels or syllables they were attached to (Goldsmith, 1976); secondly, there are segmentless tones, toneless segments and rules that affect tones or segments separately (Williams, 1976; Yip, 1980). These facts suggest that tones are primarily a suprasegmental feature, independent from segmental representation at a phonological level.

Using autosegmental theory, Goldsmith (1976), based on the 'tonology' of Igbo, a west African tonal language, proposed a 'multilinear phonological analysis in which different features may be placed on separate tier' (1979: 202). The main arguments are:

- Tones and segments are on separate tiers, and are therefore independent of each other.
- Phonological rules link tones to appropriate TBUs (tone-bearing units) to produce the final phonetic form.
- There are only level tones. The contour tones can be derived from a linear sequence of two different level tones. Therefore, a rising tone is a linear sequence of a low level tone and a high level tone.
- There can be one to one, one to many (assimilation), many to one (contour tones), one to none (floating feature), and none to one

(featureless segment) relationship between segments and tonal features.

Putonghua tones have been regarded as a compulsory syllable component, though there is debate on what the tone-bearing units in Putonghua are (i.e. syllables, rhymes, moras or vowels) (for syllable and tone association, see Wang, 1967; for syllable and rhyme association, see Bao, 1990; for syllable and mora/vowel nucleus association, see Woo, 1969; Duanmu, 1990). Wan and Jaeger (1998) offered a composite account of the relationship between tones and segments:

> … in lexical representations, tones are autosegmental and are inherently stored with the entire phonological form of the word, either in an unlinked form, or specifically linked with vowels or other aspects of the phonological form. During the phonological derivation of the forms, however, they may become delinked and more, spread, be added or deleted differentially from the segments of the word. Finally, the configuration of tones which has resulted after all phonological processes have applied must be relinked with segments, so that tones can be phonetically realised on voiced segments in appropriate syllables, typically on vowels or other sonorants which can carry pitch. (1998: 424)

2.11 Issues of Controversy

There are a number of controversies over some issues concerning the description of the Putonghua phonological system. Among these issues of controversy are:

- The phonetic nature of Putonghua consonants. For example, the sound that /ɹ/ represents is sometimes described as an approximant /ʐ/ (e.g. Wu, 1991) and sometimes as /r/ (e.g. Duanmu, 2000). The sound that /x/ represents is sometimes described as a uvular /χ/ (Norman, 1988). One explanation for the confusion with /x/ is that when the sound is pronounced in combination with some vowels, such as /ʌ/ and /u/, friction occurs between the uvular and the back of the tongue, which may make the sound resemble a uvular sound. There is also disagreement about the labels used in the description of sounds: Ladefoged and Maddieson (1996) argued that retroflex sounds should be labelled as being flat post-alveolars while alveolo-palatal sounds should be palatalised post-alveolars.

- The phonetic nature of Putonghua vowels. Some Putonghua vowels have several variants and there is disagreement on their surface values. For example, whether /ɿ/ and /ʅ/ should be considered as allophones of /i/ or as phonemes. These two vowels have a very restricted occurrence. /ɿ/ occurs only after /ts/, /tsʰ/ and /s/; /ʅ/ occurs only after retroflex /tʂ/, /tʂʰ/, /ʂ/ and /ʐ/. Duanmu (2000) also summarises the controversy on the mid and low vowels.
- The nature of weak stress, i.e. whether 'weakly stressed syllables' should be considered as a type of tone sandhi or as toneless syllables (see Duanmu, 2000).
- The nature of medial glides, i.e. whether the vowels /i/ and /u/ in diphthongs /ia/, /iɛ/, /ua/, /uo/ and triphthongs /iɑo/, /iou/, /uae/ and /uei/ should be considered as semi-vowels, especially when they occur at syllable-initial position. They have been traditionally labelled as 'medial' sounds or 'prenucleus glides' between the syllable-initial consonant and the following vowel (Xu, 1980; Lin & Wang, 1992)
- The specification of Putonghua syllable structure, which is related to the issue of the status of /i/ and /u/ in diphthongs and triphthongs. Yin (1989) and Wang (1989) suggested these sounds should be considered as part of the onset rather than part of the coda. In their framework, a syllable is represented as Figure 2.3.

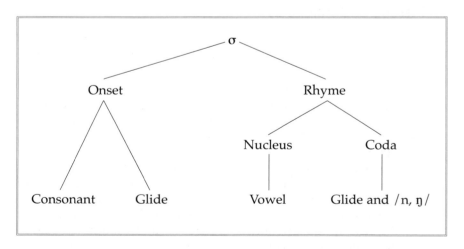

Figure 2.3 Putonghua syllable structure proposed by Yin (1989) and Wang (1989)

Duanmu (1990) proposed a three-slot approach, which he believes is applicable to all Chinese dialects (Figure 2.4).

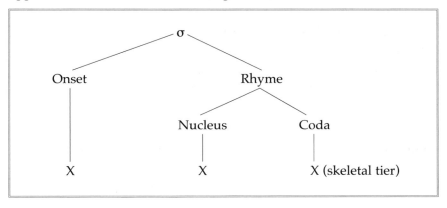

Figure 2.4 Putonghua syllable structure proposed by Duanmu (1990)

The labels and symbols adopted in this book are those widely used in the literature in the discussion of Putonghua. The implications of the alternative descriptions and arguments for interpreting developmental patterns of phonological acquisition of Putonghua children will be discussed in connection with data analyses in the following chapters.

2.12 Differences between Putonghua and Guoyu in Taiwan

There are a number of case studies of phonological acquisition of Mandarin-speaking children from Taiwan (e.g. Li, 1977; Jeng, 1979; Shiu, 1990). Mandarin is officially called *Guoyu* in Taiwan (literally, 'national language'). Important differences exist between Taiwan Mandarin and Putonghua. For example, rhotacisation and weak stress occur less frequently in Taiwan Mandarin than in Putonghua (Chen, 1999). The phonological contrast between the alveolar fricative and affricates /s, ts, tsʰ/ and the retroflex fricative and affricates /ʂ, tʂ, tʂʰ/ tends to disappear in Taiwan Mandarin. The contrast between syllable-final consonants /n/ and /ŋ/ also tends to disappear, especially in codas /in/ vs. /iŋ/ and /ən/ vs. /əŋ/ (Kubler & Ho, 1984). There are tonal differences in Putonghua and Guoyu (Yip, 1980). In a recent survey on pronunciation differences in the norms of Putonghua in mainland China and Taiwan Mandarin (Q. Li, 1992), 23% of 3500 most common characters were found to have different pronunciations. These differences between Putonghua and Taiwan Mandarin should be born in mind when relevant studies are compared.

2.13 Differences between Putonghua Phonology and English Phonology

Differences between the phonology of Putonghua and that of English are summarised in Table 2.4. These differences will be referred to when the developmental phonological patterns of Putonghua-speaking children are compared to those of English-speaking children.

Table 2.4 Differences between Putonghua and English phonology

	Putonghua	*English*
Tones	4 tones	none
Syllable-initial consonants	p, pʰ, t, tʰ, k, kʰ m, n f, s, ç, x, ʂ l, ɹ ts, tsʰ, tç, tçʰ, tʂ, tʂʰ	p, b, t, d, k, g m, n θ, ð, f, v, s, z, ʃ, ʒ, h w, j l, ɹ tʃ, dʒ
Syllable-initial clusters	none	p b t d k g f θ ʃ + l r j w s+ m n p t k l w s+ p t k + l r j w
Syllable-final consonants	n, ŋ	m, n, ŋ p, b, t, d, k, g θ, ð, f, v, s, z, ʒ, ʃ tʃ, dʒ l, ɹ
Vowels	i, u, y, o, ɤ, A, ə, ɛ, ɚ ae, ei, ɑo, oʊ, iA, iɛ, uA, uo, yɛ iɑo, ioʊ, uae, uei	i, ɪ, ɛ, æ, ʌ, a, ɒ, ɔ, ʊ, u, ɜ, ə eɪ, əʊ, aɪ, aʊ, ɔɪ, ɪə, ɛə, ɔə, ʊə (eɪə, əʊə, aʊə, ɔɪə)
Syllable structure	$C_{0-1} V C_{0-1}$	$C_{0-3} V C_{0-4}$

Phonological Acquisition of Normally Developing Children. I: Cross-sectional Study

3.1 Introduction

This chapter reports a normative, cross-sectional study of 129 normally developing Putonghua-speaking children. The age of phoneme acquisition, and the error patterns associated with the phonemes are identified. It is expected that the developmental patterns of the Putonghua-speaking children would reflect an interaction of universal tendencies and language-specific constraints. Specific hypotheses regarding the individual aspects of the phonology, based on the description in Chapter 2 and discussion in Chapter 11, are proposed:

(1) *Order of phoneme acquisition*
- Nasals would be acquired earlier than orals, and stops earlier than fricatives. This pattern, predicted by Jakobson (1941/1968), is already supported by the existing studies of Cantonese-, Italian-, Turkish-, Spanish- and English-speaking children (for Cantonese data, see So & Dodd, 1995; for Italian, see Bortolini & Leonard, 1991; for Turkish, see Topbas, 1997; for Spanish, see Jimenez, 1987; Acevedo, 1988; for English, see Olmsted, 1971; Prather *et al.*, 1975).
- Marked features, such as aspiration and affrication, would be acquired later than the default and unmarked features of the language (for aspiration, see So & Dodd, 1995; for affrication, see Olmsted, 1971; Prather *et al.*, 1975).

(2) *Error patterns*
Young children were expected to deaspirate and stop within a syllable, and assimilate and delete some syllable components such as syllable-initial and syllable-final consonants at syllable level.

(3) *Tones*
The acquisition of tones would be completed early, probably due to its capacity in differentiating lexical meaning and fulfilling children's communicative intentions.

(4) *Vowels*

Children would make fewer vowel errors compared with syllable-initial consonant errors, probably because vowels are compulsory components of syllables in Putonghua.

The chapter begins with a review of the previous findings on the phonological acquisition of Mandarin in Section 3.2, followed by Section 3.3 on the data collection method. Section 3.4 explains how the data analysis is carried out and Section 3.5 reports the results. The interpretation and implications of the results can be found in Section 3.6. The last section summarises the findings in this normative, cross-sectional study.

3.2 Previous Studies

A small number of studies have been carried out to describe the phonological development of Mandarin-speaking children.

Chao (1951/1973)

Chao's study (1951/1973) presented the earliest description of phonological acquisition of Mandarin-speaking children. In his study, he provided a detailed analysis of the consonant and vowel repertoires of the phonological system of a girl who was acquiring Mandarin as first language in the USA. At the age of 2;4, the child's consonant inventory consisted of 11 phonemes (i.e. three pairs of unaspirated and aspirated voiceless plosives /p, pʰ, t, tʰ, k, kʰ/ and two nasals /m, n/ and three fricatives /f, s, h/. The child had only mastered one nasal ending /n/ and tended to replace /ŋ/ with /n/ at syllable-final position. Her acquisition of vowels was characterised by inconsistencies and rapid changes between stages in her phonological system. Among the observed patterns of vowel acquisition were (1) diphthongs tended to be realised as simple vowels; (2) the sounds /i, u, y/ in diphthongs and triphthongs went through the stages of deletion and addition before their stabilisation. Given the fact that the study was based on one child only, however, few generalisations can be made from Chao's study. Another weakness of his study was that his transcription was based on Chinese National Romanisation system,[1] which was not accurate enough to record the minor differences between target sounds and realisations.

Li (1977)

In this study, Li analysed the speech data of one boy aged 2;0–3;0 and one girl aged 1;1–1;8. Both children were learning Mandarin in Taiwan. The main research findings were: (1) the acquisition of suprasegmentals preceded that of segments; (2) the order of acquisition of consonants generally followed 'laws of irreversible solidarity' proposed by Jakobson, i.e. stops before fricatives; stops and fricatives before affricates, and front before back consonants (for details, see section 1.2.1.2); (3) final consonants tended to be deleted at the early stage of acquisition; (4) the simple vowels /A, i, u/ were acquired error-free; and (5) the diphthongs tended to be replaced by the simple vowels. However, perhaps because the study was mainly set out to test Jakobson's hypothesis on language universals, the age of phoneme acquisition was not mentioned in the study.

Jeng (1979)

This study saw another attempt to test the applicability of Jakobson's laws of irreversible solidarity in the acquisition of Mandarin phonology. Two boys aged 0;2–1;8 and 1;3–2;7, who were acquiring Mandarin in Taiwan, provided the speech data for his study. Similar to Li (1977), Jeng found that the acquisition of suprasegmental features preceded that of segmental features. The consonants that were acquired earliest were /p, t, k, ts/, followed by nasals, aspirated stops, fricatives except /f/, and approximant /r/; /f/ was the last sound to appear. The four vowels /A, aʊ, i, e/ occurred earliest, while /u, y, o/ appeared later. Though Jeng used the terms of 'emergence' and 'stabilisation' in his description, he did not define the criteria involved.

Su (1985)

Su investigated the early phonological development of Mandarin in two Mandarin–Taiwanese bilingual children aged 1;5–2;4 and 1;2–1;11 respectively. In this study, the children were able to produce stops and nasals accurately when the data collection was complete. The frequent error patterns included: replacing aspirated consonants with unaspirated consonants, and replacing affricates with stops rather than fricatives of the same place of articulation. Su proposed that the second error pattern might be related to the high frequency of occurrence of affricates in Mandarin. As to the vowels, /A/ was the first vowel to be acquired, followed by /i/, which in turn was followed by /u/. Almost all the diphthongs and triphthongs were not stabilised by the completion of data collection. The children tended to delete part of diphthongs or triphthongs when they failed to produce them accurately. Su's study captured the characteristics of early phonological development of Mandarin in bilingual children.

Hsu (1987)

Hsu carried out a small-scale cross-sectional longitudinal study to examine the phonological development of 28 children aged 1;0–6;0 who were acquiring Mandarin Chinese in Taiwan. Two-thirds of the parents spoke Taiwanese as the first language and the other third spoke various Chinese dialects. Among the consonants acquired by the age of 20 months were /p, m, t, k/, while the children aged 4;4–6;0 still made errors with the consonants /f, n, tʂ, tʂʰ, ʂ, ɹ, ts, tsʰ/. Vowels, Hsu argued, were more difficult to acquire than most of the consonants. Similarly to Su (1985), he also found that the simple vowels /ʌ/ and /i/ emerged first around the age of 1;1. By the age of 1;6, the children had all the simple vowels except /y/, which presented difficulties even to the children aged 6;0. The diphthongs emerged almost as early as the simple vowels, but only five diphthongs /ae, aʊ, ia, iɛ, ua/ became stabilised by the age of 6;0. The first triphthong which was stabilised was /uae/ at the age of 1;9, followed by /iao/ at the age of 2;7–3;0. /uei/ and /ioʊ/ did not stabilise among the children aged 5;1–6;0. Despite the scale of the study, the generalisation of Hsu's findings were undermined by the following factors: (1) it was not clear whether the children in his study were acquiring Mandarin as first language or monolingually; (2) he did not clarify his criteria in defining when a sound would be considered 'emerged', 'established' or 'acquired'; (3) the stages in his description of acquisition of consonants and vowels were not justified and seemed arbitrary. For example, it was not clear why he analysed the acquisition of consonants in the age bands of 1;0–1;8, 1;8–2;6, 2;6–3;2, 3;4–4;0 and 4;4–6;0. There were gaps in the age bands which were missing in the description.

Shiu (1990)

Shiu described the phonological development of a boy aged 1;0–3;0 and a girl aged 0;7–2;4 again in the framework of language universals. Though exposed to more than one dialect, both children were primarily acquiring Mandarin as their first language during the observation period. Shiu (1990) analysed their phonological development in accordance with four stages in their syntactic development and used phonetic accuracy and consistency in children's realisations as an explicit criterion for acquisition. The early acquisition of /p/ and /m/ was found to be followed by the establishment of the labial-dental contrasts between /p/ and /t/, and /m/ and /n/. This was in agreement with Jakobson's postulation on the first and second consonant split (i.e. the first contrast within the consonantal system is between nasal and oral; the second between labial and dental). However, the earlier acquisition of /k, kʰ/ than /t/ in one child and the simultaneous acquisition of these sounds in the other child contradicted Jakobson's claim on the early acquisition of front consonants compared to back consonants. Apart from investigating the order of phoneme acquisition in relation to Jakobson's 'laws of irreversible solidarity', Shiu also systematically identified a number of error patterns evident in the children's speech. Among the error patterns found were fronting, backing, stopping, aspiration, deretroflexion, denasalisation, gliding, assimilation, deletion, reduplication, and metathesis. However, the chronology of these error patterns was not clear.

All these studies made one common claim, that is, Chinese children's phonological development is influenced by the structure of the language and is different from that of children of other linguistic backgrounds. However, most of these studies were based on diary records of one or two subjects. Such data do not allow generalisations concerning age or order of acquisition, nor identification of developmental error patterns in Chinese children's speech.

3.3 Method

3.3.1 Cross-sectional study as a data collection approach

A cross-sectional study approach was adopted in this study of normally developing children. In a typical cross-sectional study, a number of children would be selected from several age bands and a large sample would be collected from these children. The assumption underlying a cross-sectional study is that if a sufficient number of subjects are sampled, a typical developmental pattern that minimises individual differences in the rate and patterns of development will be established (see Ingram, 1989a, for the methodological issues of cross-sectional design). The purpose of this type of study is usually to present a representative picture of children's development over a certain period and to establish norms for the rate and patterns of development for children of a particular age. The norms may be used either for cross-linguistic comparison or for identifying children with speech and language difficulties.

Cross-sectional studies have strength in that it is feasible to make generalisations on the developmental characteristics of the children, based on the extensive data collected, with statistical analysis. These generalisations, or norms, can be further referred to in judging whether a child follows a typical developmental path, or deviates from normal development. Generally speaking, it is easier to conduct and control a cross-sectional study than longitudinal research. The size of the sample in cross-sectional studies is essential. Ideally, the larger the size is, the more representative the finding will be in statistical terms. However, since a large size of sample will impose an enormous transcription and analysis task on the researcher, the size of the sample is usually decided in the light of the research questions. The weaknesses of cross-sectional study are that it is unable to trace a sequential developmental pattern of a particular child and individual differences are often overlooked. Therefore, the findings are only probabilistic statements regarding the rate and pattern of development. These strengths and weaknesses of cross-sectional studies should be taken into account in the data interpretation.

3.3.2 Participants

In the study reported in this chapter, the phonological acquisition of 134 children aged 1;6–4;6 was assessed. The children were recruited from five nurseries in Beijing. Nursery records and parental reports ensured that all of the children were acquiring Putonghua as their first language, and had no intellectual or hearing impairment. A preliminary analysis of the data revealed that five children had very atypical speech errors and were therefore excluded from the present normative data analysis. The 129 children were divided into six age groups of six month intervals. The subject information is given in Table 3.1.

A balanced distribution was achieved between boys and girls within each age group. Altogether there were 61 girls and 68 boys. Among the children, 68 were from the nursery attached to Beijing Normal University (BNU) and 61 from the District nursery. Among the children from the BNU nursery, 22 children aged 3;1–4;6 were learning English, a language whose phonology is significantly different from Putonghua (see further in 2.12). These children had attended English classes on Sundays regularly for between six months and one year. Apart from four hours in these classes, they had some English practice with their parents at home. Nineteen children from the same nursery who had no English training background were also sampled.

Table 3.1 Subject information in the cross-sectional study of normally developing children

Age group	Sum	Girls	Boys	English	Non-English
1;6–2;0	21	10	11		
2;1–2;6	24	11	13		
2;7–3;0	21	11	10		
3;1–3;6	26	13	13	6	8
3;7–4;0	26	11	15	10	6
4;1–4;6	11	5	6	6	5
Total	129	61	68	22	19

Note: 'English' and 'non-English' columns are children who have attended English classes and those who have not.

3.3.3 Materials

Picture-naming and picture-description tasks were used to collect speech samples. For the picture-naming task, 44 words were selected to sample all the tones and phonemes in each legal word position (see Appendix 1). The word list included 39 nouns likely to be known by young children (e.g. nose, apple, bird, bed, sun). Four phrases (thank you, bye-bye, brush teeth, wash face) frequently used with young children in daily interactions were included in the picture-naming task. One colour term was also used (red). High quality colour drawings that were attractive to children were prepared. The drawings were laminated on A5 white cards. Five pictures of scenes incorporating most of the objects and actions in the picture-naming task were also prepared. Since the information on the frequency distribution of Putonghua phonemes in speech is not available, the choice of target words and phrases was primarily motivated by their familiarity to young children and imageability for producing the pictures. Thus the frequency of phonemes in the test varied. Appendix 2 summarises the frequency distribution of syllable-initial consonants, vowels, syllable-final consonants, tones, tone sandhi, weak stress and rhotacisation in the picture-naming task.[2]

3.3.4 Procedure

The children were assessed individually in a quiet room at their nursery. If a child failed to say the target word in the picture naming task, the examiner would offer semantic or contextual prompts. If it was impossible to elicit a spontaneous production of the target word, the child would be asked to imitate the examiner. Imitated responses were noted on the record form. If the child produced the wrong word, the examiner would ask the child to say the word again. Up to three attempts were made to elicit the correct pronunciation of the word. Repetitions were noted on the record form.

The children were also asked to describe what they saw in the five scene pictures, by which continuous speech data were sampled. The children were asked either 'Can you tell me what's happening here?' or 'What's funny about this picture?'. Each session lasted between 10 and 15 minutes and was audiotaped using a Sony professional micro recorder.

3.3.5 Imitated production

Although efforts were made to use the most common words and phrases in the picture-naming task, the objective of sampling all the phonemes in each legal syllable position and tones meant that some of the words and phrases used may be less familiar to some children than others. There were occasions when a child failed to produce the target word spontaneously, probably for the following reasons apart from performance factor:

- The target word was beyond the child's conceptual and lexical ability and therefore the task of accessing an appropriate lexical representation distracted the child from fulfilling the phonological task; or
- the child was actively using an avoidance strategy when s/he found certain sounds too difficult to pronounce (Macken & Ferguson, 1983).

In the present study, the children were asked to imitate the examiner when they failed to produce the target word or phrase spontaneously. The five most frequently imitated words were /ny xae/ ('*girl*', 25.6% of children), /çin/ ('*heart*', 25.6%), /tɕʰyn tsi/ ('*skirt*', 21.7%), /nan xae/ ('*boy*', 20.9%), and /çi liɛn/ ('*wash face*', 16.2%). The five least frequently imitated words were /tɕʰiou/ ('*ball*', 0.02%), /çiɑo tɕʰi tʂʰɤ/ ('*car*', 0.02%), /çi kuA/ ('*watermelon*', 0.04%), /ɚ tuo/ ('*ear*', 0.04%), and /ʂua ia/ ('*brush teeth*', 0.05%).

Imitated responses were taken into account only when the age of phone emergence was calculated, since the focus was children's articulation ability. When age of phoneme stabilisation, i.e. phonological accuracy, was calculated, imitated responses were excluded. It should be noted that the frequency of occurrence of imitated responses decreased with age. The mean frequency and standard deviation of occurrence of imitated responses for each age group in the sample was: 1;6–2;0: 12.04 (6.01); 2;1–2;6: 6.79 (4.11); 2;7–3;0: 4.42 (2.92); 3;1–3;6: 2.73 (2.61); 3;7–4;0: 1.27 (1.48); 4;1–4;6: 0.81 (0.88). Statistical analysis showed that there was a significant age effect in the frequency of occurrence of imitated responses (one-way ANOVA: $F_{(5, 120)} = 28.7599$, $p < 0.001$).

There were some words that some children, especially those in the younger age groups, failed to produce spontaneously, for conceptual, lexical or cultural reasons.

3.4 Data Analysis

The data from the picture-naming and picture description tasks were transcribed, using IPA. Incomplete responses (use of a shortened word, similar to the use of 'plane' for 'airplane' in English) were marked and excluded in the data analysis. Recordings from 20 children were independently transcribed by another phonetician to check transcription reliability. The inter-transcriber reliability for syllable-initial word-initial consonants, syllable-initial within-word, syllable-final word-final, syllable-final within-word consonants and vowels was 97.6%, 94.6%, 98.1%, 98.5%, and 97.8% respectively.

The following quantitative and qualitative measures were derived from the children's speech:

- *Phoneme emergence:* A phoneme was considered to have emerged when 90% of the children in an age group produced the sound at least once, irrespective of whether it was the correct target. This measure determined when the children were able to articulate each sound.

- *Phoneme stabilisation:* Each phoneme occurred in the sample once or several times. Since there was a certain amount of inconsistency in children's production, a criterion was needed to derive the age of phoneme stabilisation. A sound was considered stable when the child produced the sound correctly on at least two of three opportunities. When 90% of the children in an age group achieved an accuracy rating of at least 66.7% (i.e. 2/3) for a phoneme, the phoneme would be considered to have been stabilised by that age group. To balance various actual occurrences of phonemes in the children's speech, the following accuracy rating formula was applied (Shriberg & Kwiatkowski, 1982; Shriberg *et al.*, 1997):

Accuracy rating = the number of times of a phoneme produced correctly / the number of opportunities for phoneme production × 100%

Since phoneme development is a continuum ranging from the initial stage of being able to articulate a sound in isolation to the final stage of being able to articulate a sound both phonetically and phonologically accurately, it is important to define the terms and criteria in describing phoneme acquisition. Following So and Dodd's study (1995), this study adopted a 90% criterion in determining age of acquisition. Data on 75% of the age groups are also presented for comparison with other studies (e.g. Prather *et al.*, 1975). Another reason for setting up a 90% criterion is that the prevalence figure for phonologically delayed and disordered children is reported to be about 10% of the normal population (National Institute on Deafness and Other Communication Disorders, 1994).

- *Error patterns:* The consistent differences between children's realisations and target forms are described as error patterns. The
  importance of error patterns lies in that they can be understood
  as children's simplifying strategies. Therefore, they are a useful
  descriptive tool in describing and classifying the substitution
  patterns in the children's speech. In the data, if 10% of the children of the same age group were found to use the same phonemes
  (in terms of place or manner of articulation) to replace certain target
  sounds, that error pattern would be recorded. The percentage of
  the children in each age group using that error pattern was
  calculated to show the developmental tendency of the error pattern
  involved.

- *Percentage of Consonants in Error (PCE):* PCE for each child was
  calculated by the formula (the number of times phonemes are produced in error/the total number of phonemes in the sample ×
  100). (cf. *Percentage of Consonants Correct* proposed by Shriberg &
  Kwiatkowski, 1982).

- *Comparison of connected and single word speech:* Many researchers
  assume that children would make more errors in continuous speech
  than in single word speech because connected speech is linguisti-
  cally more complex (e.g. constructing sentences) (Shriberg *et al.*,
  1997). It is necessary to test this assumption to determine which
  speech mode is more indicative of phonological ability. The production of all of the words elicited in both contexts by 18 children
  (three from each age group) was compared.

3.5 Results

3.5.1 Overview of speech errors

Errors were classified into three types: syllable-initial consonant;
syllable-final consonant; and vowel errors. The mean number of all types
of errors decreased with age (see Table 3.2). Compared to the mean error
of 30.76 in the youngest age group, the oldest group's mean error was
only 7.45. The proportion of syllable-initial consonant errors in the total
number of errors was greater than that of vowel and syllable-final
consonant errors. The proportion of syllable-initial error increased with
age range while the proportion of vowel errors decreased, suggesting
vowel acquisition was complete earlier than that of syllable-initial consonants.

Table 3.2 Overview of speech errors in different age groups

Age group	1;6–2;0	2;1–2;6	2;7–3;0	3;1–3;6	3;7–4;0	4;1–4;6
Total number of errors	646	625	347	354	229	82
Mean	30.76	26.04	16.52	13.61	8.81	7.45
% Syllable-initial error	65.8	69.6	72.9	70.1	73.8	79.3
% Syllable-final error	14.2	12.8	10.7	17.8	17.0	9.8
% Vowel error	20.0	17.6	16.4	12.1	9.2	10.9

3.5.2 Emergence of syllable-initial consonants

By 4;6, 90% of the children were able to articulate all the 21 syllable-initial consonants (Table 3.3). Among the first sounds produced by 90% of the children were nasals; alveolar stops; alveolo-palatal fricatives and affricates; and the velar stop and fricative. The two alveolar affricates and the alveolar approximant appeared last. In terms of features, some unaspirated sounds emerged earlier than their aspirated pairs (e.g. /k/ earlier than /kʰ/); some unaspirated sounds emerged more or less simultaneously with aspirated pairs (e.g. /ts/ and /tsʰ/). The six affricates occurred later than the stop /t/ which has the same place of the articulation. However, the continuants at the same place of articulation did not necessarily appear before the affricates. For example, /ts/ and /tsʰ/ emerged later than /s/, but /tʂ/ and /tʂʰ/ emerged earlier than /ʂ/. The three alveolo-palatals emerged very early in the children's speech.

Table 3.3 Age of emergence of syllable-initial consonants in the cross-sectional study

	90% *Criterion*	75% *Criterion*
1;6–2;0	t, tʰ, k, m, n, x, tɕ, tɕʰ, ɕ	t, tʰ, k, m, n, f, s, x, tɕ, tɕʰ, ɕ, pʰ, p
2;1–2;6	f, s, tʂ	ʂ, tʂ, tʂʰ, kʰ
2;7–3;0	p, l	ts, l
3;1–3;6	pʰ, kʰ, tʂʰ	ɹ, tsʰ
3;7–4;0	ʂ	
4;1–4;6	ts, tsʰ, ɹ	

3.5.3 Stabilisation of syllable-initial consonants

The age of stabilisation of syllable-initial consonants is summarised in Table 3.4. The stabilisation of phonemes in Putonghua phonology, compared with their age of emergence, can be categorised into the following three groups:

- phonemes which were stabilised as soon as the child was able to articulate them. These phonemes were basically error-free, e.g. /t, m, p/;
- phonemes which took a relatively short period to become stabilised after the child was able to articulate them, e.g. /n/, f, x/; and
- phonemes which took a long time to become stabilised after the child was able to articulate them, e.g. /tɕ, tɕʰ, s/.

Table 3.4 Age of stabilisation of syllable-initial consonants in the cross-sectional study

	90% Criterion	*75% Criterion*
1;6–2;0	t, m	t, tʰ, m, n, x
2;1–2;6	n	p, pʰ, k, kʰ, ɕ, tɕ, tɕʰ
2;7–3;0	p, tʰ, f, x, ɕ	f
3;1–3;6	k, kʰ	
3;7–4;0	pʰ	
4;1–4;6	l, s, ɹ, tɕ, tɕʰ	l, s, ʂ, ɹ
>4;6	ʂ, tʂ, tʂʰ, ts, tsʰ	tʂ, tʂʰ, ts, tsʰ

3.5.4 Vowels

Vowels emerged very early in development. The youngest group of children were able to pronounce all of the simple vowels. Vowel errors were classified into the following categories (see Table 3.5).

Table 3.5 Percentage of children using error patterns affecting vowels in different age groups (%)

Age group	Triphthong reduction	Diphthong reduction	Substitution	Assimilation
1;6–2;0	67	67	71	10
2;1–2;6	63	58	83	4
2;7–3;0	48	38	76	0
3;1–3;6	23	19	50	0
3;7–4;0	23	19	42	0
4;1–4;6	22	9	45	0

- *Triphthong reduction:* Triphthongs were often reduced to diphthongs (in most cases) or sometimes to simple vowels. The middle vowel, the main vowel in Putonghua triphthongs, was maintained and one of the other vowels was deleted. This error pattern was the most evident for the triphthong /iɑo/: 48 children (37%) reduced this triphthong. Of these children, 37 (29%) used /ia/ and only 11 (8%) used /ɑo/. The second most frequently reduced triphthong was /uei/ (10% of the children): the most frequent reduction form was /ei/ (7% of the children).
- *Diphthong reduction:* Diphthongs were often reduced to simple vowels. The vowel retained was the louder and more sonorant vowel of a diphthong. The children tended to produce the second element of ongliding diphthongs when the reduction took place. For example, 12% of the children realised /ua/ as /A/ once or several times in their speech production and none of them realised it as /u/. The first element of offgliding diphthongs was most often maintained. Thus, more children replaced /ɑo/ with [A] than with [o].
- *Vowel substitution:* Some of the children substituted vowels at the same time when they deleted consonants (34.7% of vowel substitutions). When a syllable-final consonant was deleted, the vowel sometimes became lengthened and very frequently ended with /ɛ/. As a result, a simple vowel in the target syllable would turn into a diphthong ending with [ɛ] (e.g. /xin/ as [xiɛ]), a diphthong would turn into a triphthong ending with [ɛ] (e.g. /lian/ as [liaɛ]). Other vowel substitution errors were not systematic.
- *Assimilation:* This error pattern was found in the speech of a very small group of children, when they replace the vowel of a syllable with another vowel of an adjacent vowel.

3.5.5 Tone

Tonal errors were rare, even in the youngest group of children. Only two tonal errors were observed in the entire data corpus and they were produced by children in the youngest age group. The two tonal errors were [ɕiɛ4] for /ɕiɛ2/ and [uan2] for /uan3/. Five children in the youngest age group and three children in the second youngest age group occasionally used citation tones when tones should be adjusted according to tone sandhi rules. As Li and Thompson (1977) pointed out, a child who is able to adjust tones in single word context may not necessarily have acquired the tone sandhi rule. It is likely that s/he manages to learn the single words as adjusted forms without being aware of tone sandhi rules. An analogy is that an English-speaking child who uses 'went' may know little about the past tense. Alternatively, the scarcity of tone sandhi errors in the study may be an artefact of the cross-sectional design, in that tone sandhi rules may be acquired during a very short period of time and a cross-sectional study is unable to capture such rapid changes. A longitudinal study is needed to trace the development of tones.

3.5.6 Weakly stressed syllables

Data concerning the acquisition of weakly stressed syllables are shown in Table 3.6. Weakly stressed syllables were evident in 57% of the youngest group of children's speech. Only 36% of the oldest group were able to pronounce the tones of all the 13 weak stresses correctly. Almost all of the errors were associated with pitch level and duration. Of the 'affix' weak syllable type, 42.3% of the total errors occurred when weakly stressed syllables were deleted, for example, [pi2] for /pi2 tsi0/. The remaining errors involved pitch level and intensity: the children either used citation tone of /tsi3/, i.e. the falling-rising tone, or lengthened the syllable. Of the other three weak stress syllable types, most of the errors (93.4%) occurred when children used the citation tone (i.e. the pitch level of the syllable when pronounced individually), e.g. /toʊ2 fA0/ was realised as [toʊ2 fA4].

Table 3.6 Percentage of children using weak stress in different age groups (%)

				Percentage correct			
Age group	*Emerge*	*50%*	*60%*	*70%*	*80%*	*90%*	*100%*
1;6–2;0	57	5	0	0	0	0	0
2;1–2;6	88	8	4	4	0	0	0
2;7–3;0	100	57	38	29	10	5	0
3;1–3;6	100	77	69	62	19	4	0
3;7–4;0	100	96	88	77	58	38	15
4;1–4;6	100	100	100	91	73	45	36

Note: 'Emerge' column is the percentage of the children who were able to produce the target weak stress once or several times.

3.5.7 Rhotacisation

Only 57 % of the youngest group used the rhotacised form once or several times (see Table 3.7). However, over 90% of the children over 2;0 and all the children over 3;6 used rhotacised forms. The rhotacised feature was not acquired 'across the board'. With four words which are always rhotacised in adult speech, some children rhotacised some of them while using non-rhotacised forms for the others.

Table 3.7 Percentage of children rhotacising target words in different age groups (%)

Age group	Emerge	uan	mən	çiŋçiŋ	xua	niao	çywnmao	tçitşʰɤ	nyxae	nanxae	yantçʰyan
1;6–2;0	57	10	14	14	14	10	5	0	43	19	33
2;1–2;6	92	13	29	25	25	4	4	0	67	83	42
2;7–3;0	95	10	24	29	43	14	14	0	71	76	52
3;1–3;6	96	19	38	42	42	12	4	4	85	85	62
3;7–4;0	100	19	42	62	85	19	31	4	96	92	62
4;1–4;6	100	18	27	45	73	18	18	9	100	91	91
Total	90	15	30	36	46	12	12	10	76	74	54

Note: 'Emerge' column is the percentage of the children who were able to produce rhotacisation once or several times.

3.5.8 Error patterns

3.5.8.1 Error patterns affecting syllable-initial consonants

The error patterns affecting consonants at syllable-initial position can be generalised into three groups: assimilation, deletion and systematic substitution. Table 3.8 summarises the data.

The most typical realisations of these error patterns are outlined below:

- *Assimilation*. Assimilation occurs when one or more distinctive features of a sound are transferred to an adjacent sound. The transference can take place both within a syllable and across syllables and is thus highly context-sensitive. Twenty-one percent of the children harmonised a syllable-initial consonant with another consonant and 17% of the children nasalised syllable-initial consonants. Both progressive and regressive assimilation were found in the data.

Table 3.8 Error patterns affecting syllable-initial consonants and percentage of children using these patterns in different age groups (%)

	Percentage of children using error patterns (%)							Most common error types and percentages of children in all age groups
	1;6–4;6	1;6–2;0	2;1–2;6	2;7–3;0	3;1–3;6	3;7–4;0	4;1–4;6	
Assimilation	43	86	42	52	39	8	11	IC of one syllable harmonises with IC of another syllable; 21%, e.g. çiaŋ. tçiao: daŋ. tao IC harmonises with final consonant by being nasalised; 17%, e.g. çi.lien: çi.nien; yɛ.liaŋ: yɛ.niaŋ IC harmonises with final velar by being velarised; 2%, e.g. tsuaŋ: xuaŋ
IC deletion	37	81	58	29	15	15	33	IC deletion before high vowels /i/, /y/ & /u/; 37%, e.g. tsuei: uei; tɕʰyn: yn /l/ deletion; 16%, e.g. lien: ien; liaŋ: iaŋ
Fronting	87	91	100	91	85	81	89	Retroflex fricatives and affricates become alveolars; 77%, e.g. ʂ: s; tʂ: ts; tʂʰ: tsʰ Alveolo-palatal fricatives & affricates become post-alveolars; 36%, e.g. ɕ: ʃ; tɕ: tʃ Velar stops become alveolar stops; 16%, e.g. k: t; k: d; kʰ: tʰ
Backing	70	91	96	67	58	54	44	Alveolar affricates and fricative become post-alveolar; 65%, e.g. tʃ/dʒ; s: ʃ Fricatives become a glottal fricative; 5%, e.g. f: h; ʂ: h; x: h

	Percentage of children using error patterns (%)							Most common error types and percentages of children in all age groups
	1;6–4;6	1;6–2;0	2;1–2;6	2;7–3;0	3;1–3;6	3;7–4;0	4;1–4;6	
X-velarisation	48	76	71	48	31	27	22	X-velarisation occurs before a high vowel /u/; 24%, e.g. şu: xu; X-velarisation occurs before a high vowel /i/ & [y]; 23%, e.g. çi: xi; /f/ becomes X-velarised; 8%, e.g. fA: xA; fei: xei
Stopping	63	95	92	76	50	46	11	tç/tçʰ/tʂ/tʂʰ/ts/tsʰ: t/d/tʰ; 63%; x: k/g; 22%; ç/n/l/ʂ: t/d; 13%
Affrication	34	67	29	24	27	4	0	s/ʂ/ç: tʃ/dʒ; 34%; ç: tç/tçʰ; 22%
Deaspiration	56	48	88	67	50	46	44	tʂʰ: tʂ; 21%; tçʰ:tʃ; 20%; tʂʰ/tsʰ/tʰ: t/d; 16%; tçʰ: tç; 8%; kʰ: k; 5%; pʰ: p; 2%
Aspiration	32	24	46	43	27	12	0	t: tʰ; 15%; ç/tç: tçʰ; 15%; k: kʰ; 3%
Gliding	28	43	33	57	23	12	0	ɹ: lj; 28%

- *Deletion.* Syllable-initial consonant deletion was very common in the youngest group. It happened most frequently before the vowels /i/, /y/ and /u/. For example, a number of the children deleted /l/ in the target word /liɛn/ and /ts/ in /tsuei/.

- *Fronting.* While the most typical fronting pattern is the realisation of target velar sounds as alveolars in English-speaking children, only 16% of the Putonghua-speaking children in this study have used this pattern. The majority of the children (77%) fronted the retroflex sounds by realising them as alveolars and 36% replaced the alveolo-palatals with post-alveolars, which do not exist in Putonghua phonology.

- *Backing.* Backing occurs when the place of articulation moves backwards. This type of errors is rarely reported in the studies of other languages. However, in terms of the percentage of children, it is the second most frequent error pattern used by Putonghua-speaking children: 65% of the children substituted post-alveolars for alveolars. For example, /sua/ was realised as [ʃua].

- *X-velarisation.* X-velarisation was another frequent form of backing, and so frequent that it has been categorised as a group of its own for clarity: 48% of the children used [x], a velar fricative, to replace other fricatives and affricates. In most cases, X-velarisation occurred either before the vowel /u/ or before the vowels /i/ or /y/.

- *Stopping.* The most common type of stopping (63%) in the data was the use of stops of the same place or nearest place of articulation in the place of affricates.

- *Affrication.* Opposite to stopping, affrication took place when stops were replaced by affricates. This type of errors occurred in the speech of a relatively small number of the children (34%), compared with the error pattern of stopping.

- *Deaspiration and aspiration.* Deaspiration (56%) occurred significantly more frequently than the error pattern of aspiration (32%) and was often associated with other error patterns such as stopping and fronting. Among all the aspirated sounds, the aspirated retroflex /tʂʰ/ and alveolo-palatal /tɕʰ/ were most frequently deaspirated while /pʰ/ was rarely deaspirated.

- *Gliding.* /ɹ/ was replaced with [j] by 28% of the children. Apart from this type of substitution, 4 % of the children replaced /ɹ/ with the liquid [l].

3.5.8.2 Error patterns affecting syllable-final consonants

In Putonghua, there are only two possible syllable-final consonants and both of them are nasals, /n/ and /ŋ/. These two syllable-final consonants occurred very early in the children's inventory. In the data, all the children in the youngest age group were able to articulate these two phonemes. The five error patterns associated with these two syllable-final consonants were /n/ deletion, /ŋ/ deletion, replacing /n/ with [ŋ], replacing /ŋ/ with [n] and syllable-final consonant addition. Examples are listed in Table 3.9.

Table 3.9 Percentage of children using error patterns affecting syllable-final consonants (%)

	Examples	*Percentage of children*
/n/ deletion	/san/→ [sa]	57
/ŋ/ deletion	/pʰiŋ/→ [pʰi]	29
Replacing /n/ with [ŋ]	/san/→ [saŋ]	55
Replacing /ŋ/ with [n]	/pʰiŋ/→ [pʰin]	3
Syllable-final consonant addition	/niɑo/→ [niɑŋ]	6

The two most frequent error patterns were /n/ deletion and replacing /n/ with [ŋ], used by 57% and 55% of children respectively. /ŋ/ deletion was ranked the third most common error pattern. The other two error patterns, syllable-final consonant addition and replacing /ŋ/ with [n] rarely occurred. It is worth noting that all the syllable-final consonants in the children's speech were 'legal' nasal consonants. No other consonant occurred in syllable-final position even among the youngest age group.

3.5.9 Comparison of connected and single word speech

The children's speech accuracy in continuous speech was comparable to their accuracy in the picture-naming task. Of the 18 children compared, seven gave more correct responses in picture-description than they did in picture-naming; five gave the same number of correct responses in both modes; and six gave more correct responses in picture-naming (see Table 3.10). A t-test (p = 0.714) indicated there was no significant difference between the two speech samples in terms of the number of correct responses.

Table 3.10 Comparison of speech production in picture-naming and picture-description tasks*

Age	Sex	Number of shared syllables in both tasks	Number of correct syllables	
			Picture-naming	*Picture-description*
2;0	F	24	9	11
2;0	M	9	2	2
2;0	M	12	7	7
2;3	M	30	13	13
2;3	M	34	21	22
2;4	F	26	15	18
2;8	M	20	12	18
2;8	F	21	13	10
2;9	F	29	16	17
3;1	M	30	25	21
3;2	F	26	17	19
3;3	M	44	38	38
3;9	F	29	28	26
3;9	F	41	27	29
3;10	M	31	29	29
4;1	F	41	38	34
4;1	M	30	28	27
4;2	F	43	42	41

Note: The comparison is based on 18 children randomly selected from all age groups.

3.5.10 Variables

The effect of age, gender, and exposure to English on children's PCE (i.e. percentage of consonants in error) was investigated.

Age: ANOVA shows that there was a significant age effect on children's PCE score ($F_{5, 120} = 38.648$, $p < 0.001$). Tukey HSD post-hoc tests show that young age groups tended to be significantly different from each other. The results are summarised in Table 3.11.

Table 3.11 Multiple comparisons of PCE among different age groups

Age group I	Age group II	Mean differences	Significance
1;6–2;0	2;1–2;6	0.1177	0.000
	2;7–3;0	0.1884	0.000
	3;1–3;6	0.2304	0.000
	3;7–4;0	0.2753	0.000
	4;1–4;6	0.2935	0.000
2;1–2;6	2;7–3;0	0.0070	0.041
	3;1–3;6	0.1127	0.000
	3;7–4;0	0.1577	0.000
	4;1–4;6	0.1759	0.000
2;7–3;0	3;1–3;6	0.0420	0.004
	3;7–4;0	0.0869	0.005
	4;1–4;6	0.1051	0.010
3;1–3;6	3;7–4;0	0.0450	0.326
	4;1–4;6	0.0631	0.266
3;7–4;0	4;1–4;6	0.0182	0.990

Gender: MANOVA (group: boys vs. girls × conditions: six age groups) results does not reveal significant difference between girls and boys for PCE (Pillais test: $F_{(1, 127)} = 0.0902$; $p = 0.325$; Wilks test: $F_{(1, 127)} = 0.9098$; $p = 0.325$). Nor is there a significant interaction between age and gender for PCE ($F_{(5, 1, 117)} = 0.38$, $p = 0.863$).

Exposure to English: ANOVA finds no significant difference for PCE between the children who had second language learning experience and the group who had not ($F_{(1, 35)} = 2.122$, $p = 0.154$).

3.6 Discussion

As described in Chapter 2, Putonghua syllables have four possible elements: tone, syllable-initial consonant, vowel, and syllable-final consonant. Analyses of speech samples from 129 monolingual Putonghua-speaking children, aged 1;6–4;6, suggest that Putonghua-speaking children acquired these elements in the following order: tonal acquisition were completed first; then syllable-final consonants and vowels; and syllable-initial consonants were completed last. The phonetic acquisition of the 21 syllable-initial consonants was complete by 3;6 for 75% of children. By 4;6 the children were able to use the syllable-initial consonants correctly on two thirds of occasions (with the exception of four affricates). Simple vowels emerged early in development. However, triphthongs and diphthongs were prone to systematic errors. Tonal errors were rare. In contrast, the acquisition of 'weak stress' and 'rhotacised feature' was incomplete in the oldest children assessed. Similar to children acquiring other languages, Putonghua-speaking children showed the tendency of structural and systemic simplifications in their production. Differences in the error patterns used by the children acquiring Putonghua and the children speaking other languages were evident. For example, syllable-initial consonant deletion and backing, which are considered atypical error patterns in English, existed in the speech of the children acquiring Putonghua. While the effect of age was significant on the children's PCE, gender and exposure to English were found to have little influence on the children's phonological acquisition during the stage investigated.

3.6.1 Phoneme acquisition

The order of phoneme acquisition in Putonghua provides evidence for and against various theories of acquisition. Jakobson's (1941/1968) law of irreversible solidarity predicts that nasals should be acquired before orals, front consonants before back consonants, and stops before fricatives. The Putonghua-speaking children acquired nasals before orals, and stops before fricatives. However, front consonants (/p, p^h, m, /f/) were acquired at about the same stage as back consonants (/k, k^h, x, ŋ/). The three alveolo-palatal sounds (/tɕ, $tɕ^h$, ɕ/), which are very rare in the world's major languages, were acquired relatively early (75% of children by 2;6). These data do not support Jakobson's proposal that the frequency of a phoneme across the world's languages reflects the order of acquisition of the phoneme.

The last 10 phonemes to be acquired in Putonghua include all the three retroflex sounds, all the six affricates and both liquids. The late acquisition of these sounds, which were believed to be difficult to articulate and perceive (Locke, 1983), supports the hypothesis that biological constraints affect the order of phoneme acquisition. However, a closer comparison of the age of *emergence* of syllable-initial consonants and the age of *stabilisation* of these consonants (see Tables 3.3 and 3.4) casts some doubt on the role of articulatory constraints. Some of the late-stabilised sounds *emerged* very early in the children's speech. In the youngest age group, 90% of the children were able to articulate the affricates /tɕ/ and /$tɕ^h$/ once or several times. By 2;6, 90% of the children were able to utter the retroflex /tʂ/ and alveolar fricative /s/. However, it was not until the children were aged over 4;0 that they began to use these sounds consistently correctly. The delay between emergence and stabilisation indicates that articulatory constraints were not a major factor in the phonological acquisition.

3.6.2 Feature acquisition

There was a clear developmental sequence of feature acquisition. The features of aspiration, affrication and retroflex were acquired last. Late acquisition of affrication has been reported for a variety of languages. English-speaking children acquired the two affricates in English (i.e. /tʃ/ and /dʒ/) later than other phonemes (Olmsted, 1971; Prather *et al.*, 1975). So and Dodd (1995) also found that Cantonese-speaking children acquired the two affricates later than all the other phonemes. Timm (1977, cited in Locke, 1983) found that in Russian the affricate /tʃ/ ranked eighth of the 33 consonants in terms of error scores.

However, it is premature to conclude that affrication is a marked feature. Locke (1983) discussed the research into other languages that have a different pattern of affrication acquisition. For example, two affricates were among the first group of phonemes to be acquired in Japanese (Yasuda, 1970, cited in Locke, 1983). Battacchi *et al.* (1964, cited in Locke, 1983) also reported the early acquisition of the affricate /tʃ/ by Italian children.

The discrepancies associated with the acquisition of a particular feature such as affrication highlight the possibility of the influence of the ambient language on acquisition. The cross-linguistic differences also reflect the explanatory inadequacies of the theoretical concept of markedness or default features. The current theories are able to explain acquisition order similarities. However, they do not account for cross-linguistic differences.

3.6.3 Error patterns

The error patterns used by the children acquiring the Putonghua phonological system distinctively revealed both universal tendencies and language-specific constraints on acquisition. Structural simplifications such as assimilation, deletion, and reduction, and systemic substitutions such as stopping, fronting, backing, gliding were evident in Putonghua-speaking children's speech sample. These error patterns are similar across languages. Table 3.12 compares the error patterns used by Putonghua-, Cantonese-, English- and Italian-speaking children. Despite discrepancies in terminology and analysis method, the structural simplification error patterns are very similar. There are noticeable cross-linguistic differences, however, in the systemic substitution error patterns. Some of these differences can be attributed to the language-specific phonological characteristics.

Table 3.12 Error patterns used by more than 10% of Putonghua-, Cantonese-, English- or Italian-speaking children of different age groups

	Putonghua	Cantonese (So & Dodd, 1995)	English (Grunwell, 1982)	Italian (Bortolini & Leonard, 1991)
1;6–2;0	Assimilation; IC deletion; Fronting ʂ→s; Backing ts→tʃ; X-velarisation; Triphthong reduction; Diphthong reduction; Stopping ts→t; Final n deletion; Final ŋ deletion; Affrication; Deaspiration; Aspiration; n→ŋ; Gliding ɹ→j	Cluster reduction; Assimilation; Stopping f/s/ts/tsʰ; Fronting kʰ→t; Deaspiration; /h/ deletion; Affrication	Reduplication; Consonant harmony; Final consonant deletion; Cluster reduction; Fronting of velars; Stopping; Gliding r→w; Context sensitive voicing	Assimilation; Weak syllable deletion; Closer reduction; Metathesis; Epenthesis; Liquid deviation; Obstruent devoicing; Spirantisation
2;1–2;6	Assimilation; IC deletion; Fronting ʂ→s; Backing ts→tʃ; X-velarisation; Triphthong reduction; Diphthong reduction; Stopping ts→t; Final n deletion; Final ŋ deletion; Affrication; Deaspiration; Aspiration; n→ŋ; Gliding ɹ→j	Cluster reduction; Assimilation	Final consonant deletion; Cluster reduction; Fronting of velars; Stopping; Gliding r→w; Context sensitive voicing	
2;7–3;0	Assimilation; IC deletion; Triphthong reduction; Diphthong reduction; Final n deletion; Fronting ʂ→s; Backing ts→tʃ; X-velarisation; Stopping ts→t; Affrication	Cluster reduction; Assimilation; Stopping f/s/ts/tsʰ; Fronting kʰ→t; Deaspiration; Affrication; Deaffrication	——————; Stopping /v ð z tʃ dʒ/; ɵ→f; Fronting ʃ→s; Gliding r→w; Context sensitive voicing	

	Putonghua	Cantonese (So & Dodd, 1995)	English (Grunwell, 1982)	Italian (Bortolini & Leonard, 1991)
2;7–3;0 cont.	Final ŋ deletion n→ŋ Deaspiration Aspiration Gliding ɹ→j	--------	Stopping /v ð/	
3;1–3;6	Assimilation IC deletion Triphthong reduction Diphthong reduction Final n deletion Final ŋ deletion n→ŋ Fronting ʂ→s Backing ts→tʃ X-velarisation Stopping ts→t Affrication Deaspiration Aspiration Gliding ɹ→j	Cluster reduction Stopping f/s/ts/tsʰ Fronting kʰ→t Deaspiration	-------- ə→f Fronting of /tʃ dʒ ʃ/ Gliding r→w	
3;7–4;0	IC deletion Triphthong reduction Diphthong reduction Final n deletion n→ŋ Fronting ʂ→s Backing ts→tʃ X-velarisation Stopping ts →t Deaspiration Aspiration Gliding ɹ→j	Cluster reduction Stopping	-------- ə→f ð→d/v Palatalisation of /tʃ dʒ ʃ/ Gliding r→w	
4;1–4;6	IC deletion Triphthong reduction Diphthong reduction Final n deletion n→ŋ Fronting ʂ→s Backing ts→tʃ X-velarisation Stopping ts→t Deaspiration	--------	--------	

The six aspirated/unaspirated paris of phonemes in Putonghua allowed exploration of the acquisition process of the distinctive feature of aspiration. While deaspiration and aspiration error patterns were both evident, deaspiration was more prevalent (The six aspirated/unaspirated pairs of phonemes in Putonghua allowed 56% of the children de-aspirated). Although the children continued to deaspirate phonemes throughout the age groups described, aspiration was suppressed earlier. Cantonese-speaking children's use of aspiration and deaspiration error patterns is similar to Putonghua children's (So & Dodd, 1995). These patterns suggest that children acquire the unmarked before the marked member of a pair irrespective of languages. These findings support the existence of universal tendencies in cross-linguistic phonological acquisition.

Some error patterns, such as syllable-initial consonant deletion, indicate the children's high sensitivity to the characteristics of Putonghua phonology. Syllable-initial consonant deletion always occurred before the vowels /i/, /u/ or /y/. This pattern may reflect the flexible function of these three vowels. The vowels /i/, /u/ and /y/ can occur either as simple vowels, or as a component of diphthongs and triphthongs, such as /iɛ/ or /uei/. As mentioned in Chapter 2, the status of these vowels has been debated. Traditionally these sounds have been described as the first element of a diphthong or triphthong: they function as 'medial sounds' or 'prenucleus glides' between the syllable-initial consonant and the following vowel, having a shorter duration than the following main vowels. Several studies (e.g. Wang, 1989) have challenged this traditional description and proposed that the Putonghua syllable has a branching onset consisting of a consonant and a glide (i.e. syllable-initial consonant and /i/, /u/ or /y/). In other words, these three vowels form part of syllable-initial clusters. Therefore, the error pattern of syllable-initial consonant deletion could be considered as cluster reduction.

As reviewed in Section 1.2.1.1, the acquisition of the liquid /ɹ/ has been widely discussed in cross-linguistic studies. Bortolini and Leonard (1991) compared the acquisition of this phoneme in several languages. They discovered that /ɹ/ was frequently replaced by [l] in Italian-, Hindi-, Igbo-, Portuguese-, Quiche- and Spanish-speaking children. However, English-speaking children substituted the glide [w]. In this study, 28% of Putonghua-speaking children substituted [j], another glide, for /ɹ/. Only 4% of the children replaced the sound with [l]. Bortolini and Leonard argued that the cross-linguistic difference between English and Italian was due to the restricted use of /w/ in Italian, as well as phonetic differences in each language. However, similar restrictions do not account for

Putonghua-speaking children's use of /j/ rather than /w/. In Putonghua, /w/ and /j/ are variants of medial or pre-nucleus vowels /u/ and /i/. They are equally flexible in their combinations with other vowels or consonants. There might be other factors affecting the pattern of children's systemic simplification of speech.

3.6.4 Factors affecting systemic simplification

The acquisition of Putonghua phonology has shown that children do not always simplify their speech by replacing difficult sounds with sounds that are easier to articulate. The long delay between emergence and stabilisation of some phonemes (particularly the three alveolo-palatals) undermines the role of biological constraints on this stage of acquisition. Further, while markedness may account for some error patterns (e.g. the unidirectional replacement of aspirated sounds with unaspirated sounds), it does not account for cross-linguistic differences in the acquisition order of affricates.

The concept of functional load directly links order of phoneme acquisition to the role of those phonemes in a phonological system. However, previous proponents of functional load (e.g. Pye *et al.*, 1987) have failed to investigate the influence of aspects of phonology other than consonants on order of acquisition (So & Dodd, 1995). A simplified analysis of the impact of functional load, measuring only the load of consonants, does not explain the acquisition order of Putonghua phonemes. For example, Pye *et al.* (1987) argued that /ŋ/ has lower functional load than /m/ in English because /ŋ/ does not occur initially and thus has a smaller number of oppositions. In the same vein, /ŋ/ should also have a lower functional load than /n/ in Putonghua, since /ŋ/ does not occur word-initially in Putonghua. Consequently, children should acquire /n/ before /ŋ/. However, as shown in Table 3.9, the children made more errors on /n/. They either deleted /n/ or substituted /ŋ/. The phoneme /ŋ/, with a lower functional load, was acquired before /n/. These data suggest that Pye *et al.*'s (1987) notion of functional load is inadequate. Alternatively, the order of acquisition might be determined by the phonological saliency of a component within the language.

3.6.5 Phonological saliency

The notion of phonological saliency has been alluded to by others (e.g. Peters, 1983; Vihman, 1996), but there is no agreement on its definition. In the context of the current study, phonological saliency is used as a syllable-based, language-specific concept. It is determined and affected by a combination of several factors:

- The status of a component in the syllable structure, especially whether it is compulsory or optional; a compulsory component is more salient than an optional one.
- The capacity of a component in differentiating lexical meaning of a syllable; a component which is more capable of distinguishing lexical information is more salient than one which carries less lexical information.
- The number of permissible choices within a component in the syllable structure, e.g. 21 syllable-initial consonants would be considered less salient compared to four tonal contrasts.

With regard to Putonghua, tone has the highest saliency: it is compulsory for every syllable; change of tone would change lexical meaning; and there are only four alternative choices. Lexical information of a word in Putonghua is conveyed by both tone and phoneme sequence. Therefore, tone is crucial in differentiating lexical meaning.[3] In contrast, other syllable components are less vital: information lost by an incorrect phoneme within a phoneme sequence can be remedied to some extent by other phonemes in the sequence (e.g. in English we could guess that [lelou] means *yellow*). The phoneme sequence as a whole unit shares the task of conveying lexical meaning. Therefore, the significance of each phoneme in a sequence is less than tone.

The saliency value of vowels and syllable-final consonants is next to that of tone. Although vowels are compulsory syllable components, the relatively large number of options (21 in total including simple vowels, diphthongs and triphthongs) lowers their saliency, compared with tones. While there are only two syllable-final consonants, their saliency is undermined by their optional presence in the syllable structure.

Syllable-initial consonants, among the four Putonghua syllable components, have the lowest saliency: their presence is optional (not all syllables have syllable-initial consonants); and there is a range of 21 syllable-initial phonemes that can be used. Compared with the saliency of tones, consonants and vowels, the saliency of weak stress and rhotacised feature is much lower. Neither 'weak stress' nor rhotacised feature is a compulsory syllable component, and their value in differentiating lexical meaning is low.

The higher saliency value a syllable component has, the more accessible and noticeable it would be to children and the earlier it would be acquired. Therefore, tones, which has the highest saliency in Putonghua, were acquired earlier than syllable-final consonants and vowels. The syllable-final consonants and vowels were acquired earlier than syllable-initial consonants. The features of 'weak stress' and rhotacisation were acquired last due to their low saliency value.

The role of phonological saliency in the acquisition of various syllable components is also supported by the previous research findings. So and Dodd (1995) reported that the consonant acquisition rate of Cantonese-speaking children was more rapid compared to that of English-speaking children. Cantonese-speaking children acquired their range of consonants by 3;6. English-speaking children's phoneme repertoires were not complete until they were five-years-old (Prather *et al.*, 1975). These discrepancies in consonant acquisition rates between Cantonese and English reflect different saliency ranking of the same syllable component in the two languages (see Appendix 3 for comparison of the phonological structure of Putonghua, Cantonese, English and Xhosa). Cantonese has only 17 consonants and two clusters, while English has 24 consonants and 49 clusters. Although consonants are optional syllable components in both languages, the larger number of consonants and clusters in English lowers the saliency of each consonant. Therefore, the rate of acquisition in English is slower than that of Cantonese.

Similarly, Mowrer and Burger (1991) found that Xhosa-speaking children acquired most consonant phonemes earlier than their English-speaking counterparts. although Xhosa has 41 consonants, it has a very simple syllable structure. A typical Xhosa syllable is structured as CV. In addition, Xhosa has very few consonant clusters. Their relatively indispensable status in a syllable and lack of clusters thus contribute to the higher saliency of consonants in Xhosa and explain their early acquisition, when compared to English.

It should be noted, however, that phonological saliency as defined here is a language-specific concept. The saliency value of a particular feature is primarily determined by its role within the phonological system of the language, not by reference to other languages. Secondly, the concept of phonological saliency is different from linguistic markedness and functional load in that it is cognitive in nature and characterises the accessibility or noticeability of certain linguistic forms to children. It seems to be the case that children's are likely to acquire those phonological features which are made readily available and highly noticeable to them via the input they receive.

3.6.6 Interaction between lexical and phonological acquisition

The acquisition of weak stress and rhotacisation in Putonghua reflects interactions between lexical and phonological development. The children's tendency to use citation tones in the place of weak stress may be attributed to caretakers' often exaggerated manner of speaking in which citation tones are given to weakly stressed syllables (Li & Thompson, 1977; Erbaugh, 1992). However, it is arguable whether the acquisition of these features are rule-based or lexically motivated. Most of the children in the study made consistent errors with the weak stress syllable /tsi/ when it occurred in different syllable contexts. If the learning of weak stress took place on a word-by-word basis, different error types would have been present. Further investigation is needed to examine the interaction of phonological and lexical constraints in children's phonological and lexical development.

3.6.7 Variations in children's phonological development

The role of gender in language acquisition is a controversial issue. Some researchers argued for the existence of differences in the phonological development between girls and boys, probably due to biological differentiation between them in the rate of maturation of the left cerebral hemisphere (Kagan, 1971), in the rate of lateralisation (Buffery, 1970; 1971) or in the pattern of hemispheric development (Shucard *et al.*, 1987). Other researchers argued that there were differences between boys and girls either in the rate of language development or in the style of language acquisition as the result of differences in the language input they received (Wells, 1985).

The statistical analysis in this study confirmed the previous findings by Mowrer and Burger (1991) and Ritterman and Richtner (1979) in that there is no difference in the rate of phonological acquisition between boys and girls. No interaction is found between gender and age (cf. Wellman *et al.*, 1931; Poole, 1934). A plausible explanation is that while biological differentiation or input differences between boys and girls might result in gender-related differences in some other aspects of language development (such as semantics, syntax or pragmatics), phonological acquisition is little affected by such biological differentiation or input differences. Alternatively, the differences in the amount or quality of language input received by boys and girls are not as considerable as they used to be. Templin (1963) argued that many studies did not find gender-related difference simply because boys and girls were brought up in a increasingly similar language environment. In this study, all the children, boys and girls, are the only child in their families due to the implementation of 'one family one child' policy in China. The discrimination against girls is minimal in a metropolitan city like Beijing. The role of some variables in language development may change with changes in social and cultural environments.

The argument that exposure to two or more languages might have an impact on children's language and speech development has been supported by studies on bilingual children. Research on simultaneous bilingual children (i.e. children acquiring two languages at the same time from birth) suggests that they would follow separate paths of development from monolingual children. Ingram (1981) analysed the speech errors of a two-year-old Italian-English bilingual child and found that their error patterns were different from that of Italian or English monolingual children. Dodd *et al.* (1997) found that the phonological acquisition of young Cantonese–English bilingual children was characterised by unusual error patterns in both languages. Exposure to two or more languages also has an impact on children's phonological awareness (Campbell & Sais, 1995; Rubin & Turner, 1988; Bruck & Genesee, 1995).

It has been accepted that second language learning is strongly influenced by the learner's first language (see Ellis, 1985; Larsen-Freeman & Long, 1991). For example, the influence of L1 on L2 phonology is evident in the 'foreign' accent of second language learners (Ellis, 1985). A collateral question would be whether learning a second language in a monolingual environment would affect the phonological development of the first language?

The data analysis in this study showed that the children who had learned English did not show any significant difference from the children who have not in terms of the number of errors present in the children's speech. A possible explanation is that the amount of input was not sufficient for the expected impact on the phonological development to take place. Second language *learning* in a monolingual environment is different from second language *acquisition* in a bilingual environment in that the amount of language input is extremely impoverished in the former condition. In this study, the Putonghua-speaking children were exposed to very limited amount of English: four hours a week at school plus occasional input from their parents. It needs to be pointed out that the school teacher and the children's parents are second language learners themselves. This perhaps shows how important both the quality and quantity of language input are in language acquisition.

3.7 Summary

The cross-sectional data in this chapter established the phonological development norms for Putonghua-speaking children aged 1;6–4;6. Putonghua (Modern Standard Mandarin) syllables have four possible elements: tone, syllable-initial consonant, vowel, and syllable-final consonant. The children's errors suggested that Putonghua-speaking children completed the acquisition of these elements in the following order: tones first; then syllable-final consonants and vowels; and syllable-initial consonants last. The phonetic acquisition of the 21 syllable-initial consonants was complete by 3;6 for 75% of children. By 4;6 the children were using the syllable-initial consonants correctly on two-thirds of occasions (with the exception of four affricates). Simple vowels emerged early in development. However, triphthongs and diphthongs were prone to systematic errors. Tonal errors were rare, perhaps because of their role in distinguishing lexical meaning. In contrast, the acquisition of 'weak stress' and 'rhotacised feature' was incomplete in the oldest children assessed. Error patterns used by the children were identified. Two of these error patterns, syllable-initial consonant deletion and backing, would be considered atypical in English. Existing theories of phonological acquisition (e.g. markedness, functional load) cannot account for some of the patterns revealed. A satisfactory explanation of the findings requires more attention to the specific characteristics of the linguistic system the children are learning. It is proposed that the saliency of the components in the language system determines the order of acquisition.

The norms may be used either for cross-linguistic comparison (as in this chapter) or for assessing children in atypical circumstances (in Chapters 5, 6, 7 and 8). However, the very nature of cross-sectional data makes it difficult to make reliable estimates of the interrelationship between the age factor and developmental changes, especially those relatively small but steady changes over time. In addition, out of concerns for the feasibility of the picture-naming and picture-description task, the age group 1;6–2;0 was set up to be the youngest age group in this study. As a result, detailed information on the development of tones, vowels and some consonants, which might be acquired at an early stage, was missing. To explore these issues further, a longitudinal study on four children between 12 and 24 months was carried out and is reported in the next chapter.

Notes

1. Chinese national romanisation is an alphabetical writing system designed for Chinese in 1920s. It was later developed into *'Hanyu pinyin'* which is widely used today in China. A main difference between the two systems is that the former uses letters to spell tones, while the latter adopts diacritics.
2. The varied frequency of phonemes targeted in the data collection may have affected the results (e.g. opportunities for each phoneme) to some extent. However, as the phonemes which had the same frequency in the picture-

naming task showed different age of emergence and stabilisation, it was unlikely that the overall findings on the age of acquisition and chronology of error patterns were an artefact of the seemingly unbalanced frequency distribution. In addition, the same picture-naming task was administered in assessing the phonological development of children with speech disorders, children with hearing impairment, and twins in the following studies. Comparisons were made between the speech data of the children under study and those of normally developing children collected using the same picture-naming and picture-description tasks. Therefore, variations in the frequency of occurrence of phonemes are less likely to interfere with the assessment process and the results.

3. There are about 420 full syllables in Putonghua if the tonal differentiations are not counted and about 1300 if they are counted, according to Xiandai hanyu cidian (1979).

Chapter 4
Phonological Acquisition of Normally Developing Children. II: Longitudinal Study

4.1 Introduction

Longitudinal studies have long been claimed to be very effective in studies of age-related development and individual differences, especially in the studies of relatively small but stable development over time (Ingram, 1989a). In a typical longitudinal study, a small number of children are observed over a considerable period of time or repeatedly sampled at predetermined intervals within a long period. With other variables of an individual subject being stable over time (such as gender, socio-economic status, parents' background, etc.), researchers are able to put the collected data on one subject in parallel, comparing each observation with some earlier or later observation. If there are changes in the performance over time, researchers can make reliable estimates of the interrelationship between the age factor and changes.

While the close observation in longitudinal studies can provide a clear picture of a child's development at various stages, it is difficult to generalise the findings of such studies due to individual variations and preferences at the various stages of development. Another apparent drawback of longitudinal studies is that it is very time-consuming and slow in progress.

With these strengths and weaknesses of longitudinal studies in mind, this chapter reports on the findings from a study of four children during the age of one to two. Section 4.2 reviews the previous findings on the development of suprasegmental features of Mandarin (i.e. tones, tone sandhi, weak stress). Subject information and data collection methods are discussed in detail in 4.3 below, followed by data analysis in 4.4. Section 4.5 reports the results, which are discussed in 4.6.

4.2 Previous Studies

4.2.1 Tones

As has been described in 2.5, the four tones in Putonghua are lexical tones, for differences in tones result in different lexical meanings. However, while lexical tones are widely regarded as one of the most salient features of the Chinese languages, there is relatively little research on tonal acquisition by Chinese-speaking children. Most of the existing studies of Chinese tonal acquisition (on Mandarin, see Chao, 1951; Li & Thompson, 1977; Li, 1977; Clumeck, 1977, 1980; Su, 1985; Jeng, 1985; Hsu, 1987; Shiu, 1990; on Cantonese, see Tse, 1978; Tse, 1992) were carried out in 70s and 80s. These studies generally agreed that the acquisition of the tones precedes that of segments, and that some tones were acquired earlier than others. However, the details on the order of acquisition of tones, age of acquisition and error patterns identified in these studies differed from each other. To be specific,

- The age of acquisition of tones: Clumeck (1980) reported a study of one subject who did not finish the acquisition of tones until the age of 3;0. Shiu (1990) also found the late completion of tonal acquisition – neither of the two children in her study had acquired rising and falling–rising tones by the end of data collection when they were aged 3;0 and 2;4. However, Jeng (1979) revealed that one of his subjects was able to produce tones correctly by the age of 1;7,15 and another by the age of 1;5.
- The order of acquisition of tones: Clumeck (1977) found that the rising tones were acquired first when the subject began to use words at about the age of 1;10. Li (1977) briefly mentioned that his subject seemed to have acquired high level, rising, and high falling tones before falling–rising tones. A different order was reported by Jeng (1979). In his study, rising and falling–rising tones were acquired more or less simultaneously and without much difficulty.

4.2.2 Tone sandhi

Tone sandhi is another prominent suprasegmental feature in Putonghua. As reviewed in 2.6, there are four rules, two of which affects falling–rising tone:

- Tone 3 sandhi rule 1: a falling rising tone → a rising tone before another falling rising tone.
- Tone 3 sandhi rule 2: a falling rising tone → a falling tone before high level, rising or high falling tones.
- Tone 4 sandhi rule: a high falling tone → a low falling tone before another high falling tone.
- Morphologically conditioned sandhi rule: four lexical items (i.e. /pu4/, /i1/, /tɕ1/ and /pA1/) follow their own rules. Their citation tones will become rising before high falling tones. /i/ will become a high falling tone before all the tones except a high falling tone.

Among these four rules, tone 3 sandhi rules have received the most research attention. Chao (1951) reported that his subject only began to use tone 3 sandhi rules at the age of 2;4. Li and Thompson (1977) pointed out that the late emergence of tone sandhi rules in the children's speech might be related to the fact that tone sandhi rules, which are only applicable when two or more syllables are involved, are linked to children's ability to produce multi-word utterances. In other words, children cannot be said to be actively applying a tone sandhi rule until they have been able to produce multi-word uttrances. Besides this, they argued that children were able to learn tone sandhi rules with infrequent errors as soon as they began to produce multi-word uttrances. This argument was supported by Jeng (1979), who found his subject made very few errors where tone sandhi rules should apply. Jeng also reported that the morphologically conditioned tone sandhi rule was acquired later than tone 3 sandhi rules. Individual variations in acquiring these tone sandhi rules were reported in Shiu (1990). She found that tone 3 sandhi rules appeared in one child's speech as early as at the age of 1;1. However, the rules did not become stabilised until 2;4. The other subject in her study was able to produce the rule at the age of 1;5 and reached a certain level of accuracy by the age of 2;8. Error patterns, if any, were little described in these studies.

4.2.3 Weak stress

As reviewed in 2.7, weak stress can be described in several types:

- 'affix' type in which weak stress occurs to the affix of nouns. For example, /tsi/ 'zi' in /pitsi/ ('*nose*');
- 'reduplication' type in which the reduplicated second syllables in nouns, verbs and adjectives are weakly stressed; for example, /çinçin/ ('*star*') and /çieçiɛ/ ('*thank you*');
- 'grammatical particle' type in which particles such as /lɤ/ 'le', /pɐ/ 'ba' are weakly stressed;
- 'lexeme' type in which two lexemes, especially nouns, are combined together and the stress of the second lexeme is weakly stressed, for example, /ɚtuo/ ('*ear*'), /tʰoʊfʌ/ ('*hair*').

Li and Thompson (1977) claimed that the tones of weakly stressed syllables were often replaced with citation tones in children's speech during the process of acquisition. Shiu (1990) found an opposite pattern: in the first stage of phonological development, the accuracy of weak stress production was high in the speech of both of her subjects. However, one child's accuracy rating of weak stress plunged during the following stages while that of the other kept increasing during the observation period. Su

(1985) suggested that children might use different strategies in the substitution of full tones for weak stress, depending on different contexts. The weakly stressed syllables occurring in utterance-final particles, classifiers, particle '*de*', and nouns ending with '*tsi*' were likely to be replaced with low falling tones, while the weakly stressed syllables in disyllabic words were likely to change into citation tones.

4.2.4 Summary of previous findings

Several factors might account for the discrepancies in the reported findings:

- Different criteria were used in these studies . For example, to say a tone has been acquired can either refer to the cases when children are able to pronounce tones accurately according to the underlying representations of tones of each morpheme, or the cases when children are able to apply, at a lexical level, the phonological rules governing tone sandhi where appropriate.
- The existence of individual variations in phonological development also leads to disagreement in the above studies.
- The discrepancy in the subjects' age at onset of study in some studies (Jeng, 1979; Clumeck, 1980; Li, 1977) further affected comparability of the subjects within and across studies.
- The target language environment of the children in the studies was not the same. The children in Chao (1957) and Clumeck's (1980) studies were acquiring Mandarin in America (English-dominant, L2 environment). The children in Su (1985), Hsu (1987) and Shiu's (1990) studies were acquiring Mandarin and Taiwanese (or Hokkien, of the Southern Min dialectal group of Chinese; see further 2.1) simultaneously in Taiwan. It is arguable whether the patterns of tonal acquisition identified in the speech of children exposed to two languages are comparable to those of monolingual children.

The present longitudinal study is primarily aimed to systematically describe the patterns of acquisition of suprasegmental features in Putonghua, including lexical tones, tone sandhi and weak stress, and the patterns of acquisition of vowels and some of the consonants by young, monolingual Putonghua-speaking children in Beijing. We shall examine both the 'emergence' (i.e. first appearance) and 'stabilisation' (i.e. consistent production) of a particular feature. More specifically, the following aspects will be examined:

- the age and order of emergence and stabilisation of tones;
- the error patterns associated with tones;

- the age and order of emergence and stabilisation of tone sandhi;
- the error patterns associated with tone sandhi;
- the age of emergence and stabilisation of weak stress;
- the error patterns associated with weak stress;
- the patterns of acquisition of vowels and consonants, particularly those consonants acquired before the age of two (cf. cross-sectional study in Chapter 3).

4.3 Method

4.3.1 Participants

Four children (referred to as J.J., Z.J., H.Y. and Z.W.) were recruited in Beijing. The children were aged 1;1.15, 1;0.0, 0;10.15 and 1;2.0 at the beginning of the data collection. The data collection ended when the children reached the age of two with the exception of the fourth child (Z.W.) whose family moved abroad when she was 1;8. The subject information is summarised in Table 4.1.

Table 4.1 Subject information in the longitudinal study of normally developing children

Child	Gender	Age range	Age of four-word point	Total number of tokens in the data
J.J.	girl	1;1.15–2;0.15	1;2.0	947
Z.J.	boy	1;0.0–2;0.15	1;4.0	683
H.Y.	boy	0;10.15–2;0.15	1;2.0	890
Z.W.	girl	1;2.0–1;8.0	1;2.15	432

Note: Four-word point is defined by Vihman (1996) as the approximate beginning of lexical use.

All of the children were acquiring Putonghua monolingually as their first language. They were the only child in the family. They were healthy and had no hearing impairment according to their medical records. Their motor development was reported to be within normal range. One or both of the parents of the children were working in the University where the recruitment for this study took place. All the parents were Putonghua speakers. Two of the children were taken care of mainly by the family relatives in the day and the other two went to a private nursery.

4.3.2 Data collection

Data collection took place every 15 days. In each data collection session, the mothers were asked to talk with the children while playing together. The mothers were also asked to repeat the children's words when they could so that the target/adult forms were recorded on tape for ease of later transcription. Each session lasted about one hour. The conversation was recorded using a Sony professional micro-recorder. Mini-microphones were pinned to the children.

The mothers were trained together before the first data collection session. They were given detailed guidelines as to what they were expected to do in the data collection. This, to a certain extent, guaranteed consistency in the data collection method used for different children and between different data collection sessions for the same child.

4.3.3 Transcription

The speech samples from each session were transcribed using the International Phonetic Alphabet. Inter-transcriber reliability (on 10% of the samples) for syllable-initial word-initial, syllable-initial within-word, syllable-final word-final, and syllable-final within-word consonants was 94.3%, 92.9%, 98.5% and 98.1% respectively. Imitated productions from the children were marked in the data analysis. The unintelligible productions (i.e. the targets of these productions were not clear from the context) were also marked.

4.4 Data Analysis

Words were identified using the criteria proposed by Vihman and McCune (1994), which are briefly summarised below:

- Criteria based on context: vocalisations will be identified as words when their meanings are easily identified in contexts or by the mother, or when they are used by the child more than once with similar phonological shapes across different uses. An imitative response to a verbal stimulus is not considered as a word.
- Criteria based on vocalisation shape: vocalisations will be identified as words when they match more than two segments of the adult form, or when the prosody (in the present study, the tone) of the vocalisations matches the adult target.

- Criteria based on relation to other vocalisations: vocalisations will be recognised as words when vocalisations are instances of imitation produced with apparent understanding, when all instances of vocalisations share the same phonological shape, or when all uses of vocalisations occur in contexts which plausibly suggest the same word.

Although the data collection took place before or very closely to the onset of speech, the present study was limited to the analysis of the children's productions when the children had attempted to produce at least four or more different adult words in two subsequent sessions (i.e. the four-word point defined by Vihman (1996: 249) as the approximate beginning of lexical use). Table 4.1 lists the age of the four-word point for each child. A maximum of 50 tokens were transcribed for each recording. The target words the children were attempting were identified based either on the mothers' repetition of the children's vocalisations or the contexts. The words whose target adult forms were ambiguous would be marked. Unlike the previous cross-sectional study, imitated responses were included in the data analysis, following Ferguson and Farwell's arguments (1975: 422). The main reasons for including imitated responses were:

- very little data would be available if imitated utterances were excluded, since a very high percentage of the utterances produced by children aged 1;0–2;0 are imitation;
- technically, no simple definition of imitation is feasible, because children of this age band can 'repeat' or 'imitate' adult forms after a considerable interval or they may include some elements not present in the adult model in their imitation.

It should be noted that the range of words recorded and transcribed did not guarantee opportunities for the child to attempt all the features. Since the data were collected spontaneously, the occurrence of the target features (whether a child would have a chance to use a feature or how many times a feature would occur) varied from one child to another and from one data collection session to another. Therefore, the mere non-existence of a feature in children's production did not mean that the child could not produce it. This needs to be taken into consideration when interpreting the results.

4.5 Results

4.5.1 Vowels

The age of emergence of Putonghua vowels (i.e. the age when a vowel was produced phonetically correctly in a lexical item for the first time) in the speech of the four children was presented in Table 4.2. Because the nature of spontaneous speech, not all the Putonghua vowels were sampled. The fact that vowels carry a heavy lexical load made difficult the identification of children's realisations in which target vowels were substituted. If the target word of such a realisation was unclear, the realisation had to be excluded in the data analysis.

Table 4.2 Age of emergence of vowels in the longitudinal study (in year; month, day)

Vowels	J.J.	Z.J.	H.Y.	Z.W.
i	1;3	1;4	1;5	1;2.15
y	1;3.15	1;7	1;8.15	1;6
u	1;2.15	1;4	1;2	1;3
ɤ	1;5.15	1;9	1;2	1;2.15
o	1;7.15	1;9	no data	1;7.15
ʌ	1;2	1;4	1;2	1;2.15
ɚ	1;7.15	1;7	no data	no data
ae	1;5.15	1;8	1;4.15	1;5.15
ɑo	1;4	1;7	1;3	1;5
ei	1;2.15	1;7	1;2	1;3
oʊ	1;3	1;8	1;5	1;4.15
ia	1;3.15	1;8	1;4	1;3.15
iɛ	1;3.15	1;8.15	1;2.15	1;2.15
ua	1;5.15	1;7.15	1;2.15	1;3.15
uo	1;7.15	1;9.15	1;8	1;5
yɛ	1;10	no data	no data	1;6.15
iɑo	1;3.15	1;6.15	1;6.15	1;5.15
ioʊ	1;3.15	1;4.15	1;5.15	1;3.15
uae	1;6.15	1;9.15	1;5.15	1;6
uei	1;4.15	1;8	1;6	1;3.15
Mean age of emergence of simple vowels	1;4.15	1;6.9	1;3.27	1;4.2
Mean age of emergence of diphthongs	1;5	1;7.24	1;3.27	1;4.12
Mean age of emergence of triphthongs	1;4.15	1;7.3	1;5.26	1;4.18

Despite these methodological difficulties as well as individual differences, some patterns were identifiable in the development of vowels in the children. Among the simple vowels, the central low vowel /A/ and back high vowel /u/ were the earliest to emerge in the four children; the retroflex vowel /ɚ/ and the back vowel /o/ seemed to be the last simple vowels to emerge in the children's output. Among diphthongs, /ei/ was the first to emerge for all the children, and /yɛ/ the last. Among triphthongs, /iou/ emerged first in three children's speech, while /uae/ was the last for three children. Among the four children, Z.J. was the slowest in learning the simple vowels, diphthongs and triphthongs.

4.5.2 Consonants

Tables 4.3 and 4.4 show the age of emergence and stabilisation of consonants. If a sound occurred in a child's realisation of a meaning unit, the sound would be considered as 'emerged' irrespective of whether it was the correct target. A sound was 'stabilised' when the child produced the sound phonologically correctly on at least two of three opportunities. By the end of the data collection (J.J., Z.J. and H.Y. were 24 months old and Z.W. 20 months old), syllable-initial consonants /p, t, m/ and syllable-final consonants /n, ŋ/ had become stabilised in the speech of all the children. There were variations in the emergence of sounds: while J.J. and H.Y. were found to have produced all the Putonghua sounds except two sounds once or several times, Z.J. had never used the sounds /pʰ, kʰ, ʂ, tɕʰ, tʂʰ, tsʰ/. Most of the aspirated sounds were missing from his repertoire. Z.W., whose data collection ended at the age of 1;8, had never produced the sounds /pʰ, tʰ, kʰ, ɹ, tɕʰ, tʂʰ, tsʰ/ in his speech.

Table 4.3 Four children's phonetic inventories at different age

Age	*J.J.*	*Z.J.*	*H.Y.*	*Z.W.*
1;2			m	m
1;2.15	k, ŋ		p	t, n-
1;3	p		t	
1;3.15	t, m			s, x
1;4		t		p
14.15	n-, -n	ŋ	ŋ	ŋ
1;5	tɕ	p	l	ʂ
1;5.15	tʰ, x, ɕ		n-	ɕ, tʂ, ts, -n

Table 4.3 *cont.*

Age	J.J.	Z.J.	H.Y.	Z.W.
1;6	f			f, l
1;6.15	ts	m, n-		k, tɕ
1;7	s, tsʰ	s	k	
1;7.15	pʰ, l,ɹ			
1;8		tɕ, -n	pʰ, tʰ, s, x, tɕ, -n	
1;8.15		x, ts	ɕ	No data
1;9		k, ɹ		No data
1;9.15		l	f	No data
1;10	ʂ	tʂ	kʰ	No data
1;10.15	tʂ	f	tsʰ	No data
1;11		tʰ	ʂ, tʂ	No data
1;11.15		ɕ	ts, tɕʰ	No data
2;0	tʂʰ			No data
2;0.15				No data
Missing phonemes	kʰ, tɕʰ	pʰ, kʰ, ʂ, tɕʰ, tsʰ, tʂʰ	ɹ, tʂʰ	pʰ, tʰ, kʰ, ɹ, tɕʰ, tʂʰ, tsʰ

Note: '-n' = syllable-final consonant /n/; 'n-'= syllable-initial consonant /n/.

Table 4.4 Four children's phonemic inventories at different age

Age	J.J.	Z.J.	H.Y.	Z.W.
1;2				
1;2.15				
1;3				
1;3.15				t
1;4				
14.15	m, ŋ			ŋ
1;5				m
1;5.15				-n
1;6		p		

Table 4.4 *cont.*

Age	J.J.	Z.J.	H.Y.	Z.W.
1;6.15	-n	t		p, k1;7
	m			
1;7.15				
1;8	p, t	-n, ŋ	m	
1;8.15				No data
1;9		n-	t, -n, ŋ	No data
1;9.15				No data
1;10				No data
1;10.15	ç		l, tç	No data
1;11				No data
1;11.15				No data
2;0			p	No data
2;0.15				No data
Missing phonemes	pʰ, tʰ, k, kʰ, n-, f, s, x, ʂ, l, ɹ, tɕ, tɕʰ, tʂ, tʂʰ, ts, tsʰ	pʰ, tʰ, k, kʰ, f, s, x, ʂ, l, ɹ, tɕ, tɕʰ, ɕ, tʂ, tʂʰ, ts, tʂʰ	pʰ, tʰ, k, kʰ, n-, f, s, x, ʂ, ɹ, tɕʰ, ɕ, tʂ, tsʰ, ts, tsʰ	pʰ, tʰ, kʰ, n-, f, s, x, ʂ, l, ɹ, tɕ, tɕʰ, ɕ, tʂ, tʂʰ, ts, tsʰ

Note: '-n' = syllable-final consonant /n/; 'n-'= syllable-initial consonant /n/.

4.5.3 Tones

4.5.3.1 Emergence of tones

　　Table 4.5 summarises the age at which the four Putonghua tones emerged in the children's speech. A tone was considered to have emerged when a child could produce it at least once either in his spontaneous speech or in imitation.

　　In terms of emergence, high level and high falling tones were earliest and they both existed in all the children's speech data collected at the time when the children began to produce first words (4-word point). Rising tone existed in two children's first words (Z.J. and Z.W.), yet it emerged about one month later than high level and high falling tones in the other two children. Falling–rising tone was the last to emerge in all the four children.

Table 4.5 Age of emergence of tones

	J.J.	*Z.J.*	*H.Y.*	*Z.W.*
High level tone	1;2*	1;4*	1;2*	1;2.15*
Rising tone	1;3	1;4*	1;3	1;2.15*
Falling–rising tone	1;4	1;7	1;5	1;4.15
High falling tone	1;2*	1;4*	1;2*	1;2.15*

Note: '*' marks the age when the child uttered a recognisable meaningful word for the first time.

4.5.3.2 Age of stabilisation

A certain amount of inconsistency in children's speech production as well as fluctuation (termed reduction and regression by Ferguson and Farwell, 1975) in their overall language development was always a possibility. In addition, opportunities for each tone in the speech sample were not always equal. Consequently, a criterion was needed to determine the level of stability in the children's production. A tone was considered to become stabilised only when it satisfied all of the following standards:

- its accuracy rating in the spontaneous speech sample reached 66.7% level (accuracy rating = the number of times of a tone produced correctly / the number of opportunities for the tone in the sample × 100%);
- its accuracy rating in all the subsequent speech samples remained as high as or higher than 66.7%. This minimised the effect of regression;
- if there was only one opportunity for a tonal feature in the speech data recorded at a given time, the data would be excluded in deriving the age of stabilisation in case the child produced it solely on a formulaicly learned basis (e.g. '*thank you*'). This particular criterion was even more important when applied to tone sandhi and weak stress (see 4.5.2 and 4.5.3 below).

Tables 4.6 summarises the age of stabilisation derived using the 66.7% criterion. It was clear that high level tones were the first to be stabilised, followed by high falling tones. There were variations in the order of stabilisation of rising and falling–rising tones. Falling–rising tones were stabilised earlier than rising tones in two children, at the same time as rising tones in another child and later than rising tones in yet another child. The differences between the age of stabilisation of these two tones were small. The maximum interval between the age of stabilisation of falling–rising tones and rising tones was one month and a half in Z.W.'s productions.

Table 4.6 Age of stabilisation of tones

	J.J.	Z.J.	H.Y.	Z.W.
High level tone	1;4	1;5.15	1;2.15	1;2.15
Rising tone	1;7	1;8.15	1;8	1;6
Falling–rising tone	1;6.15	1;9.15	1;8	1;4.15
High falling tone	1;4.15	1;7	1;4	1;4.15

Differences between the age of emergence and stabilisation of each tone in each child were compared to examine the time it took for a feature to reach a certain level of phonological accuracy. The mean lengths of time between the age of emergence and that of stabilisation for high level, rising, falling–rising, and high falling tones were one, four, two, and two-and-a-half months, respectively.

4.5.3.3 Patterns of tonal errors
Some tones seemed to replace a certain tone more often than others in the children's speech (see Table 4.7).

Table 4.7 Frequency of occurrence of tonal error patterns (%)

Target	Realisation	J.J.	Z.J.	H.Y.	Z.W.
High level tone	rising	25.8	34.8	81	25
	falling–rising	54.8	17.4	81	0
	high falling	19.4	47.8	83.8	75
Rising tone	high level	40	68	56.5	62.5
	falling–rising	51.1	20	17.4	18.8
	high falling	89	12	26.1	18.8
Falling–rising tone	high level	35.6	35.9	54.2	73.3
	rising	44.4	46.2	20.8	67
	high falling	20	17.9	25	20
High falling tone	high level	77.5	70.8	80	83.3
	rising	10	16.7	14.3	0
	falling–rising	12.5	12.5	57	16.7

Note: The frequency of occurrence is calculated by the following formula: the number of times of a particular type of substitution/the total number of the occurrence of errors for a tone × 100%. Shaded cells highlight the most frequent substitution pattern for a tone.

Specifically,

(a) High level tones: three children preferred to use high falling tones to replace high level tones, while one child (J.J.) used falling–rising tones to replace high level tones in most cases.
(b) Rising tones: three children used high level tones to replace rising tones most frequently, while one child (J.J.) used falling–rising tones.
(c) Falling–rising tones: two children (H.Y. and Z.W.) preferred to replace falling–rising tones with high level tones while the others (J.J. and Z.J.) preferred to replace falling–rising tones with rising tones.
(d) High falling tones: All the children showed a preference to replace high falling tones with high level tones when an error occurred.

In general, high level tones seemed to be used in an 'unmarked' sense and were most frequently employed to replace other tones. Child J.J. seemed to be different from other children in her strategy: she preferred to use falling–rising tones to replace high level and rising tones in most cases.

4.5.4 Tone sandhi

4.5.4.1 Age of emergence and stabilisation of tone sandhi

As summarised in Chapter 2, Tone sandhi rules can be described in four types according to the tones involved and the conditions in which tone sandhi takes place. The age of emergence and stabilisation (using 66.7% criteria) of various types of tone sandhi is listed in Table 4.8. The age when the children reached 90% in the accuracy rating is also given for reference.

Table 4.8 Age of emergence and stabilisation of tone sandhi

		J.J.	Z J.	H.Y.	Z.W.
Tone 3 sandhi 1	Emergence	1;9	1;10	1;10.15	1;6
	Stabilisation (66.7%)	1;9	1;10	1;10.15	1;6
	Stabilisation (90%)	1;9	1;10	1;10.15	1;6
Tone 3 sandhi 2	Emergence	1;7.15	1;8	1;7	1;6
	Stabilisation (66.7%)	1;8	1;9	1;9.15	1;6
	Stabilisation (90%)	1;8	1;10.15	1;11	1;6
Tone 4 sandhi	Emergence	1;7.15	1;9	1;6	1;6
	Stabilisation (66.7%)	1;7.15	1;9	1;8.15	1;6
	Stabilisation (90%)	1;7.15	1;9	1;8.15	1;6
M conditioned sandhi	/pu/ emergence*	1;4	1;6.15	1;11	1;6
	/pu/ stabilisation (66.7%)	1;4	1;6.15	1;11	1;6
	/pu/ stabilisation (90%)	1;4	1;6.15	1.11	1;6

Note: /pu/ means 'no'.

It is difficult to speculate on the order of emergence and stabilisation of tone sandhi among the four children, partly because of the nature of the spontaneous data. There was little data on morphologically conditioned tone sandhi except the tone sandhi associated with the negative morpheme /pu/, due to the late acquisition of these lexical items. However, it is clear from the table that there was very little gap between the age of emergence and the age of stabilisation (66.7% criterion). It seemed that the tone sandhi rules were established very quickly once they emerged. This is confirmed by the comparison of two types of accuracy rating in the following section.

4.5.4.2 Accuracy rating of tone sandhi realisation

Two types of accuracy rating were calculated:

- One was the overall accuracy rating of tone sandhi (= the number of times tone sandhi is applied correctly in the speech sample/the number of opportunities when tone sandhi should be applied in the speech sample × 100%).
- The second was the accuracy rating of tone sandhi after tone sandhi rules have emerged in the children's production (= the number of times tone sandhi is applied correctly in the speech sample after the emergence of tone sandhi/the number of opportunities when tone sandhi should be applied after the emergence of tone sandhi × 100%).

Table 4.9 summarises the two types of accuracy rating. Two children (Z.J. and Z.W.) assigned all the correct tones where tone sandhi applied and the other two children (J.J. and H.Y.) showed less proficiency with Tone 3 sandhi rule 2 and Tone 4 sandhi. Not surprisingly, the second type of accuracy rating was higher than overall accuracy.

Table 4.9 Accuracy rating of tone sandhi (%)

		J.J.	Z.J.	H.Y.	Z.W.
Tone 3 sandhi 1	Overall accuracy 1	100	100	100	100
	Overall accuracy 2	100	100	100	100
Tone 3 sandhi 2	Overall accuracy 1	77.4	100	65.4	100
	Overall accuracy 2	81.5	100	65.4	100
Tone 4 sandhi	Overall accuracy 1	67.6	100	64	100
	Overall accuracy 2	88.5	100	72.7	100
M conditioned sandhi	Overall accuracy 1	82.4	100	100	100
	Overall accuracy 2	100	100	100	100

4.5.4.3 Error patterns in tone sandhi realisation

A tone sandhi error refers to the difference between the child's realisation and the target tonal pattern, where tone sandhi applies.

- Tone 3 sandhi rule 1: no errors were found for this type of tone sandhi in the speech of the four children.

- Tone 3 sandhi rule 2: two children (Z.J. and Z.W.) made no errors; among the errors made by J.J., 66.7% of them occurred when the target tones were replaced by citation tones, that is, falling–rising tones; among the errors made by H.Y., 75% were substitution of citation tones for the target tones.

- Tone 4 sandhi rule: two children (Z.J. and Z.W.) made no errors; among the errors made by J.J., 63.6 % occurred when the target tones were replaced by citation tones, that is, high falling tones. Other errors occurred when high level tones were used to replace high falling tones. H.Y. made very few errors: in three cases he used citation tones, and in one case he used rising tones.

- Morphologically conditioned tone sandhi: no errors occurred, though this may be due to the few opportunities for this type of tone sandhi in the spontaneous data collected.

4.5.5 Weak stress

4.5.5.1 Age of emergence and stabilisation of weak stress and accuracy rating

As reviewed in 2.7, there are several types of weak stress. The age of emergence and stabilisation of various types of weak stress is summarised in Table 4.10. As early as 1;2, three children could produce weak stress in the reduplication type correctly on one or several occasions (i.e. emergence). Yet they still had not stabilised the use of weak stress in the reduplication type by the end of the data collection (about the age of 2;0). The weak stress in affix and lexeme types emerged later than that of the reduplication type. However, stabilisation of the weak stress in the first two types took a shorter time than that of the reduplication type (Table 4.10). Since there were very little data on grammatical particles, the weak stress of grammatical particle type was excluded in the analysis. Fluctuation in the accuracy rating characterised the children's production of weak stress.

Table 4.10 Age of emergence and stabilisation of weak stress

		J.J.	Z.J.	H.Y.	Z.W.
Affix	Emergence	1;7	1;8	1;5	1;6
	Stabilisation (66.7%)	1;11.15	1;8	1;11	1;6.15
	Stabilisation (90%)	not yet	1;9	1;11	1;6.15
Lexeme	Emergence	1;5.15	1;4.15	1;6	1;7
	Stabilisation (66.7%)	1;9.15	1;6.15	1;11.15	fluctuating
	Stabilisation (90%)	1;9.15	fluctuating	not yet	fluctuating
Reduplication	Emergence	1;2	1;5.15	1;2	1;2.15
	Stabilisation (66.7%)	fluctuating	fluctuating	fluctuating	fluctuating
	Stabilisation (90%)	fluctuating	fluctuating	fluctuating	fluctuating

Note: The children whose accuracy rating had not reached 66.7% or 90% are marked by 'not yet'; the children whose accuracy rating has reached 66.7% or 90%, but showed a tendency of fluctuation and had lower accuracy rating than 66.7% or 90% in the speech samples collected later are marked by 'fluctuating'.

4.5.5.2 Error patterns in weak stress realisation

Using citation tones for syllables with weak stress was the most common error pattern used by the children, especially for the reduplication type. Using other tones in place of weak stress also occurred in the data, but rather sporadically compared to the use of citation tones (Table 4.11).

Table 4.11 Frequency of occurrence and percentage of error patterns with weak stress

		J.J.		Z.J.		H.Y.		Z.W.	
		N	%	N	%	N	%	N	%
Affix type	Citation	5	45.5	0	0	0	0	0	0
	High level	2	18.2	1	50	1	50	0	0
	Rising	0	0	0	0	0	0	0	0
	Falling–rising	0	0	0	0	0	0	0	0
	High falling	4	36.4	1	50	1	50	1	100

Table 4.11 *cont.*

		J.J.		Z.J.		H.Y.		Z.W.	
		N	**%**	**N**	**%**	**N**	**%**	**N**	**%**
Lexeme type	Citation	2	33.3	4	66.7	3	37.5	2	100
	High level	2	33.3	0	0	2	25	0	0
	Rising	1	16.7	1	16.7	1	12.5	0	0
	Falling–rising	0	0	0	0	0	0	0	0
	High falling	1	16.7	1	16.7	2	25	0	0
Reduplication	Citation	56	70	14	87.5	53	93	24	100
type	High level	13	16.3	0	0	2	3.5	0	0
	Rising	1	1.3	1	6.3	0	0	0	0
	Falling–rising	0	0	0	0	0	0	0	0
	High Falling	10	12.5	1	6.3	2	3.5	0	0

Note: Shaded cells highlight the most frequent error patterns.

4.5.6 Summary of findings

Acquisition of segments:
Unaspirated stops (i.e. /p, t/) and three nasals (/m, -n, ŋ/) seemed to be stabilised earlier than other sounds in the children's speech. /n/ was acquired earlier at syllable-final position than syllable-initial position. Acquisition of vowels was relatively error-free though subject to individual variations. The central low vowel /A/ and back high vowel /u/ occurred earliest in the children's production of first words. The retroflex vowel /ɚ/ and the back vowel /o/ seemed to be the last simple vowels to emerge in the children's production. Among diphthongs, /ei/ was acquired first by four children, and /yɛ/ last. Among triphthongs, /iou/ was acquired first in three children's production, while /uae/ was acquired last by three children.

The order of acquisition of tones:
- Age of emergence: high level and high falling tones emerged first, followed by rising tones. Falling–rising tones were the last to emerge.
- Age of stabilisation using 66.7% criterion: high level tones were stabilised first, followed by high falling tones. Rising and falling–rising tones were the last.

Error patterns in tonal acquisition:
When an error occurred, the most frequent substitute for high falling tones was high level tones in all the children; the most frequent substitute for rising tones was high level tones in three children and falling–rising

tones in one child. Two children showed a preference for replacing falling–rising tones with high level tones, while the other two children preferred rising tones. Three children frequently used high falling tones to replace high level tones and one child used falling–rising tones in the place of high level tones.

Tone sandhi:
Individual differences and the nature of spontaneous data made it difficult to generalise on the order of acquisition of various types of tone sandhi rules. Nevertheless, the data suggested that morphologically conditioned sandhi seemed to emerge and become stabilised earlier than other types of tone sandhi (it was first in three children), and Tone 3 sandhi rule 1 was the last to emerge and become stabilised in two children. The age of emergence and stabilisation of tone sandhi rules was very close. Two children's accuracy ratings of all the four tone sandhi rule were as high as 100%. When an error occurred, the children usually used citation tones where tone sandhi should have applied.

Weak stress:
Weak stress emerged early in the children's speech, yet its acquisition was still not completed around the age of two. Fluctuation in accuracy rating characterised the process. Using citation tones for weakly stressed syllables, where the pitch of weakly stressed syllables should be adjusted according to the preceding tones, was the most common error pattern among the children.

4.6 Discussion

4.6.1 Vowels and consonants

As the age of emergence of vowels identified in this study shows, some vowels emerged as early as tones at the four-word point (when the children were supposed to be at the beginning of lexical use), though the acquisition of some vowels such as /ɚ, yɛ/ seemed to fall behind. Similar to the findings reported in Jeng (1979) and Shiu (1990), /y/ emerged later than /i, u/. This finding, together with the fact that the back vowel /u/ was among the first group of vowels to occur in the children's speech (cf. Jeng, 1979), contradicted Jakobson's prediction on the early acquisition of front vowels with regard to back vowels (1941/1968).

Though differences between the mean age of emergence of three types of vowels (i.e. simple vowels, diphthongs, triphthongs) were not striking, triphthongs seemed to emerge slightly later than diphthongs and simple vowels in the speech of all but one child, and diphthongs seemed to emerge later than simple vowels in all the children. This confirmed the findings reported in the cross-sectional study (Chapter 3), in which more children made errors with triphthongs and diphthongs than with simple vowels.

The age of stabilisation of consonants was comparable to the finding in the cross-sectional study. In the cross-sectional study, 90% of the children in the age group of 1;6–2;0 had stabilised syllable-initial consonants /t, m/ and syllable-final consonants /n, ŋ/. The syllable-initial consonant /p/, which was mastered by all of the children by the completion of the data collection in this longitudinal study, was not acquired by 90% of the children in the cross-sectional study until 3;0. The difference might be an artefact of the picture-naming task used in the cross-sectional study. In the picture-naming task, the phoneme /p/ appeared only once and the lexical item in which /p/ appeared happened to be the first one in the picture-naming task. This perhaps led to a lower rate of responses for this item than others. /p/ occurs in common words such as /pApA/ (*'papa'*), and there is no apparent reason that it should present particular difficulty to children.

The age of emergence of consonants in the longitudinal study was much earlier than the age identified in the cross-sectional study (see Table 3.5). Two children (J.J. and H.Y.) had nearly complete repertoires. Dodd (1995) also reported that the phoneme repertoires found in the longitudinal study consisted of more phonemes than those found in the cross-sectional study. A plausible explanation for the difference is that the children's development was accelerated as a result of the bi-weekly sessions in which parents made an effort to elicit their speech. Another explanation is that the difference may be due to different types of speech sample collected in the longitudinal study and cross-sectional study. Since the spontaneous speech sample was collected in the longitudinal study, the children had the opportunity to partially control topics and content and produce familiar words, and were subject to less stress and nervousness than they would have in the picture-naming task in the cross-sectional study.

4.6.2 Tone

In this study, the age of emergence recorded the first time a child was able to articulate a feature such as a tone, and the age of stabilisation reflected when a child was able to produce a tonal feature with a certain degree of phonological accuracy and consistency (i.e. 66.7% accuracy rating). Not surprisingly, the age of stabilisation in most cases was older than the age of emergence, indicating that the children completed the phonetic mastery of tones earlier than the completion of phonological learning. However, the gap between the age of emergence and that of stabilisation of the four tones was marginal, suggesting Putonghua-speaking children had relatively little difficulty in acquiring tones. This can be attributed to the high phonological saliency of Putonghua tones, as argued in 3.6.5.

When a tonal error occurred, there were several explanations. The child might be learning on an item-by-item basis. S/he might perceive tones in adults' words incorrectly; or perceive tones correctly, but produce the tone incorrectly. If the learning of tones takes place merely on an item-by-item basis, there would be random occurrence of tonal errors in the children's productions. However, the analysis of tonal errors suggested that there seemed to be patterns concerning which tone substitutes for another. For example, when an error occurred, the most frequent substitute for high falling tones was high level tones in all the children; the most frequent substitute for rising tones was high level tones in three children and falling–rising tones in one child; the most frequent substitute for falling–rising tones was high level tones in two children while it was rising tones in two children; the most frequent substitute for high level tones was high falling tones in three children and falling–rising tones in one child.

Although it is possible that a tonal error occurred because the child made an incorrect association between a tone and a segment on a lexical basis, it is very likely that most of the errors were systematic, and were the result of children's simplification strategies (cf. 3.5.6, the discussion on weak stress error). If the children were believed to have a more active role in acquiring their phonological system, and to have underlying representations resembling those of the adult, then the errors could be viewed as children's attempt to simplify the production process by replacing the target with an alternative representing less difficulty to them (Stampe, 1973; Ingram, 1986).

The patterns on tonal acquisition identified here raise two specific questions: Why is one tone acquired earlier than another? Why is tonal acquisition completed earlier than that of segments?

4.6.2.1 Why is one tone acquired earlier than another?

Though different measures (for example, age of emergence and age of stabilisation) gave a slightly different order of acquisition of the four tones, high level tones seemed to be the first tones to be acquired by the children, followed by high falling tones. Rising and falling–rising tones were acquired last. This was more or less in agreement with Li and Thompson's findings (1977), i.e. high level and high falling tones were acquired before rising and falling–rising tones in Mandarin.

A number of explanations have been offered relating to the order of acquisition of tones. Li and Thompson (1977) proposed a 'hypothesis of difficulty' and emphasised the role of articulatory and perceptual constraints in the order of acquisition of tones. They reviewed several studies on the production and perception of tones and argued that in terms of ease of articulation and perception rising tones were more difficult than high falling tones. Their argument was also supported by the oft-cited observation that high falling tones have greater frequency of occurrence in the world's languages than rising tones, and a sound or feature with high distribution frequency in the world's languages would be acquired early (Jakobson, 1941/1968). Research evidence on the degree of markedness of tones also suggested that falling pitch movement was a natural gesture of speech production and required less physiological effort than rising tones, and therefore would be acquired earlier than rising pitch (for a summary, see Vihman, 1996). These arguments explained well why high falling tones were acquired earlier than rising and falling–rising tones. However, they could not explain why high level tones were acquired earliest among the four tones.

The early acquisition of high level tones might be accounted for in terms of features. In traditional descriptions of Putonghua tones, each contour tone such as rising, falling, and falling–rising tones were considered as distinct units in the same way as high level tones. In an autosegmental account of the tonal inventory (see 2.10), in contrast, there is only one unit of default specification: level tones. The contour tones are a linear sequence of two or several different level tones: a rising tone is a linear sequence of a low level and high level tones; a falling–rising tone is that of a mid level, low level and high level tones and a high falling tone is that of high level and low level tones. Children's acquisition would be a process of replacing a default value with a language-specific value (Dinnsen, 1997). The high level tone, according to the autosegmental account, which only consists of default feature, would therefore be acquired first by Putonghua-speaking children. The substitution patterns of tones in the children's productions also confirmed the status of high level tones as a default specification. As the analysis of tonal error patterns shows, high level tones were preferred to other tones in most cases when tonal errors took place in the children's production. This explanation may also account for the findings in other cross-linguistic studies of tonal acquisition. Tse's study (1978) on Cantonese tonal acquisition reported that among the nine tones in Cantonese (i.e. 6 level tones and 3 contour tones), all the level tones were acquired earlier than contour tones and that high falling tones preceded rising tones (cf. A. Tse, 1992).

Alternatively, the early acquisition of high level tones can be accounted for in terms of alignment between high level tone and stress (Duanmu, personal communication). It is proposed that every syllable has a stress which tends to be aligned with high level tones. In Putonghua, every full syllable is stressed, so perhaps it is natural for the children to align the syllable with high level tones, which results in early acquisition of high level tones.

It is conceivable that tonal acquisition is subject to a number of factors. The de-component of contour tones as a sequence of default level tones and alignment between high level tone and stress might explain why level tones are acquired early. The relative unmarkedness of high falling tones as opposed to rising and falling–rising tones within the context of contour tones might explain why high falling tones are acquired earlier than other contour tones.

4.6.2.2 Why is tonal acquisition completed earlier than segments?

Acquisition of tones was completed earlier than that of segments (vowels and consonants), though some of the phonemes might be acquired at the same time as some tones. By the end of data collection, all of the children in the study had stabilised the tonal contrasts and had been able to use tone sandhi appropriately. In contrast, only five phonemes (i.e. /p, t, m, n, ŋ/) had become stabilised in the children's production. Acquisition of vowels was relatively error-free but subject to individual variations. While all of the children were able to produce the central vowel /A/ at the beginning of the four-word point stage, two vowels /ɚ/ and /yɛ/ had not been mastered by two children by the end of the data collection. The similar pattern, i.e. tonal acquisition was completed earlier than segments, have been reported for Cantonese (Tse, 1978). The early acquisition of tonal features as opposed to segmental features in Putonghua- and Cantonese-speaking children can be well explained in terms of the high saliency value of tones. In these two languages, tones contrast word meanings, and have a limited number of options and are compulsory syllable components, which make tonal information highly accessible and noticeable to children.

Several other hypotheses have been proposed to interpret the earlier acquisition of tones. Firstly, prosodic features, such as pitch variation, are believed to be perceptually salient to infants. Research findings have suggested that infants are sensitive to the suprasegmental aspect prior to the segmental aspect of speech (for a summary, see Quigley & Paul, 1984.) However, how such perceptual saliency leads to early production in the early stages of phonological development is not known, though it has been suggested that inaccurate perception may be the source of some speech errors (Eilers & Oller, 1976).

Secondly, Allen and Hawkins (1980) have proposed a physiological account. While tonal contrasts are realised largely by changes in fundamental frequency, which originates in the larynx, segmental contrasts have to involve a wider range of articulatory processes using both glottal, supraglottal and durational mechanisms. In addition, the realisation of segmental contrasts requires different degrees and kinds of co-ordination between different mechanisms. This may slow down the acquisitional process of segmental contrasts.

However, physiological factors cannot be the sole factor contributing to the early acquisition of tonal contrasts as compared to segmental contrasts. It has been repeatedly reported that non-native speakers of tonal languages have more difficulty with tones than segments (e.g. Guo, 1993). Among the four tones, rising-falling tones are the most difficult for non-native speakers of Putonghua. Most of the errors were related to non-native speakers' inaccurate mastery of relative pitch variation. If the order of acquisition is determined by physiological factors alone, tones should present less difficulty to non-native speakers of tonal languages (as well as native speakers) than segments.

The ease with which native speakers acquire tonal features as opposed to non-native speakers cannot be explained by language representation in the brains of tonal language speakers. Gandour (1998) reviewed the contemporary aphasia literature on tonal languages and concluded that language representation in the brains of tonal language speakers was essentially the same as that in non-tonal language speakers. Tones, similar to segments, appeared to be lateralised to the left hemisphere in speakers of tonal languages. This suggests that early tonal acquisition cannot be related to hemispheric specialisation.

Another possible factor influencing the order of acquisition may be the degree of complexity of contrasts and rules involved. The patterns of prosodic features are far more limited than that of segments in a tonal language (Vihman, 1996). The complexity of segmental contrasts to be learned may therefore influence the length of time of acquisition. The relationship between the complexity of rules involved and the ease of acquisition is shown in Demuth's study (1993) on the acquisition of the grammatical tonal system of Sesotho. She found that while rule-assigned tones on subject markers were generally acquired by the age of two, the underlying tonal representations on verb roots would take a longer time. The reason was, she argued, '... that the richness and pervasiveness of tone sandhi rules in grammatical tone languages like Sesotho produces recoverability problems, making the mapping between surface and underlying representations a more difficult and prolonged undertaking' (1993: 299).

4.6.3 Tone sandhi

Instances of tone sandhi began to emerge in the children's data after the children were able to produce multi-syllabic phrases. The data seemed to suggest that morphonologically conditioned tone sandhi was acquired earlier than tone 3 sandhi rules, which are phonologically conditioned. Three out of four children were able to stabilise morphologically conditioned tone sandhi earlier than other tone sandhi rules. For example, when the children acquired the negation word /pu4/, 'no', they made no error in applying the relevant tone sandhi rule (i.e. high falling tones will become high rising before high falling tones). They produced the syllable /pu4/ as /pu2/ in the phrases /pu2 tuei4/ '*not correct*' and /pu2 kʰan4/ '*not look*', as opposed to /pu4/ in the phrases /pu4 ɕiaŋ3/ '*not think*' and /pu4 tʰiŋ1/ '*not listen*'. In contrast, some errors occurred with tone 3 and tone 4 sandhi rules, when the children used citation tones where tone alterations were expected.

The early stabilisation of morphologically conditioned tone sandhi might be related to the fact that the rule only applies to several lexical items. In contrast, tone 3 and tone 4 sandhi are dependent on phonological phrasing which is in turn dependent on syntax. In acquiring a phonological system, a child is believed to be actively constructing the rules of the phonology from his or her mental lexicon (e.g. Dodd, 1995). Consequently, a simpler rule would be derived and learned earlier than a more complicated rule.

It is questionable, however, whether the children are aware of these rules and consciously apply them in their production. There are two possibilities. Since the children listen to the words or phrases to which tone sandhi has been applied where appropriate right from the start (though no systematic data are available on tone sandhi in motherese), they might learn the expected tonal alteration as an individual and independent combination on a lexical basis. If that is the case, children would have made random tone sandhi error. Another possibility is that the children acquired the rules first and applied the rules where appropriate. If this is the case, children would be expected to frequently replace the tones involved with citation tones of the syllables when errors occurred. The analysis of error patterns of tone sandhi showed that the citation tones were the major substitutes when the children made errors with tone sandhi. This seems to suggest that the children are learning tone sandhi actively.

4.6.3 Weak stress

The weak stress of the reduplication type emerged early, perhaps because reduplicated words, as one of the major production forms in the early stage of language development (Grunwell, 1982), developed earlier than other types of words using weak stress. Yet it took the children a longer time to master the phonological use of weak stress in reduplication than the other two types of weak stress. None of the children stabilised weak stress in reduplication in their speech by the end of data collection (i.e. when they were about two years old). This is perhaps related to the fact that it is relatively 'acceptable' to give stress to the second syllable in reduplicated words which should be weakly stressed, while it is extremely rare to stress the weakly stressed syllable in either affix or lexeme type. A closer examination of parental speech in child-parent interaction is needed to examine whether adults are more likely to give citation tones to weakly stressed syllables in reduplication than the other two types of weakly stressed syllables.

Using citation tones for the weakly stressed syllable was a dominant error pattern in the children's production of the target weak stress. This tendency is clearly demonstrated in children's realisation of weak stress in the reduplication type. The normative study on the acquisition of weak stress in the 129 children aged 1;6–4;6 (see Chapter 3) also found that citation tones were used in most cases when errors occurred to weak stress in lexeme and reduplication types. Among the errors for the affix type of weak stress, half were weakly stressed syllable deletion and the other half occurred when the children substituted citation tones and lengthened syllables. The use of citation tones may, again, be related to parental input, in which citation tones of reduplicated syllables often took the place of weak stress. Alternatively, the systematic error patterns could be evidence for the argument that the children were actively learning and applying the rules in acquiring stress, similar to tonal acquisition (cf. Klein, 1984).

4.6.4 Individual differences

A considerable amount of individual variations was evident among the children in their rate and style of acquisition of tones, tone sandhi,

weak stress, and segments as well as error patterns in their early phonological development. For example, on tonal acquisition, while all the
children appeared to stabilise high level tones firstly and high falling
tones secondly, there were variations in the order of stabilisation of rising
and falling–rising tones among the children: two children seemed to
acquire falling–rising tones earlier than rising tones, one child had the
opposite pattern and one child stabilised these two tones at about the
same time. On tone sandhi, one child was able to produce nearly all types
of tone sandhi appropriately by 1;6, while the other three did so at about
the age of 1;9, 1;10 and 1;11. A greater degree of variability was also found
in the acquisition of weak stress in terms of age of emergence and
stabilisation.

There are a number of possible sources of individual variations. Firstly,
individual variation might arise as the result of the data collection
method. Since the study was aimed to collect the children's spontaneous
speech data, there was no guarantee that each feature examined in the
study had an opportunity to appear in the children's production. Also,
the frequency of occurrence of each feature may vary from one child to
another, which might affect the comparability of the age of emergence
and stabilisation of the features involved to some extent.

Secondly, children's preference for different strategies in acquisition
might result in individual variations. Some children were found to have
a tendency to avoid using features which they could not yet produce
accurately, while some seemed to be less aware of the inaccuracy of their
output and attempted to produce the features in question (Menn & Stoel-
Gammon, 1995). Therefore, the former group of children might be found
to have a relatively higher accuracy rating of a particular feature and the
latter might have a lower accuracy rating. The children also varied in
their preferences for certain sounds and features and in the way they
used their preference to replace target forms. This is evident in the substitution patterns associated with the acquisition of various features in
the present study. For example, when a tonal error occurred, high level
tones were used most frequently to replace other tones by three children.
In contrast, one child (J.J) showed a preference to use falling–rising tones
to replace other tones.

Finally, individual variations reflect the different in the input children
are exposed to. The type of input children receive may affect the way
they acquire a particular feature. The influence of input on the acquisition of Mandarin tones was reported in Clumeck (1977). In his study, one
child produced rising tones earlier than the other three tones when he
began to use words based on adult models at about the age of 1;10,

perhaps as the result of high frequency of occurrence of rising tones in the speech of the child's caretaker. However, such a claim on the relationship between input and individual variations is still tentative, since some studies failed to find input effects (e.g. Leonard *et al.*, 1980).

4.7 Summary

In this chapter, a longitudinal study of four children between the age of 0;10 and 2;0 is reported. This study complements the cross-sectional study reported in Chapter 3 with corroborating evidence on the age and order of phoneme acquisition and error patterns. It also highlights the developmental patterns of suprasegmental features such as tone, tone sandhi and weak stress. The two studies together, cross-sectional and longitudinal, provide normative data on the acquisition of phonology by Putonghua-speaking children, which can be used not only for cross-linguistic comparison but also for the assessment of phonological disorders in children in exceptional developmental circumstances.

Chapter 5
The Phonological Systems of Putonghua-speaking Children with Functional Speech Disorders

5.1 Introduction

The cross-sectional and longitudinal studies reported in Chapters 3 and 4 described the order and age of tonal and phoneme acquisition and identified developmental error patterns of normally developing Putonghua-speaking children. These normative data provide a useful tool for assessing phonological development of Putonghua-speaking children and identifying phonological disorder. The primary aim of the present chapter is to describe the phonological systems of Putonghua-speaking children whose speech disorders have no known organic cause.

Speech disorders in Putonghua-speaking children are rarely reported in the literature. Prevalence figures for developmental speech disorders in English-speaking children range from 3% to 10% (Kirkpatrick & Ward, 1984; Enderby & Philipp, 1986) and almost 70% of children attending paediatric speech-language therapy clinics are speech (not language) disordered (Weiss *et al.*, 1987). In China, terms such as 'phonological impairment' or 'speech disorder' are rarely known in hospitals, nurseries or schools. During informal interviews with teachers when recruiting participants for this study, it was found that there was an awareness of the existence of late-speakers and children with low speech intelligibility. However, most teachers associated speech difficulties with laziness and believed that the children would 'grow out of' the problem by themselves.

The study reported in this chapter is designed with the following research questions in mind:

(1) What are the characteristics of the speech of Putonghua-speaking children who are identified as having speech intelligibility difficulties?
(2) Can four subgroups of children with the following linguistic symptomatology be identified?

Articulation disorder – consistent distortion of a phone either in isolation or in any phonetic context.

Delayed development – use of non-age-appropriate error patterns and/or restricted phonetic or phonemic inventories.

Consistent disorder – use of error patterns not used by more than 10% of children.

Inconsistent disorder – variable production of more than 40% of the items produced in identical linguistic contexts on three occasions in one assessment session.

(3) How does the speech of Putonghua-speaking children with disordered phonology differ from that of normally developing Putonghua-speaking children?

(4) How does the speech of Putonghua-speaking children with disordered phonology differ from that of speech disordered children speaking other languages?

5.2 Method

5.2.1 Participants

Fourty-eight children aged 2;8–7;6 were identified initially by nursery and school teachers as having atypical speech development. Three screening tests (Appendices 4, 5 and 6) were subsequently administered: pure tone audiometry, oromotor examination (Ozanne, 1992), Visual-Motor Integration Test (VMI, Beery, 1989). To limit the study to children with 'functional' phonological disorders, the following criteria were used:

- normal hearing;
- no abnormalities in oral structure;
- no learning problems as assessed by VMI;
- no behavioural problems reported by nursery/school teachers;
- normal language comprehension reported by nursery/school teachers.

Five children from the teachers' initial referral were excluded (one had a hearing impairment; one was suspected of autism; two performed poorly on VMI; and one was suspected of behaviour disorder). Speech from another 10 children was considered to be within the normal range of phonological development. They were assessed but the data from these ten children were excluded in the analyses in this chapter (cf. Chapter 6). Another boy presented an interesting case. He had been previously assessed in the cross-sectional study and his speech development was considered normal at the time. However, he was later referred by his teacher as having 'speech difficulties', when children with speech disorders were sampled. He (Child 12) is included in this study. The comparison between his phonological systems assessed at different time can be found in Chapter 6.

The findings on the speech of 33 children (nine girls and 24 boys) are now reported. Figure 5.1 illustrates subject distribution over the age bands. All the children were acquiring Putonghua as their first language, though some of them had been exposed to English either in English lessons in schools or tutoring at home. None of the children had siblings. The children attended school and nurseries in Beijing.

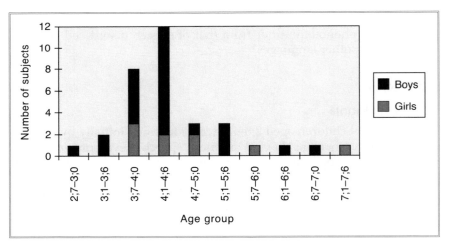

Figure 5.1 Subject distribution over the age band in the speech disorder study

5.2.2 Procedure

The children were assessed individually in a quiet room at their nurseries or schools, using the same tasks as in the cross-sectional normative study in Chapter 3. Each child was first asked to name the objects or actions in 44 pictures three times and then to describe what is happening in five pictures. The children's speech was audiotaped using a Sony professional micro-recorder. It should be pointed out that in order to assess the consistency of production the children were specifically asked to name each picture three times. This is rarely done in existing studies of developmental speech disorders (see further discussion in

1.3.1) and consequently inconsistent disorder is not widely recognised (cf. McCormack & Dodd, 1998).

5.2.3 Data analysis

The speech samples from the picture-naming and picture-description tasks were phonetically transcribed, using IPA. Inter-transcriber reliability (on 18.5% of the data) for syllable-initial word-initial, syllable-initial within-word, syllable-final word-final, and syllable-final within-word consonants were all above 96%.

The following quantitative and qualitative measures were derived from the children's speech:

- *Percentage of Consonants in Error (PCE):* PCE for each child was calculated by the formula (the number of times phonemes are produced in error/the total number of phonemes in the sample × 100). (cf. Percentage of Consonants Correct proposed by Shriberg & Kwiatkowski, 1982).
- *Total number of error patterns:* An error pattern had to occur at least twice in different lexical items to be included.
- *Total number of missing consonants in phonetic inventory:* The number of consonants missing from the child's phonetic inventory.
- *Z scores:* Calculated for the three measures described above by comparing to the normative data. For example, Z score for PCE is the difference between PCE and mean PCE of the children of the equivalent age band in the normative sample divided by standard deviation. Z scores were used to (a) compare the children with speech disorders and normally developing children of the same age, (b) compare the children of different ages with the same type of speech disorder.
- *Phonetic inventory:* All the sounds produced at least once in the speech sample, irrespective of whether they were the correct targets.
- *Phonemic inventory:* All the sounds produced both phonetically and phonologically correctly on at least two of three opportunities.
- *Error patterns:* Error patterns were classified as either age-appropriate, delayed or unusual. An error pattern had to be used at least twice to be included.
  - ∗ *Age-appropriate error patterns:* Error patterns used by at least 10% of the children in the same age band in the normative sample.
  - ∗ *Delayed error patterns:* Error patterns used by less than 10% of the children in the same age band in the normative data, but appropriate for younger children.
  - ∗ *Unusual error patterns:* Error patterns not found among more than 10% of the normally developing children.

- *Inconsistency rating:* Comparison of the three productions of each of the 44 words. The number of words with two or three different productions was expressed as a percentage of the total number of words produced three times. When a child's production alters between correct targets and developmental errors, this type of variation is considered as by-product of children's normal development. Therefore, this type of variation was not counted as an inconsistent production. In other words, if a child sometimes produced a phoneme correctly and sometimes incorrectly yet consistently (for example, /k/ always realised as [t] or [k]), this phoneme would not be considered as having an inconsistent realisation. In contrast, a range of error forms used for the same phoneme in the same phonetic context may reflect acquisition difficulties (Dodd, 1995). Dodd (1995) considers an inconsistency score of more than 40% indicative of inconsistent disorder.

5.3 Results

Using Dodd's (1995) classification system, one child (3%) was diagnosed to have an articulation disorder, 18 (54.5%, mean age 4;8, Standard deviation 10 months) had delayed development, eight (24.2%, mean age 4;3, SD 9 months) had consistent disorder, six (18.2%, mean age 3;8, SD 4 months) had inconsistent disorder.

5.3.1 Quantitative data

5.3.1.1 Overview of the results

Children's age, gender, Z score for PCE, Z score for the total number of error patterns, Z score for the number of missing consonants, and inconsistency rating are summarised in Table 5.1. Comparison of these measures between the subgroups of speech disorder is presented below.

Table 5.1 Speech disordered children's Z score for PCE, Z score for the total number of error patterns, Z score for the number of missing consonants, inconsistency rating, and diagnosis

Child	Age	Gender	Z_1	Z_2	Z_3	Inconsistency	Diagnosis
1*	7;6	F	−0.13	−1.05	1.00	14	Articulation
2	3;7	F	1.81	1.71	0.33	30	Delay
3	3;8	F	4.01	4.34	1.41	27	Delay
4	3;11	M	2.24	3.14	5.89	21	Delay

Table 5.1 *cont.*

Child	Age	Gender	Z_1	Z_2	Z_3	Incon-sistency	Diagnosis
5	4;0	M	2.04	0.76	2.56	21	Delay
6	4;1	M	2.83	1.65	5.29	34	Delay
7	4;2	M	1.19	0.84	2.43	9	Delay
8	4;3	F	2.93	1.39	5.20	21	Delay
9	4;3	M	1.67	4.89	1.00	32	Delay
10	4;4	M	2.83	3.27	6.71	34	Delay
11	4;5	F	1.28	−0.24	1.00	25	Delay
12	4;6	M	0.02	1.39	−0.43	23	Delay
13*	4;7	M	1.98	2.46	2.43	28	Delay
14*	5;0	F	−0.25	1.65	−0.43	30	Delay
15*	5;2	M	2.69	1.92	3.86	11	Delay
16*	5;6	M	0.92	0.57	3.86	16	Delay
17*	5;7	F	0.50	−0.51	−0.43	14	Delay
18*	6;1	M	0.21	0.03	1.00	18	Delay
19*	6;7	M	0.04	0.30	−0.43	18	Delay
20	2;8	M	3.27	4.69	2.72	28	Consistent D
21	4;1	M	1.10	0.57	1.00	14	Consistent D
22	4;2	M	3.44	3.81	5.20	33	Consistent D
23	4;2	M	1.03	1.92	2.43	30	Consistent D
24	4;3	M	0.45	4.35	1.00	24	Consistent D
25	4;6	M	2.59	4.62	5.29	16	Consistent D
26*	4;8	F	4.38	6.24	8.14	32	Consistent D
27*	5;6	M	0.86	0.03	1.00	26	Consistent D
28	3;2	M	−0.19	−0.75	0.39	58	Inconsistent D
29	3;6	M	3.18	1.93	3.07	49	Inconsistent D
30	3;7	M	8.88	8.62	10.33	76	Inconsistent D
31	3;11	M	8.01	9.12	10.23	49	Inconsistent D
32	3;11	M	6.77	3.38	7.00	60	Inconsistent D
33	4;0	M	2.05	2.90	1.44	55	Inconsistent D

Notes: Z_1: Z score for PCE; Z_2: Z score for the total number of error patterns; Z_3: Z score for the total number of missing consonants. Consistent D: consistent disorder; Inconsistent D: inconsistent disorder. Z scores of the children marked by '*' are computed on the basis of means and SD of the age group of 4;0–4;6 in the normative study.

5.3.1.2 Statistical analyses of differences between subgroups

PCEs and inconsistency ratings of each subgroup of speech disordered children are provided in Table 5.2.

Table 5.2 Means and standard deviations of PCE and inconsistency rating of four subgroups of speech disorders

Subgroups	*Means (Standard deviations)*	
	PCE	*Inconsistency rating*
Articulation*	7.0	14
Delayed development	15.1 (9.3)	22.8 (8.1)
Consistent disorder	25.9 (11.1)	25.2 (7.2)
Inconsistent disorder	38.8 (11.3)	57.6 (10)

Note: Since there is only one child in this subgroup, no standard deviation is given for this subgroup.

Statistical analyses showed that there were significant differences in the measures of PCE and inconsistency scores between the three subgroups (non-parameteric Kruskal–Wallis Test: $H = 8.497$, $df = 2$, $p = 0.014$ for PCE; $H = 14.537$, $df = 2$, $p = 0.001$ for inconsistency rating). *Post hoc* Mann–Whitney Testing indicated:

- a significant difference in PCE between the delay and inconsistent disorder subgroups ($p = 0.000$);
- a significant difference in inconsistency rating both between the delay and inconsistent disorder subgroups ($p = 0.000$), and between the consistent disorder and inconsistent disorder subgroups ($p = 0.002$). However, there is no significant difference in inconsistency rating between the delay and consistent disorder subgroups.

5.3.1.3 Z score distribution

Figure 5.2 illustrates the distribution of Z scores of the participants arranged in the order of degree of inconsistency. Three measures represent Z scores of PCE, the total number of error patterns and the number of missing consonants, respectively. Since the normative data did not examine the children older than 4;6, the reference means and standard deviations in calculating Z scores for children older than 4;6 in this study are those of 4;0–4;6 – the oldest age group in the normative sample. Therefore, caution should be taken in referring to Z scores of Children 1, 13–19, 26, and 27. As Figure 5.2 shows, while the participants with low inconsistency had relatively lower Z scores, the participants with high inconsistency had a wider range of Z score distribution.

Figure 5.3 illustrates Z score distribution of participants in each subgroup. There were no substantial differences between the three subgroups (i.e. delay, consistent disorder and inconsistent disorder subgroups) except that the inconsistent disorder subgroup covered wider range of Z scores than the other two subgroups.

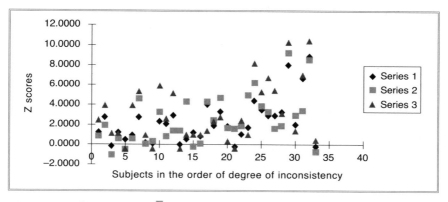

Figure 5.2 Three Z scores distribution of speech disordered children in the order of degree of inconsistency

Note: Series 1: Z score for PCE; Series 2: Z score for the total number of error patterns; Series 3: Z score for the number of missing consonants in phonetic inventory.

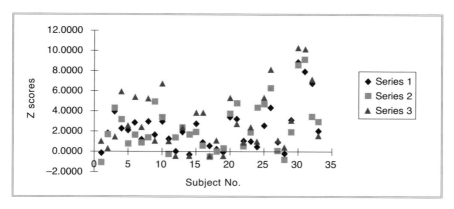

Figure 5.3 Three Z scores distribution over four subgroups of speech disorders

Note: Series 1: Z score for PCE; Series 2: Z score for the total number of error patterns; Series 3: Z score for the number of missing consonants in phonetic inventory.

5.3.2 Qualitative data: Diagnostic classification

5.3.2.1 Error patterns

Tables 5.3 and 5.4 summarise the error patterns used by the delay, consistent disorder and inconsistent disorder subgroups.

Table 5.3 Error patterns used by the subgroup of delayed development

Normal error patterns	2	3	4	5	6	7	8	9	10	11	12	13	14	15	16	17	18	19
Consonant assimilation								*			*			*			*	
Syllable initial deletion			*	*						*		*		*	*			
Fronting: /ʂ/ → [s]	*		*	*	*	*	*	*	*	*	*	*	*	*	*	*		*
/ɕ/ → [ʃ/ʂ]																		
/k/ → [t]			*							*				*			*	
Backing: /s/ → [ʂ]			*					*			*	*	*					
Stopping: /ts/ → [t]	*	*	*		*		*	*	*	*				*			*	
/s/ → [t]	*																	
/x/ v [k]							*			*								
Affrication: /ɕ/ → [tɕ]						*			*		*							
Deaspiration: /tʰ/ → [t]			*															
Aspiration: /t/ → [tʰ]			*															
X-velarisation		*	*														*	
Gliding			*		*	*	*					*		*	*			
Final /n/ deletion			*	*	*		*	*					*					
Backing: /n/ → [ŋ]			*					*										
Final /ŋ/ deletion							*											
Triphthong reduction																		
Diphthong reduction																		

Note: Shaded cells are delayed error patterns for a particular child. Typical examples are given next to each error pattern.

Table 5.4 Error patterns used by the subgroups of consistent and inconsistent disorders

Normal error patterns	Consistent disorder								Inconsistent disorder					
	20	21	22	23	24	25	26	27	28	29	30	31	32	33
Consonant assimilation	*		*					*		*				
Syllable initial deletion		*	*	*		*			*	*		*	*	
Fronting: /ʂ/→ [s]			*		*		*		*	*				*
/ç/→ [ʃ/ʂ]	*													*
/k/→ [t]								*						*
Backing: /s/→ [ʂ]	*													*
Stopping: /ts/→ [t]	*		*						*	*	*	*		*
/s/→ [t]										*		*		
/x/→ [k]			*							*				
Affrication:/ç/→ [tç]	*				*				*			*		*
Deaspiration:/tʰ/→ [t]	*	*								*			*	
Aspiration: /t/→ [tʰ]														
X-velarisation	*				*		*						*	
Gliding	*	*	*		*	*		*					*	*
Final /n/ deletion	*			*			*		*		*			
Backing: /n/→ [ŋ]										*				
Final /ŋ/ deletion	*										*			
Triphthong reduction	*						*							
Diphthong reduction							*							
Unusual error patterns														
Final consonant addition				*	*						*			
Syllable initial addition												*		
Vowel change					*				*		*	*		

Table 5.4 *cont.*

Unusual error patterns	Consistent disorder								Inconsistent disorder					
	20	21	22	23	24	25	26	27	28	29	30	31	32	33
/ŋ/→ [n]	*						*							
/ts, tʂ/→ [k]	*	*				*			*				*	
/k/→ /ts, tʂ/			*					*						*
/tɕ/→ [ɕ]; /ts/→ [s]							*				*			
/k/→ [p]									*	*				
/ts/→ [tɕ]					*								*	
											ç→t	f→p	t→k	ʂ→k
											p→tɕ	tʂ→p		ʂ→f
											ʂ→l	t→p		
												p→f		
												p→tʂ		
												tɕ→n		

Note: Shaded cells are delayed error patterns for a particular child. Individual unusual error patterns are listed for the children with inconsistent disorder.

5.3.2.2 Individual profiles

Each child's phonological system is described below. The children in each subgroup are arranged in age order. Unless stated, phonetic and phonemic inventories were age-appropriate, and vowels, syllable-final consonants and tones were error-free. Appendix 7 describes the production variability of two children in the inconsistent disorder subgroup.

Articulation subgroup

Child 1 (7;6, female)
- Substituted [θ] for /s/. [θ] is not a Putonghua phoneme.
- /ts/ and /tsʰ/ realised as [t] or [tʰ] (e.g. /tsae/ [tae]; /tsʰae/ [tʰae]).

Delayed development subgroup

Child 2 (3;7, female)
- 1 delayed error pattern – stopping: /ɕ/ as the stop [t] (e.g. /ɕi/ [ti]; /ɕiɛ/ [tiɛ]).

Child 3 (3;8, female)
- Delayed phonetic and phonemic development.
- 4 phones (/k, s, kʰ, tsʰ/) missing from her phonetic inventory.
- 10 phonemes (/f, k, kʰ, l, s, ʂ, tʂ, tʂʰ, ts, tsʰ/) missing from her phonemic inventory.

Child 4 (3;11, male)
- Delayed phonetic development.
- 6 phones (/pʰ, ʂ, tʂ, tʂʰ, ts, ts/) missing from his phonetic inventory.

Child 5 (4;0, male)
- Delayed phonemic development.
- 7 phonemes (/kʰ, l, ɹ, ʂ, tʂ, tʂʰ, tsʰ/) missing from his phonemic inventory.

Child 6 (4;1 male)
- Delayed phonetic development.
- 4 phones (/l, ɹ, ts, tsʰ/) missing from his phonetic inventory.
- 1 delayed error pattern – gliding (/ɹ/ realised as [j], e.g. /ɹoʊ/ [joʊ]).

Child 7 (4;2, male)
- 2 delayed error patterns:
  - (a) gliding (/ɹ/ realised as [j], e.g. /ɹoʊ/ [joʊ]);
  - (b) affrication (fricatives, especially /ʂ/, realised as affricates, e.g. /ʂua/ [tsua]).

Child 8 (4;3, female)
- Delayed phonetic development.
- 4 phones (/tʂ, tʂʰ, ʂ, ɹ/) missing from her phonetic inventory.
- 1 delayed error pattern – stopping (/x/ replaced by stop [k], e.g. /xua/ [kua]).

Child 9 (4;3, male)
- Delayed phonemic development.
- 7 phonemes (/tɕ, tɕʰ, ʂ, tʂ, tʂʰ, ts, tsʰ/) missing from his phonemic inventory.
- 1 delayed error pattern: final consonant /ŋ/ deletion (e.g. /tʂʰ uaŋ/ [tsʰua]).

Child 10 (4;4, male)
- Delayed phonetic development.
- 5 phones /tʂ, ʂ, ts, tsʰ, ɹ/ missing from his phonetic inventory.
- 1 delayed error pattern – affrication (e.g. /ɕiɛ/ [tɕiɛ]).

Child 11 (4;5, female)
- Delayed phonemic development.
- 5 phonemes (/k, l, ʂ, tʂ, tʂʰ/) missing from her phonemic inventory.
- 1 delayed error pattern – stopping (/x/ realised as [k], e.g. /xua/ [kua]).

Child 12 (4;6, male)
- 1 delayed error pattern – affrication (/ɕ/ realised as [tɕ], e.g. /ɕiɛ/ [tɕiɛ]).

Child 13 (4;7, male)
- Delayed phonetic and phonemic development.
- 2 phones (/tʂʰ, ɹ/) missing from his phonetic inventory.
- 7 phonemes (/l, s, ɹ, ʂ, tʂ, tʂʰ, ts/) missing from his phonemic inventory.
- 1 delayed error pattern – gliding (/ɹ/ realised as [j], e.g. /ɹoʊ/ [joʊ]).

Child 14 (5;0, female)
- Delayed phonemic development.
- 2 phonemes (/ts, ʂ/) missing from her phonemic inventory.
- 1 delayed error pattern -- /n/ deletion at syllable-final position with vowel changes (e.g. /pʰin/ [pʰiɛ]).

Child 15 (5;2, male)
- Delayed phonetic and phonemic development.
- 4 phones (/k, l, ɹ, tsʰ/) missing from his phonetic inventory.
- 6 phonemes (/k, l, ɹ, tʂʰ, ts, tsʰ/) missing from his phonemic inventory.
- 4 delayed error patterns:
  (a) affricate-stopping (affricates realised as stops, e.g. /tsʰae/ [tae]);
  (b) fronting (/k/ realised as [t], e.g. /kua/ [tua]);
  (c) gliding (/ɹ/ realised as [j], e.g. /ɹoʊ/ [joʊ]);
  (d) consonant assimilation (e.g. /pʰiŋ kuo/ [pʰiŋ puo]).

Child 16 (5;6, male)
- Delayed phonetic and phonemic development.
- 6 phonemes (/k, kʰ, l, ɹ, tʂ, tsʰ/) missing from his phonemic inventory.
- 3 delayed error patterns:
  (a) fronting (/k/ realised as [t], e.g. /kua/ [tua]);
  (b) gliding (/ɹ/ realised as [j], e.g. /ɹoʊ/ [joʊ]);
  (c) /l/ syllable-initial deletion.

Child 17 (5;7, female)
- Delayed phonemic development.
- 3 phonemes (/ʂ, tʂ, tsʰ/) missing from her phonemic inventory.
- 2 delayed error patterns:
  (a) fronting retroflexes as alveolars (e.g. /ʂua/ [sua]);
  (b) X-velarisation (/tsʰ, tʂʰ/ velarised, e.g. /tsʰae/ [xae]; /tʂʰuɑŋ/ [xuɑŋ]).

Child 18 (6;1, male)
- Delayed phonemic development.
- 3 phonemes (/k, ts, tsʰ/) missing from his phonemic inventory.
- 3 delayed error patterns:
  - (a) affricate-stopping (affricates realised as stops, e.g. /tsʰae/ [tae]);
  - (b) fronting (/k/ was fronted as [t], e.g. /kaŋ/ [taŋ]);
  - (c) consonant assimilation (e.g. /pʰiŋ kuo/ [pʰiŋ puo]).

Child 19 (6;7, male)
- Delayed phonemic development.
- 3 phonemes (/ʂ, tʂ, tʂʰ/) missing from his phonemic inventory.
- 1 delayed error pattern: fronting retroflexes as alveolars (e.g. /ʂua/ [sua]).

Consistent disorder subgroup

Child 20 (2;8, male)
- 2 unusual error patterns:
  - (a) syllable-final nasal /ŋ/ realised as [n] (e.g. /pʰiŋ/ [pʰin]);
  - (b) affricates /tɕʰ, tʂ/ realised as [k] (e.g. /tɕʰyn/ [kyn]; /tʂuo/ [kuo]).

Child 21 (4;1, male)
- 1 delayed error pattern – gliding.
- 1 unusual error pattern: /tʂ, tʂʰ/ realised as velar stops [k] or [kʰ] (e.g. /tʂəŋ/ [kəŋ]; /tʂʰuaŋ/ [kʰuaŋ]) .

Child 22 (4;2, male)
- Restricted phonetic and phonemic inventories.
- 3 phones (/tʂʰ, tsʰ, ɹ/) missing from his phonetic inventory.
- 10 phonemes (/tʰ, x, k, kʰ, s, ɹ, tɕʰ, ʂ, tʂʰ, tsʰ/) missing from his phonemic inventory.
- 2 unusal error patterns:
  - (a) nasalising weakly stressed syllables (e.g. /pi tsi/ [pi dʒɐⁿ]; /kʰuae tsi/ [kuae dʒɐⁿ]);
  - (b) /k/ realised as [tʂ] (e.g. /kɤ/ [tʂɤ]; /kao/ [tʂao]).

Child 23 (4;2, male)
- Restricted phonetic inventory.
- 2 phones (/tʂ, l/) missing from his phonetic inventory.
- 1 unusual error pattern – [n] added at syllable-final position (e.g. /tʂuo/ [tʰun]).

Child 24 (4;3, male)
- 2 unusual error patterns:
  - (a) substituting [tɕiɛ] for the weakly stressed syllable [tsi].
  - (b) [n] and [ŋ] added at syllable-final position.

Child 25 (4;6, male)
- Restricted phonetic and phonemic inventories.
- 4 phones (/ɹ, ʂ, tʂ, ts/) missing from his phonetic inventory.
- 7 phonemes (/ɕ, s, ɹ, ʂ, tʂ, tʂʰ, ts/) missing from his phonemic inventory.
- 2 unusual error patterns:
  - (a) substituting [kʰɤ] for the weakly stressed syllable /tsi/.
  - (b) realising /ts/ and /tʂʰ/ as [k] or [kʰ] (e.g. /tsuei/ [kuei]; /tsae/ [kae]; /tʂʰuo/ [kuo]; /tʂʰɤ/ [kʰɤ]).

Child 26 (4;8, female)
- Restricted phonetic and phonemic inventories.
- 6 phones (/kʰ, ɹ, ʂ, tʂ, tʂʰ, tsʰ/) missing from her phonetic inventory.
- 9 phonemes (/kʰ, l, ɹ, tɕ, ʂ, tʂ, tʂʰ, ts, tsʰ/) missing from her phonemic inventory.
- 2 unusual error patterns:
  - (a) replacing /ŋ/ with [n] (e.g. /uaŋ/ [an]);
  - (b) realising affricates as fricatives of the same place of articulation (e.g. /tsʰae/ [sae]; /tɕiao/ [ɕiao]).

Child 27 (5;6, male)
- Restricted phonetic and phonemic inventories.
- 1 phone (/kʰ/) missing from his phonetic inventory.
- 4 phonemes (/k, kʰ, ʂ, ts/) missing from his phonemic inventory.
- 1 unusual error pattern: /k, kʰ/ realised as [tʂ] (e.g. /kɤ/ [tʂɤ]).

Inconsistent disorder group
Child 28 (3;2, male)
- Restricted phonetic and phonemic inventories.
- 4 phones (/s, p, tsʰ, ɹ/) missing from his phonetic inventory.
- 7 phonemes (/p, tʰ, s, ɹ, tʂ, tʂʰ, tsʰ/) missing from his phonemic inventory.
- Variable productions for vowels (e.g. /ɹou/ as [iou], [ou] or [iao]; /tɕʰyn tsi/ as [tʰui tsi], [tʰyɛ tsi] or [tʰiɛ tsi]).
- Variable productions for initial consonants (e.g. /ʂu/ as [xu], [fu] or [ʂu]).

Child 29 (3;6, male)
- Restricted phonetic and phonemic inventories.
- 6 phones (/s, tʂ, kʰ, tʂʰ, ʂ, ts/) missing from his phonetic inventory.
- 10 phonemes (/tʰ, ɕ, kʰ, l, s, tɕʰ, ʂ, tʂ, tʂʰ, tsʰ/) missing from his phonemic inventory.
- Variable productions for syllable-initial consonants. Examples:
  - (a) /ʂu/ realised as [tsu], [tu], or [su];

    (b) /tʂuo/ realised as [kuo] or [tsuo];
    (c) /kʰuae/ realised as [uae], [pae] or [kʰuae];
    (d) /xua/ realised as [kua] or [ua].

Child 30 (3;7, male)
- Restricted phonetic and phonemic inventories.
- 11 phones (/tʰ, k, kʰ, pʰ, s, tɕʰ, ʂ, tʂ, tʂʰ, ts, tsʰ/) missing from his phonetic inventory.
- 15 phonemes (/tʰ, x, ɕ, k, kʰ, pʰ, l, s, tɕ, tɕʰ, ʂ, tʂ, tʂʰ, ts, tsʰ/) missing from his phonemic inventory.
- Restricted syllable sturcture: V or CV.
- Frequent occurrence of reduplications: substituting [tia], [tɕia] or [tɕɐ] for a large number of different syllables while retaining the original tones (e.g. /tʌŋ1/ [tia1]; /tʂʰuaŋ2/ [tia2]; /tɕʰyn2 tsi0/ [tɕia2 tɕɐ0]).
- Frequent occurrence of assimilation: adjacent syllables sharing the same initial consonant and sometimes the same vowel (e.g. /ɕiaŋ tɕiao/ [tiɑ tiɑo]; /nan xan/ [nia nia]; /tsae tɕiɛn/ [tʂA tʂiaŋ]).
- A number of deviant substitutions: [p] for /k/; [t] for [ɕ]; [l] for /ʂ/.
- Frequent variable productions. Examples:
    (a) /ɕin/ realised as [iŋ], [tia], or [tin];
    (b) /tsʰae/ realised as [sae], [xae], [tʰia], or [tsuo];
    (c) /ɕywn mɑo/ realised as [ia mɑo], [in mɑo], or [tA mɑo].

Child 31 (3;11, male)
- Restricted phonetic and phonemic inventories.
- 10 phones (/f, kʰ, pʰ, l, s, ɹ, ʂ, tʂ, ts, tsʰ/) missing from his phonetic inventory.
- 14 phonemes (/n, f, ɕ, k, kʰ, pʰ, l, s, ɹ, ʂ, tʂ, tʂʰ, ts, tsʰ/) missing from his phonemic inventory.
- Many deviant substitutions (e.g. /pʰiŋ/ [tiŋ]; /niao/ [tɕiao]; /fA/ [pA]; /tʂuo/ [puo]; /ny/ [niou]; /nan/ [yan]; /mən/ [mein]; /ʂuei/ [jei]).
- Variable productions for initial consonants (especially with /ɕ/ and /k/) and vowels. Examples:
    (a) /ɕin/ realised as [təŋ], [xin] or [tən];
    (b) /kua/ realised as [pA] or [tua].

Child 32 (3;11, male)
- Restricted phonetic and phonemic inventories.
- 7 phones (/kʰ, l, s, ɹ, ʂ, tʂʰ, tsʰ/) missing from his phonetic inventory.
- 12 phonemes (/tʰ, x, k, kʰ, l, s, ɹ, ʂ, tʂ, tʂʰ, ts, tsʰ/) missing from his phonemic inventory.

- Variable productions for syllable-initial consonants, particularly /s, ṣ, tṣ, tṣʰ/. Examples:
  (a) /ṣ/ deleted, velarised as [x], or realised as [f], (e.g. /ṣuei/ as [xuei] or [uei]; /ṣua/ as [xua] or [ua]; /ṣu/ as [fu] or [xu]);
  (b) /tṣ/ deleted or realised as [k], [ts], or [ṣ], (e.g. /tṣuo/ as [kuo] or [uo]; /tṣi/ as [tsi] or [ṣ]);
  (c) /tṣʰ/ deleted or velarised as [x], (e.g. /tṣʰuaŋ/ as [xuaŋ] or [uaŋ]).
  d) /s/ deleted, velarised as [x], or realised as [ts] or [k], (e.g. /san/ as [tsan], [ian] or [san]; /suan/ as [kuan] or [xuan]).

Child 33 (4;0, male)
- Restricted phonemic inventory.
- 6 phonemes (/ç, k, l, ɹ, ṣ, ts/) missing from his phonemic inventory.
- Variable productions for syllable-initial consonants, especially /ç, k, ṣ/. Examples:
  (a) /ç/ deleted or realised as [tç], [tçʰ], [p], (e.g. /çiŋ/ as [tçiŋ] or [in]; /çin/ as [tçin], [tçʰin] or [pin]);
  (b) /k/ realised as [t], [p], (e.g. /kuo/ as [tuo], [kuo] or [puo]; /kuən/ as [kɤ], [tuən] or [kuən]);
  (c) /ṣ/ realised as [k], [kʰ], [t], [s], [x], [ts], (e.g. /ṣu/ as [ku], [tɤ] or [kʰɤ]; /ṣou/ as [sou], [tou] or [ṣou]; /ṣuei/ as [tsuei] or [xuei]).

5.4 Discussion

The study reported in this chapter examined the phonological systems of 33 Putonghua-speaking children with speech disorders using both quantitative and qualitative measures. The analyses indicated that the children could be categorised into four subgroups: one child had an articulation disorder, 18 were delayed in their phonological development, eight had consistent phonological disorder, and six had inconsistent phonological disorder. The individual profiles suggested that children differed significantly in terms of the size of their phonetic and phonemic inventories, types of error patterns, and degree of inconsistency. Nevertheless, these children exhibited characteristic error patterns that allowed identification of subgroups.

5.4.1 How does the phonology of one subgroup of children differ from another?

One child had difficulty articulating /s/. There was no apparent organic cause for her impairment: there was no anatomical anomaly and she passed oro-motor, hearing and VMI screening tests. A neurological disorder (a dysarthria) would affect articulation of a range of sounds rather than only one sound (Dodd, 1995). Therefore the impairment reflects a breakdown in motoric ability – mislearning of an articulatory gesture. In contrast, phonological disorders have a cognitive-linguistic basis (Bernthal & Bankson, 1998; Gierut, 1998). Articulation and phonological disorders can co-occur (Elbert, 1992; Fey, 1992). However, the relationship between the two disorders (i.e. whether they contribute to speech processing in a parallel way or in a hierarchical way, one dominating the other) needs further research.

The largest subgroup (54.5%) of children in this study had delayed phonological development. Most children in this subgroup (15 out of the 18) used one or more delayed error patterns. These error patterns were not found among more than 10% of the children of the same age band in the normative data, but frequently used by more than 10% of the children of a younger age band. While all of the 'normal' error patterns were present in the children of the youngest age group in the normative data, most error patterns were suppressed by 5;0 in the normative data. Therefore, children older than 5;0 (Children 15, 16, 17, 18 and 19) whose speech included several delayed error patterns were very straightforward cases and often associated with a severe degree of delay.

The identification of delay was less straightforward for children under four years – at this age normally developing children still make some developmental errors. In this study, three children under 4;0 were classified as delayed because their phonetic and/or phonemic inventories resembled those of younger children in the normative data. These children should have acquired some phones or phonemes at least one year earlier. It is arguable whether the size of a child's phonetic and phonemic inventories alone can be used as a criteria for assessing phonological development. There is no evidence that one sound is dependent on another for development and there are individual variations in sequences of phonetic and phonemic acquisition (Bankson & Bernthal, 1998). However, classifying these children as delayed is supported by the fact that their speech was perceived as abnormal by their caretakers and they made more errors and used more error patterns than children of the same age group as shown by Z scores (for example, Child 3's Z scores for PCE and the total number of error patterns fell more than four standard deviations above the means of the normally developing children).

Although the delayed subgroup showed slower acquisition compared to normally developing children, accumulating research evidence suggests that the differences between delayed and normally developing groups are more quantitative than qualitative in nature. Variations in rate and manner of acquisition exist among normally developing children as well (Winitz, 1969; Wells, 1985, 1986). Previous research suggests that children with delayed phonology do not differ from normally developing children on tasks that assess their understanding of their native phonological system (Dodd *et al.*, 1989), and fine motor skills (Bradford & Dodd, 1994, 1996). It therefore seems likely that children with delayed development constitute the lower range of normal development.

A range of unusual error patterns were used by the eight children with consistent phonological disorder (e.g. syllable-final consonant addition, replacing alveolar and retroflex affricates with the velar stop /k/). Some children with consistent disorder also used developmentally delayed error patterns (e.g. Children 21, 22). It is nevertheless important to classify these children as disordered rather than delayed: the existence of unusual error patterns suggests a breakdown in these children's speech processing mechanism. This breakdown is possibly the inability to accurately extract knowledge from the mental lexicon about the nature of the phonological system to be learned (Dodd *et al.*, 1989).

The children classified with inconsistent disorder (six children in total) had variable productions of more than 40% of the items when the same words were sampled in three separate trials. Their substitution patterns were unpredictable with the same target being replaced by different error sounds in the same environment. Some sounds were used interchangeably (e.g. Child 31 sometimes replaced /f/ with [p] and sometimes replaced /p/ with [f]). Vowels were also subject to error, while normally developing children rarely made vowel errors. Such error patterns suggests that inconsistent production is not due to an inability to articulate sounds. Rather, the deficit may be in the organisational use of sounds, probably in the child's ability to assemble contrastive phonological plans for words (Dodd *et al.*, 1989).

Statistical analyses suggested that there were significant differences in PCE, the total number of error patterns, the number of missing phones and inconsistency rating between the three subgroups of delay, consistent disorder and inconsistent disorder. *Post-hoc* analyses indicated that the inconsistent disorder subgroup had higher PCEs, used significantly more error patterns and had more missing phones than the delayed subgroup. However, the fact that the inconsistent disorder subgroup (mean age 3;8) was younger than the other two subgroups (delay subgroup: 4;8; consistent disorder subgroup: 4;3) made it difficult to speculate on the bases of these measurements alone on whether the inconsistent disorder subgroup is associated with severity of impairment.

Z scores were used to compare the performance of children of different ages. As illustrated in Figure 5.2 in section 5.3.1.3, the children with high inconsistency ratings had a wider range of Z score distribution, covering both high and low Z scores. This result supports McCormack and Dodd's (1998) finding that there is no continuous relationship between severity of speech errors and degree of inconsistency.

The distribution of Z score for PCE, the number of error patterns, and the number of missing consonants also has implications for identification and diagnoses of speech disordered children. If we assume 10% as a pre-valence figure (National Institute on Deafness and Other Communication Disorders, 1994), Z scores higher than 1.28 would signal a deviation from the normal population. As shown in the figures, most of the children scored higher than 1.28. In fact, if the children older than 4;6 are excluded (for the reason that the means and standard deviations are not available among the normally developing children of the same age group), only two children's Z scores fell below 1.28. All the delayed children had at least one Z score (all the three Z scores in some children) higher than 1.28. This finding is consistent with the definition of delayed development – a quantitatively slower rate of development.

5.4.2 How does disordered phonology of Putonghua-speaking children differ from that of normally developing Putonghua-speaking children?

Speech disorder is diagnosed with reference to normal development: the age of emergence and stabilisation of phonemes, error patterns and consistency. A diagnosis of delayed phonological development reflects slower acquisition (i.e. smaller phonetic and/or phonemic inventories in comparison to the children of the same age and use of one or more error patterns that should no longer be evident). The use of rules or error patterns atypical of normal development characterises the speech of children with consistent disorder. Children with inconsistent disorder have variations in their production atypical of normal development.

However, speech disordered Putonghua-speaking children showed sensitivity to the phonological system being acquired, especially the degree of phonological saliency of syllable components, similar to normally developing children (for a definition of phonological saliency, see 3.6.5). As discussed in 3.6.5, tones in Putonghua have the highest saliency, syllable-initial consonants have the lowest saliency of the four syllable components; and vowels and syllable-final consonants are in between. Despite the diversity of error types, the Putonghua-speaking children with speech disorders seldom made tone errors (see 3.6.5 and 4.6.2.2 for discussions on error-free acquisition of tones); only four children (12%) made vowel errors; and only four children (12%) used delayed error patterns affecting syllable-final consonants. Most errors affected syllable-initial consonants.

Certain sounds (e.g. velar stops /k/ and /kʰ/, retroflexes and affricates) were often absent from speech disordered Putonghua-speaking children's phonemic inventories. It is not surprising that children with speech difficulties had problems with the sounds such as retroflexes and affricates, since normally developing children also had difficulties with these sounds. This is evident both in the late acquisition of these sounds and high frequency of fronting and backing error patterns in the normative sample. However, velar stops /k/ and /kʰ/ are exceptional. While 90% of the children in the normative sample had mastered the stops by 3;6 and 90% of the children were able to articulate the unaspirated /k/ by 2;0, 13 children (39%) in the speech disordered children were still not able to use velar stops /k/ and /kʰ/ either phonologically or phonetically correctly.

The factors that contribute to breakdown in the phonological processing of certain sounds, especially sounds which are otherwise acquired early in the normative sample, are not known. Ingram (1989b) made a similar observation for disordered English-speaking children, finding persistent problems with the production of fricatives and affricates in the speech of some English-speaking children with speech disorders. Although affricates are acquired late by English-speaking children, some fricatives are acquired early (Prather *et al.*, 1975; Dodd, 1995). Mohring (1931) suggested that those phonemes with which children with speech disorders had least difficulty would be acquired earlier by normally developing children than phonemes they found difficult. Therefore, the order of acquisition of phonemes in normally developing children could be identified by looking at the phonemes prone to error in children's disordered speech. The fact that disordered Putonghua-speaking and English-speaking children make errors with phonemes that are acquired early by normally developing children does not support this suggestion.

5.4.3 How does disordered phonology of Putonghua-speaking children differ from that of children speaking other languages?

Stoel-Gammon (1991: 27–8) noted that 'published studies of developmental phonological disorders have focused almost exclusively on young British and American children, thereby precluding the possibility of making firm statements regarding universal patterns'. This study on speech disordered Putonghua-speaking children, together with other cross-linguistic studies (for a review, see 1.3.1; for Italian data, see Bortolini & Leonard, 1991; Portugese data, see Yavas & Lamprecht, 1988; for Swedish data, see Nettelbladt, 1983), provides evidence concerning some universal patterns of speech disorder. Subgroups of speech disorders (articulation, delayed development, consistent disorder and inconsistent disorder) have been observed in English (Dodd *et al.*, 1989), Cantonese (So & Dodd, 1994), Spanish (Goldstein, 1996), Turkish, (Topbas, 1997) and German data (Fox, 1997). Studies of phonologically disordered bilingual children (Cantonese–English, Dodd *et al.*, 1997; Punjabi–English, Holm *et al.*, 1999; Italian–English, Holm & Dodd, 1999) also support the existence of four subgroups: the bilingual children had similar surface error characteristics in both their languages despite the influence of the ambient phonology of the language.

Nevertheless, irrespective of the languages being learned, there is evidence that children with speech disorders show sensitivity to the structure of the language being learned. Speech disordered children speaking one language may present with error patterns which are considered 'typical' or 'atypical' relative to the normal patterns of that language. In other words, what error patterns should be considered unusual and used as criteria for diagnosis varies from one language to another. For example, while 'backing' at syllable-initial position is considered an atypical error pattern in Cantonese-speaking children (So & Dodd, 1994), it is frequently found in normally developing Putonghua-speaking children. Therefore, a Cantonese-speaking child using a backing error pattern would be considered disordered, but a Putonghua-speaking child would not.

In general, the characteristics of speech disordered Putonghua phonology are similar to those of English-speaking children (Grunwell, 1982; Stoel-Gammon & Dunn, 1985; Stoel-Gammon, 1991). These characteristics are:

- Persisting error patterns. Error patterns which are prevalent in young children persisted beyond age-appropriate levels.
- Unusual error patterns rarely found among normally developing children.
- Variability/inconsistency in production. Variability in normally developing children is common when a child varies between an incorrect and correct form. Speech disordered children (especially the subgroup of inconsistent disorder) had a range of incorrect realisations for the same target sounds in the same context.
- Restricted phonetic or phonemic inventories. Most of speech disordered children have limited phonetic or phonemic inventories.

- Systematic sound or syllable preference. Some sounds or syllables are preferred to other sounds or syllables in children's productions and used as substitutes for other sounds or syllables. This often leads to many homonymous productions and low intelligibility. Child 30 is a typical example. In his production, [tia] and [tɕia] replaced a number of syllables including /tʌŋ/, /tʂʰuaŋ/, /ʂuei/, /tɕʰyn/, /tʰae/, etc.

5.5 Summary

In this chapter, the phonological development of 33 children with functional speech disorders is described. Among the children, one child had an articulation disorder, 18 had delayed development, eight consistently used unusual error patterns, and six children's speech was characterised by inconsistency of production. The analyses lead to the following conclusions:

- Cross-linguistic evidence was provided for four-subgroup diagnosis system (articulation, delay, consistent disorder, and inconsistent disorder) – a combined linguistic and psycholingusitic approach in categorising heterogeneous speech disordered children.
- A number of qualitative and quantitative measurements in screening phonologically disordered Putonghua-speaking children were suggested and their effectiveness in diagnoses of speech disorders was evaluated.
- Patterns found in speech disordered Putonghua-speaking children were compared with normally developing children. Both normally developing children and speech disordered children show sensitivity to the phonological system of the language being learned. However, phonemes which are problematic for disordered children are not necessarily the same phonemes acquired late by normally developing children. This not only indicates the atypical nature of disordered children, but also suggests that further research is needed to examine the factors that contribute to the breakdown in the speech-processing chains of speech disordered children.
- Putonghua-speaking children with disordered speech are sensitive to the structure of the ambient language. They also share the characteristics common to speech disordered children speaking other languages. These characteristics are persisting delayed error patterns, unusual error patterns, variability, restricted phonetic or phonemic inventories, and systematic sound or syllable preference.

The present chapter provides perhaps the first comprehensive account of the disordered phonology of Putonghua-speaking children. The next chapter will examine the development and change over time in the disordered phonology of Putonghua-speaking children.

Chapter 6
Development and Change in the Phonology of Putonghua-speaking Children with Functional Speech Disorders

6.1 Introduction

In the previous chapter, the phonological systems of 33 Putonghua-speaking children with speech disorders were examined using both quantitative measures (PCE, tonal number of error patterns, total number of missing consonants in phonetic inventory and inconsistency) and qualitative measures (phonetic inventory, phonemic inventory and error patterns). The study reported in the present chapter is a follow-up to the one in Chapter 5. The focus here is on the issue of development and change over time in the disordered phonology of Putonghua-speaking children. As discussed in 1.3.2, there is disagreement regarding when developmental speech disorders emerge and whether speech disorder in young children spontaneously resolve (Compton, 1976; Fletcher, 1990; Ingram, 1989b; McReynolds, 1988; cf. Leahy & Dodd, 1987). Yet, data on the origin of developmental speech disorders is difficult to obtain. By the time children are suspected of having speech disorders, their early speech development is beyond close inspection. Data on the spontaneous resolution of speech disorders is also difficult to get, since the children will be involved in treatment programmes once they are referred to speech and language therapy services.

However, because speech and language therapy services are yet to be established in China, Putonghua-speaking children with speech disorders receive no speech and language therapy intervention. This less than ideal situation in fact provides a rather unique opportunity to document the development of disordered phonology in the absence of intervention, which may shed light on the course of development of speech disorders in children.

The specific research questions addressed by the study reported in this chapter are:

- What changes in developmental patterns characterise phonological impairment in Putonghua-speaking children in terms of qualitative measures and quantitative measures?
- Do the changes in developmental patterns of different subgroups of speech disorders (articulation disorder, delayed phonological development, consistent disorder and inconsistent disorder) differ?

6.2 Method

6.2.1 Participants

Of the 33 children with speech disorders who were studied in Chapter 5, six (three with delayed development, two with consistent disorder and one with inconsistent disorder) from the same nursery were assessed for a second time after an average interval of 11 months (11.29 ± 4.03 months). Recall that the 33 children included one boy (coded as Child 12 in chapter 5) who had been previously assessed in the cross-sectional study and whose speech development was considered normal at the time. He was later referred by his teacher as having 'speech difficulties', when speech disordered children were sampled. The assessment (Chapter 5) revealed that his phonological development was delayed. The data from the two assessments of this particular child (the first time as part of the cross-sectional study and the second time when he was diagnosed as having a delayed phonology) are included in the present analysis (referred to as Child A in this chapter).

All the children were acquiring Putonghua as their first language and attended nurseries in Beijing. None of the children had siblings. None of the children had hearing impairment as detected by pure tone audiometry, abnormalities in oral structure as assessed by an oromotor examination (Ozanne, 1992), learning problems as assessed by the Visual-Motor Integration test (Beery, 1989), behavioural difficulties or language comprehension problems as reported by teachers and parents or observed by researchers. Information about the children's age and gender is summarised in Table 6.1.

6.2.2 Procedure

The children were assessed individually in a quiet room at the nursery, using the same picture-naming and picture-description tasks that were used in the cross-sectional normative study in Chapter 3 and speech disorder study in Chapter 5. The target words in the picture-naming task sampled all the consonants, vowels and tones in Putonghua phonology.

The children were first asked to name the objects or actions in 44 pictures three times, with each trial separated by another activity. The children were then asked to describe what was 'funny' in another set of pictures (e.g. a panda eating watermelon in bed). The children's speech was audiotaped using a Sony professional micro-recorder.

The speech samples from the picture-naming and picture-description tasks were transcribed using IPA. Inter-transcriber reliability (on all of the samples) for syllable-initial word-initial, syllable-initial within-word, syllable-final word-final, and syllable-final within-word consonants was 95.0%, 94.6%, 98.6% and 97.2%, respectively.

6.2.3 Data analysis

The following quantitative and qualitative measures were derived for the two assessments of each child. All of them have been used and defined in the speech disorder study reported in the previous chapter.

- *Percentage of Consonants in Error (PCE):* PCE for each child was calculated by the formula (number of times phonemes are produced in error / total number of phonemes in the sample × 100).
- *Z score for PCE:* Calculated by the formula (the difference between PCE and mean PCE of the children of the equivalent age band in the normative sample divided by standard deviation). The Z scores were used to compare children with speech disorders and normally developing children of the same age.
- *Phonetic inventory:* All the sounds produced at least once in the speech sample, irrespective of whether it was the correct target.
- *Phonemic inventory:* All the sounds produced correctly on at least two of three opportunities.
- *Error patterns:* Similar to the speech disorder study, each error pattern was classified as either age-appropriate (if used by at least 10% of the children in the same age band in the normative sample), delayed (if used by less than 10% of the children in the same age band in the normative data, but appropriate for younger children) or unusual (if not found among more than 10% of the normally developing children).
- *Total number of error patterns:* Consistent differences between children's realisations and target sounds. An error pattern had to occur at least twice in different lexical items to be included.
- *Inconsistency rating:* Comparison of the three productions of the 44 words. The number of words with two or three different productions was expressed as a percentage of the total number of words produced three times.

6.3 Results

Group trends in development and change for the seven children are examined as a whole in terms of PCE, Z score for PCE, the number of error patterns, phonetic and phonemic inventories, and error patterns.

6.3.1 Severity scores

The children's PCE, the total number of error patterns identified, Z score for PCE, and inconsistency rating are summarised in Table 6.1. Statistical analyses showed that there was a significant decrease between the two assessments in terms of PCE, the total number of error patterns and inconsistency rating. (Wilcoxon Two-related Sample Signed Ranks Test: $T = 1$, $n = 7$, $p = 0.028$ for PCE; $T = 0$, $n = 7$, $p = 0.043$ for the total number of error patterns; $T = 0$, $n = 7$, $p = 0.028$ for inconsistency rating.)

Table 6.1 Results of quantitative analysis for seven children in the two assessments

Child	Gender	Age	PCE	Error pattern	Z score for PCE	Inconsis-tency rating	Classi-fication
A	boy	3;3	17.82	3	0.621	10.0	Normal
		4;6	7.93	3	0.023	22.7	Delay
B	girl	4;3	24.81	4	2.932	20.5	Delay
		5;0	6.03	1	−0.305*	14.0	Normal
C	girl	3;8	43.41	10	4.014	27.1	Delay
		4;5	24.69	9	2.912	23.0	Delay
D	girl	3;3	24.45	7	1.595	29.5	Delay
		4;5	15.22	5	1.279	25.0	Delay
E	girl	2;2	32.16	11	0.763	35.1	Consistent D
		3;7	25.37	5	1.813	30.2	Consistent D
F	boy	2;8	42.91	14	3.275	28.0	Consistent D
		3;5	20.16	7	0.965	21.0	Consistent D
G	boy	3;11	76.20	10	8.012	48.8	Inconsistent D
		4;5	55.10	11	8.155	47.6	Inconsistent D

Note: 'Consistent D': consistent disorder; 'Inconsistent D': inconsistent disorder. The Z score for child B was computed with reference to the means and standard deviation of the age group of 4;0–4;6, the oldest age group in the normative study.

6.3.2 Phonetic and phonemic inventories

Table 6.2 compares the missing phones and phonemes in the phonetic and phonemic inventories of each child in the first and second assessment. The size of six children's phonetic and phonemic inventories increased over time. This is in agreement with the changes reflected in quantitative measures of PCE and Z scores. Yet Child G showed the opposite tendency in the development of his phonemic inventory: 6 phonemes he had mastered in the first assessment were not present in his inventory at the second assessment. In other words, he appeared to have 'lost' six phonemes over time. 'Loss' of phonemes was also found in another two children: Child A lost two phonemes; Child C lost three phonemes.

Statistical analyses showed that there was a significant increase in the size of the phonetic inventory between the two assessments (Wilcoxon Two-related Sample Signed Ranks Test: $T = 0$, $n = 7$, $p = 0.018$). However, there was no significant increase in the size of the phonemic inventory between two assessments (Wilcoxon Two-related Sample Signed Ranks Test: $T = 5.50$, $n = 7$, $p = 0.149$). Although the children had increased the number of speech sounds in their phonetic repertoire, they had not significantly increased their contrastive use.

Table 6.2 The missing phones and phonemes in seven children's phonetic and phonemic inventories in the two assessments

Child	*Sample 1*	*Sample 2*
A phone	s, ts	none
phoneme	k, kʰ, s, tʂʰ, ts	ʂ, tʂ, tʂʰ
B phone	ʂ, ɹ, tʂ, tʂʰ	none
phoneme	p, ʂ, ɹ, tʂ, tsʰ, tʂʰ	tʂ,tʂʰ
C phone	k, kʰ, ɹ, s, tsʰ	ɹ, tʂ, ts, tsʰ
phoneme	k, kʰ, f, s, x, l, tʂʰ, ts, tsʰ	ʂ, ɹ, tʂ, tʂʰ, ts, tsʰ
D phone	l, ʂ, ɹ, ts	l
phoneme	f, l, ʂ, ɹ, tɕ, tʂ, tʂʰ, ts	k, ʂ, l, tʂ, tʂʰ
E phone	p, pʰ, m, n, f, s, ʂ, l, ɹ, tɕ, tɕʰ, tʂ, tʂʰ, ts, tsʰ	tʂ
phoneme	p, pʰ, m, n, f, s, ʂ, l, ɹ, tɕ, tɕʰ, tʂ, tʂʰ, ts, tsʰ	l, tɕ, tɕʰ, tʂ, tʂʰ, ts

Table 6.2 *cont.*

Child	Sample 1	Sample 2
F phone	k^h, s, ʂ, l, ɹ, tɕʰ, tʂ, tʂʰ, ts, tsʰ	s, ʂ, l, tʂ, tʂʰ
phoneme	k, k^h, s, x, ʂ, l, ɹ, tɕʰ, ɕ, tʂ, tʂʰ, ts, tsʰ	k, s, ʂ, l, tʂ, tʂʰ, ts, tsʰ
G phone	p^h, k^h, f, s, ʂ, l, ɹ, tʂ, ts, tsʰ	p^h, k^h, s, ʂ, ɹ, tɕ, tʂʰ, ts, tsʰ
phoneme	p^h, k, k^h, n, f, s, ʂ, l, ɹ, tʂ, tʂʰ, ts, tsʰ	p^h, t^h, k, k^h, m, n, f, s, x, ʂ, ɹ, tɕ, tɕʰ, ɕ, tʂ, tʂʰ, ts, tsʰ

6.3.3 Error patterns

Eighteen 'normal' (both age-appropriate and delayed) error patterns and 13 unusual error patterns were identified (see Table 6.3).

Table 6.3 Error patterns in seven children's speech in the two assessments

	A		B		C		D		E		F		G	
	3;3	4;6	4;3	5;0	3;8	4;5	3;3	4;5	2;2	3;7	2;8	3;5	3;11	4;5
Normal error patterns														
Consonant assimilation	*	*				*			*		*	*		
Syllable initial deletion					*	*	*						*	*
Fronting:														
/ʂ/ → [s]	*		*	*			*		*		*			
/ɕ/ → [ʃ/ʂ]										*				
/k/ → [t]	*				*	*	*	*						
Backing:														
/s/ → [ʂ]	*				*	*					*			
Stopping:														
/ts/ → [t]			*		*	*	*	*	*		*		*	*
/s/ → [t]				▓	▓			▓	*	▓			▓	▓
/x/ → [k]							▓							
Affrication:														
/ɕ/ → [tɕ]	▓								*		*	*	▓	▓
Deaspiration:														
/tʰ/ → [t]					*	*			*		*			
Aspiration:														
/t/ → [tʰ]			*	▓			*							

Table 6.3 *cont.*

	A		B		C		D		E		F		G	
	3;3	4;6	4;3	5;0	3;8	4;5	3;3	4;5	2;2	3;7	2;8	3;5	3;11	4;5
X-velarisation			*	*	*				*	*	*	*		
Gliding			*								*			
Final /n/ deletion		*			*	*					*			
Backing: /n/ → [ŋ]			*	*	*				*					*
Final /ŋ/ deletion									*		*			
Triphthong reduction											*			
Unusual error patterns														
Syllable initial addition													*	
Vowel change													*	*
/ŋ/ → [n]									*	*				
/ts, tʂ/ → [k]							*		*	*				
/f/ → [p]													*	*
/tʂ/ → [p]													*	*
/pʰ/ → [t]													*	*
/tɕʰ/ → [k]									*		*			
										ç→t		ʂ→k	tɕ→n	k→p
														x→t

Note: Shaded cells are delayed error patterns for a particular child. Idiosyncratic errors are listed for Children E, F and G.

- Normal error patterns (both age-appropriate and delayed): There was a significant decrease in the number of normal error patterns identified between the first and second assessment (Wilcoxon Two-related Sample Signed Ranks Test: T = 2.00, n = 7, *p* =

0.041). Some error patterns identified in the first assessment were no longer evident in the second assessment: e.g. stopping /ts/→ [t] and final /n/ deletion in Child B. Some error patterns persisted over time even if they were no longer age-appropriate: e.g. aspiration in Child C; stopping /s/→ [t] in Child E. Four error patterns, though not identified at the initial assessment, appeared in some children's speech at the second assessment: fronting /ʂ/→ [s] in Children A, D, E and F; stopping /ts/→ [t] in Child E; affrication /ɕ/→ [tɕ] in Child A; backing /n/→ [ŋ] in Child G.

- Unusual error patterns: There was no significant change in the number of unusual error patterns identified in the first and second assessment (Wilcoxon Two-related Sample Signed Ranks Test: T = 0, n = 3, *p* = 0.317).

6.3.4 Individual profiles

Individual profiles are also presented to outline variations among the children diagnosed as belonging to different subgroups of speech disorders. Since the children made no tonal errors, tonal markers are not included in the examples.

Child A (normal → delayed)
This boy's development was considered normal when assessed at 3;3 as part of the cross-sectional study in Chapter 3. Three age-appropriate error patterns – consonant assimilation, fronting /k/ as [t] and backing /s/ as [ʂ] – were identified in his initial speech sample. When assessed again upon his teacher's insistence after 13 months, a delayed error pattern – affrication (fricatives replaced with affricates e.g. /ɕiɛ/ [tɕiɛ]) was identified. The other two error patterns identified in his second sample were age appropriate: fronting (retroflexes realised as alveolars. e.g. /ʂuei/ [suei]) and consonant assimilation.

Child B (delay → normal)
When initially assessed, this girl showed characteristics of delayed development: restricted phonetic inventory and delayed error patterns. The size of her phonetic inventory at 4;3 was equivalent to that of children aged 3;1–3;6. The error patterns she used included three age-appropriate ones: fronting (retroflexes realised as alveolars, e.g. /tʂuo/ [tsuo]); affricate-stopping (/tsʰ/ realised as stop [tʰ], e.g. /tsʰae/ [tʰae]); /n/ deletion at syllable-final position with vowel

changes in the syllable (e.g. /wan/ [wae]) and one delayed error pattern: stopping (/s/ realised as [t], e.g. /tan/ [san]). When she was assessed again seven months later, all the error patterns except fronting had been eliminated from her speech. Her phonetic inventory was complete.

Child C (delay → delay)

This girl's phonology was considered delayed at the first assessment. Her phonemic repertoire was smaller compared to that of normally developing children of the same age. She also used a wide range of error patterns such as fronting /k/ to [t] (e.g. /kua/ [tua]; /kʰuae/ [tuae]), backing alveolars as retroflexes (e.g. /san/ [ʂan]), affricate-stopping (affricates realised as [t], e.g. /tɕʰin/ [tʰin]), stopping (/s/ realised as [t], e.g. /san/ [tan]), deaspiration (e.g. /tʂʰuɑŋ/ [tsuɑŋ]), aspiration (e.g. /tuo/ [tʰuo]), X-velarisation (e.g. /fA/ [xA]), gliding (e.g. /ɹou/ [jou]), /n/ syllable-final deletion (e.g. /wan/ [wa]), and replacing /n/ with [ŋ] (e.g. /ɕin/ [ɕiŋ]). Among them, stopping /s/ as [t] was a delayed error pattern. All of these error patterns except gliding were still present in her speech when assessed seven months later. She remained delayed in her phonological development.

Child D (delay → delay)

In addition to a restricted phonemic inventory, one delayed error pattern – stopping (/x/ realised as [k], e.g. /kua/ [xua]) was evident in this girl's speech when assessed for the first time. The age-appropriate error patterns identified were: consonant assimilation, syllable initial deletion, fronting /k/ as [t] (e.g. /kuae/ [tuae]), affricate-stopping (e.g. /tsuo/ [tuo]), X-velarisation (e.g. /fA/ [xA]), and replacing /n/ with [ŋ] at syllable-final position. In the second sample, collected 12 months later, her phonology was still typical of delayed development with a restricted phonemic repertoire and the use of delayed error patterns. Some of the error patterns identified in the first sample (e.g. consonant assimilation, stopping /x/ as [k]) had been eliminated; some (e.g. fronting /k/ as [t], affricate-stopping) remained; and some error patterns were newly developed: fronting retroflexes as alveolars (e.g. /ʂui/ [sui]) and stopping /s/ as [t] (e.g. /san/ [tan]).

Child E (consistent disorder → consistent disorder)

The first assessment revealed the child's consistent use of one unusual error pattern, indicating a diagnosis of consistent disorder. The unusual error pattern was the replacement of affricates /ts, tʂ, tɕʰ/ with the velar stop /k/ (e.g. /tʂɤ/ [kɤ]). When assessed 13 months later, this unusual error pattern had been eliminated. However, she had developed another unusual error pattern – replacing /ɕ/ with [t] (e.g. /ɕiɛ/ [tiɛ]). Some of the age-appropriate error patterns identified in the first assessment such as consonant assimilation, syllable-initial deletion, and affrication were no longer evident at the second assessment.

Child F (consistent disorder → consistent disorder)
When this boy was assessed for the first time, a number of age-appropriate and unusual error patterns were identified in his speech. The unusual error patterns were: syllable-final nasal /ŋ/ realised as [n] (e.g. /pʰiŋ/ [pʰin]); and affricates /tɕʰ, tʂ/ realised as [k] (e.g. /tɕʰyn/ [kyn]; /tʂuo/ [kuo]). These error patterns were still evident in the second sample, nine months later. A new unusual error pattern, replacing /ʂ/ with [k] (e.g. /ʂu/ [ku]), was identified in his speech. Some of the normal error patterns such as affrication, X-velarisation, final /n/ deletion were no longer evident.

Child G (inconsistent disorder → inconsistent disorder)
At the first assessment, this boy's phonology resembled that of children with inconsistent disorder: inconsistency was evident in both initial consonants (especially /ɕ/ and /k/) and vowels. Examples were: /ɕ/ realised as [tɕ], [t] or [x], (e.g. /ɕin/→ [təŋ], [xin], or [tɕən]); /k/ realised as [p] or [t] (e.g. /kua/→ [pʌ] or [tua]). Many deviant substitutions affecting initial consonants and vowels were found in his speech: /pʰiŋ/ [tiŋ]; /niɑo/ [tɕiɑo]; /fʌ/ [pʌ]; /tʂuo/ [puo]; /ny/ [niʊ]; /nan/ [yan]; /mən/ [mein]; /ʂuei/ [jei]. His phonology remained inconsistent at his second assessment six months later. Many non-developmental errors were identified at the first and second assessment (e.g. /pʰiŋ/ [tiŋ]; /fʌ/ [pʌ]; /tʂuo/ [puo]; /kua/ [pʌ]; /kʰuae/ [pae]; /xae/ [tʌ]). Unlike the other six children reported in this chapter, the size of his phonemic inventory did not increase over time. Instead, some sounds which he was able to use phonemically correctly at the first assessment were no longer present in his inventory (see phoneme grids in Table 6.4 for an overall picture of the boy's inconsistent productions in the two assessments).

Table 6.4 Phoneme Grids: Child G's inconsistent productions

Child G: First assessment at the age of 3;11

	ø	x	kʰ	k	ç	tɕʰ	tɕ	ʂ	tʂʰ	tʂ	ɹ	l	s	tsʰ	ts	n	tʰ	t	f	m	pʰ	p	
p																					▓		p
pʰ																	▓						pʰ
m																				▓			m
f																			▓				f
t																		▓					t
tʰ																		▓					tʰ
n	▓						▓								▓								n
ts																		▓					ts
tsʰ																		▓					tsʰ
s											▓	▓											s
l	▓																						l
ɹ	▓																						ɹ
tʂ																		▓				▓	tʂ
tʂʰ									▓						▓								tʂʰ
ʂ	▓																						ʂ
tɕ							▓																tɕ
tɕʰ						▓																	tɕʰ
ç		▓				▓																	ç
k			▓																				k
kʰ																						▓	kʰ
x	▓																						x
ø																							ø
	ø	x	kʰ	k	ç	tɕʰ	tɕ	ʂ	tʂʰ	tʂ	ɹ	l	s	tsʰ	ts	n	tʰ	t	f	m	pʰ	p	

Production

Note: The phonemes in both left and right edges are targets. The phonemes in both upper and lower edges should be used as references for children's realisations. The shaded cells on the same horizontal line represent children's realisations of the same phoneme on several trials.

Table 6.4 *cont.*

Child G: second assessment at the age of 4;5

	ø	x	kh	k	ç	tçh	tç	ş	tşh	tş	ɹ	l	s	tsh	ts	n	th	t	f	m	ph	p	
p																						▓	p
ph																					▓		ph
m	▓																			▓			m
f																			▓				f
t																		▓					t
th																	▓						th
n	▓															▓							n
ts																		▓					ts
tsh																		▓					tsh
s																		▓					s
l	▓																						l
ɹ	▓																						ɹ
tş										▓													tş
tşh									▓														tşh
ş								▓															ş
tç							▓																tç
tçh						▓																	tçh
ç					▓																		ç
k				▓																			k
kh			▓																				kh
x		▓																					x
ø	▓																						ø
	ø	x	kh	k	ç	tçh	tç	ş	tşh	tş	ɹ	l	s	tsh	ts	n	th	t	f	m	ph	p	

Production

Note: The phonemes in both left and right edges are targets. The phonemes in both upper and lower edges should be used as references for children's realisations. The shaded cells on the same horizontal line represent children's realisations of the same phoneme on several trials.

6.4 Discussion

6.4.1 General patterns of development and changes found among seven children

In this study, the spontaneous changes in the phonological systems of seven Putonghua-speaking children with speech disorders were described using both quantitative and qualitative measures. As a group, the children showed a tendency to make statistically significantly fewer errors, use fewer error patterns and perform more consistently over time. Their phonetic inventories expanded over time although there was no significant increase in their phonemic use. There was a significant reduction in the number of normal error patterns used (including both age-appropriate and delayed error patterns) when the children were assessed for the second time. However, there was no significant change in the use of unusual error patterns.

The phenomenon of 'recidivism' (i.e. loss of phonetic and phonemic contrasts, see Smith, 1973) was evident during the course of the children's development. Child C was able to produce the phonemes /ɹ/, /ʂ/ and /tʂ/ at the first assessment, yet failed to produce them at the second assessment; Child G lost six phonemes which he had used correctly on two-thirds of occasions in the first assessment. Some error patterns which were not present in the children's phonology during the first assessment were found in the children's second assessment. This phenomenon, however, is not unique to children with speech disorders. Smith (1973) documented some patterns of change in the phonological system of a boy aged 2;2–4;0. He found that during the development the boy lost some systematic contrasts or correct forms that had already been established. The same tendency was also reported in Weiner and Wacker's (1982) observations on changes that took place over a period of one year and a half in ten normally developing children aged 3;1–3;6.

However, the extent to which a phonologically impaired child like Child G in this study failed to produce phonemes which he had used correctly at an earlier developmental stage is noticeable. One possible explanation is that the child was experiencing a 'destabilisation' developmental stage (Grunwell, 1992): a stable pronunciation pattern changes into variable production as the result of the introduction of a new pattern into the child's phonology or generalisation of phonological rules. Alternatively, recidivism of such an extent might indicate that the child's phonological difficulties have come to affect his phonological production to a greater degree.

6.4.2 Patterns of development in different subgroups

Individually, children showed significant variations in their developmental patterns. In terms of the subgroups of normal, delay, consistent disorder, and inconsistent disorder, changes that took place in the phonology of these seven children were:

- normal → delay (one child);
- delay → normal (one child);
- delay → delay (2 children);
- consistent disorder → consistent disorder (2 children);
- inconsistent disorder → inconsistent disorder (one child).

Children from different subgroups of speech disorders may follow different developmental routes as the result of different underlying deficits. Accumulating research evidence indicates that different types of speech disorders arise from different underlying deficits (Dodd & McCormack, 1995). Children who use one or more error patterns typical of the development of a younger child were classified as delayed. Previous research suggests that children with delayed phonological development do not differ from normally developing children on phonological awareness tasks that assess their understanding of their native phonological system (Dodd *et al.*, 1989), or on fine motor skills (Bradford & Dodd, 1994; 1996). Therefore, it seems likely that children with delayed development constitute the lower range of normal development. Evidence from the speech disorder study reported in Chapter 5 suggested that the differences between delayed and normally developing children are more quantitative than qualitative in nature. In other words, there is no impairment in these children's internal phonological acquisition mechanism. The delay in acquisition is more likely due to external or environmental factors such as 'inadequate exposure to language' (Savic, 1980).

If it is external factors such as insufficient language input that lead to delay in the children's phonological development, it is feasible that:

(a) children with characteristics of delayed development are those who initially follow a normal developmental path, but for environmental reasons, slow down in their rate of acquisition – as proposed by several researchers (Compton, 1976; Fletcher, 1990; Ingram, 1989b; McReynolds, 1988);

(b) children who are delayed in their phonological development may be able to catch up and follow the normal developmental path again, if the external factors that impede their phonological acquisition no longer exist;

(c)   children may remain delayed over time, if the external factors that impede their phonological acquisition are still in function.

These possibilities are reflected in the observed changes that occurred to Children A, B, C and D in this study. Child A was developing normally at the first assessment and then became delayed, falling behind children of the same age. In contrast, Child B was delayed when assessed initially but performed within normal limits at the second assessment. Children C and D remained delayed across the two assessments. However, further research is needed to confirm the direct link between the language exposure and phonological development, perhaps by monitoring the changes both in language input and in the rate of phonological development.

Compared with the delayed subgroup, children with consistent or inconsistent disorders evidenced little change in their phonological systems (e.g. Children E, F and G), perhaps due to deficits in their internal speech processing mechanism. For children with consistent disorder (i.e. children who consistently use unusual error patterns) the breakdown may lie in an impaired ability to accurately extract knowledge from the mental lexicon about the nature of the phonological system to be learned (Dodd *et al.*, 1989). For children with inconsistent disorder (i.e. children who tend to have inconsistent production of the same words in the same context) the deficit may lie in the children's ability to assemble contrastive phonological plans for words (Dodd *et al.*, 1989).

Compared to external environmental causal factors, an internal underlying deficit in children's phonological system is resistant to spontaneous change. The development and change in the phonological systems of children with such deficits were examined in terms of error patterns (i.e. strategies adopted by the children to cope with the complex task of learning how to pronounce words, Shriberg and Kwiatkowski, 1980). While little change occurred to the unusual error patterns used by phonologically disordered children over time, there was a significant reduction in the number of delayed error patterns used at the first and second assessment. Similar findings were reported in Weiner and Wacker's (1982) and Leahy and Dodd's (1987; 1995) studies. Further, unusual and delayed error patterns respond differently to treatment: unusual error patterns may be more resistant to treatment while delayed error patterns are likely to resolve spontaneously (Dodd & Iacano, 1989).

6.4.3 Clinical implications

Different underlying deficits may lead to different patterns of developmental change, suggesting that differential diagnosis has important clinical implications. The delayed subgroup has been reported to be the largest subgroup among the children with speech disorders. For example, 54.5% of the Putonghua-speaking children with speech disorders, who were randomly selected for study, belonged to the subgroup of delayed phonological development (Chapter 5). The current study indicated that the delayed development of one child, who used a small number of delayed error patterns at the first assessment, spontaneously resolved without intervention. Future research might investigate on whether the extent of early delay might predict spontaneous recovery in the largest subgroup of children with speech disorders. However, as yet it is not possible to make any firm argument concerning the early prognostic indicators of spontaneous recovery from delayed phonological development due to the limited number of children in this study.

However, the children with consistent or inconsistent disorders made relatively little progress over time, adding to the evidence that speech disorder is resistant to spontaneous change (Leahy & Dodd, 1987; Weiner & Wacker, 1982). This factor needs to be considered when deciding clients' priority for treatment. The findings also have implications for choice of treatment targets. The children with consistent disorder used some delayed error patterns at the first assessment that were eliminated by the second assessment. This finding might suggest that those aspects of the phonological system that appear to be developing non-age-appropriately do not necessarily need to be targeted in therapy. Rather, therapy might target those aspects of the system that are developing atypically. The child who made inconsistent errors at the first assessment remained inconsistent. In such cases, establishing consistency of production would seem to be an important therapeutic goal.

6.5 Summary

The studies reported in this chapter and Chapter 5 are the first systematic studies of the phonological systems of Putonghua-speaking children with functional speech disorders. They illustrate similarities as well as differences in children with speech disorders across languages. The follow-up study of seven children with disordered phonology reported in this chapter provides a unique window to the development and change of the phonological systems of these children over time and raises important professional issues regarding clinical intervention.

It is suggested that:

- Children with different underlying deficits follow different paths of development. Delayed development may be caused by external environmental factors such as the quality and amount of language input. Therefore, it can occur at any stage of children's phonological acquisition and may spontaneously resolve later. However, this does not seem to be the case for children whose speech is characterised by consistent use of atypical error patterns or inconsistent errors. These error patterns have been shown to be associated with underlying deficits in the children's internal speech processing mechanism (Dodd & McCormack, 1995). Unless these deficits are targeted in specific intervention programs, there appears to be little spontaneous change in the number of unusual phonological errors made.
- Different developmental patterns found in children with different types of speech disorders imply the need for differential diagnosis and treatment. The fact that some of the children with delayed development would resolve spontaneously without intervention and the children with consistent or inconsistent disorders would make little progress over time needs to be considered in deciding clients' priority for therapy.

Chapter 7

The Phonological Systems of a set of Putonghua-speaking Twins

7.1 Introduction

This chapter turns its attention to the phonological development of Putonghua-speaking twins. It is often mentioned in the literature that the most salient characteristic of the communication profiles of twin children is their impaired phonology (McEvoy & Dodd, 1992). However, little is known about the phonological development of twins speaking languages other than English. The hypotheses discussed in 1.3.3, i.e. whether the phonological development of twins would follow the same path as normally developing singletons, and whether twins have a dual phonological representation for some lexical items, have not been tested on twins speaking languages other than English. Putonghua-speaking twins in China are of particular interest, since the phonological systems of Putonghua and English differ markedly (for details, see 2.12). The present study of a set of Putonghua-speaking twins therefore offers cross-linguistic and cross-populational evidence for studies on children's developmental phonology.

Previous research allows hypotheses to be made about the aspects of twins' phonological system that are most likely to be at risk for atypical development. These hypotheses are partly derived from the data on singleton Putonghua-speaking children who are speech disordered (Chapters 5 and 6), and partly from descriptions of characteristics of English-speaking children who are speech disordered (e.g. syllable constraints, Dunn & Davis 1983; restricted phoneme contrasts, Leonard, 1985). Two general research questions addressed in the present study were:

(1) Would the phonological systems of the co-twins demonstrate the characteristics of delayed or disordered development? To answer this question, the twins' phonological systems, identified both in single words (picture-naming task) and connected speech (child–child interaction and child–adult interaction), were compared, using qualitative measures (phonetic and phonemic inventories, and error patterns) and quantitative measures (PCE and inconsistency rating).

It was predicted that:

- the twins would make more errors than singleton children of the same chronological age;
- the twins' error patterns would include some patterns reflecting delayed acquisition and/or some patterns that are atypical of normal development;
- the atypical patterns would reflect restricted phonemic inventory, giving rise to unusual substitution patterns that rarely occur in the speech of normally developing children.

(2)   Did the co-twins understand both the adult and their sibling's phonological forms? Data from a single word comprehension task and child–child interaction would be used to answer this question. It was predicted that the twins would have no difficulty understanding the adult form of words and that each twin would demonstrate comprehension of their sibling's mispronunciations irrespective of differences between their pronunciations.

The study reported in this chapter was a single case study. The case study approach, common to studies of child language development, has many advantages. As Platt (1988) argued, a single case study can be used to refute a universal generalisation, may be a useful source of hypotheses and can identify and demonstrate features or characteristics which need to be taken into account in any generalisation. Nevertheless, each child varies from each other in terms of developmental patterns and individual strategies (Vihman, 1996). Caution should therefore be taken in generalising the findings of a single case study.

7.2 Method

7.2.1 Participants

DN and EN were a set of identical twins (boys, aged 6;2). DN was the older twin. They did not have any other siblings. They were both attending a district nursery in Beijing and referred by their nursery teacher during the investigation on children with speech disorders. Putonghua was their first language and the language of their parents. They had little exposure to any other languages.

7.2.1.1 General development

The twins were born at 37 weeks, and weighted 2478g and 2602g respectively. Their mother experienced no problems during pregnancy. The twins were healthy and there was nothing relevant in their medical history. Their motor development was reported to be within the normal range. They had no hearing impairment as detected by pure tone audiometry, no abnormalities in oral structure as assessed by oromotor examination (Ozanne, 1992), no learning problems as assessed by Visual-Motor Integration test (Beery, 1989).

7.2.1.2 Family background

The mother of the twins worked as a shop assistant. She took leave before the children were born and did not work until the children were four years old. The father worked in a garage. The mother and grandmother were the two main caretakers of the boys before they went to the nursery at the age of four. The grandmother spoke a *Beifang* dialect (see 2.1). She visited the family at weekends. During an interview with the parents, they reported their concern about the children's language development. They noticed two years ago that their children's speech was not as intelligible as that of other children of the same age. Since then, they had tried to spend more time talking with the boys. They also asked the nursery teacher to encourage the boys to speak.

7.2.1.3 Nursery

The nursery was run by a local district council. It was a small nursery with only three teachers and about 20 children aged 1;9–6;2. The children spent one or two hours singing, doing origami, counting or story-telling in the classroom in the mornings. The rest of day was spent playing among themselves under supervision. DN and EN were the oldest among the children in the nursery. They started the nursery full-time at the age of four. They were planning to go to a primary school at the age of seven.

7.2.2 Tasks and procedures

The boys were given four tasks.

- *Picture-naming task.* Each child was asked to name 44 pictures (the cross-sectional normative and speech disorder studies used the same picture-naming task). If the child failed to say the target word in the task, semantic or contextual prompts would be offered. The children were asked to do the task three times, with each round of picture-naming separated by a free talk activity.
- *Single word comprehension.* Each child was given 44 pictures (the same pictures as in picture-naming task). When the name of an object chosen randomly was pronounced in Putonghua, the child was asked to pick out the picture in which the object was depicted within a reasonable time limit. For example, if the researcher said /ɕiɛ/, 'shoe', the child would be expected to point to the picture with

shoes in it. He would get one point if he found the target. The children's performance was recorded on an observation sheet. The children would be asked to try again if they did not find the target for the first time. The children did the task separately.

- *Child–child interaction.* The children played a question-and-answer game between themselves. They were given some pictures and encouraged to ask each other questions. For each correct answer (judged by the children themselves), they would get a building block. The child who received the most building blocks would be the winner. Some questions asked by the children were related to the objects in the pictures, such as, 'why is a banana yellow?' and 'why is the moon in the sky?'. Other questions were not related to the objects in the pictures, for examples, 'In which dynasty did people start making gunpowder?', and 'Why are monks bald?'.

- *Child–adult interaction.* Each child was engaged separately in a conversation with the researcher. The children were encouraged to initiate topics.

The assessment took place in a quiet room in the children's nursery school. In the first session, each child, in turn, was given the picture-naming task. Then the researcher had a 10-minute free conversation with each child individually (child–adult interaction). After that, the children were given the single word comprehension task individually. In the second session which took place one day later, the two children were brought together and encouraged to have conversation between themselves (child–child interaction). The conversation lasted 20 minutes. The speech samples were audiotaped using a Sony professional microrecorder.

7.2.3 Analysis

All the speech samples were transcribed using IPA. Inter-transcriber reliability for syllable-initial word-initial, syllable-initial within-word, syllable-final word-final, and syllable-final within-word consonants was 96.7%, 96.0%, 98.6% and 97.4%, respectively.

A number of measures were derived from the transcripts:

- Phonetic inventory: All the sounds produced at least once in the speech sample, irrespective of whether it was the correct target.
- Phonemic inventory: All the sounds produced correctly on at least two of three opportunities.
- Inconsistency rating: Comparison of the three productions of the 44 words in the picture-naming task.

- Percentage of Consonant in Error (PCE): PCE for each sample was calculated by the formula: the number of times phonemes are produced in error/the total number of phonemes in the sample × 100.
- Error patterns: Similar to the speech disorder study, each error pattern was classified as either age-appropriate (if used by at least 10% of the children in the same age band in the normative sample), delayed (if used by less than 10% of the children in the same age band in the normative data, but appropriate for younger children) or unusual (if not found among more than 10% of the normally developing children).

For the picture-naming task, phonetic and phonemic inventories, PCE, error patterns and inconsistency rating were derived. For the conversational speech elicited both in child–child and child–adult interaction, PCE and error patterns were derived based on the transcription of the 10-minute speech sample in each activity. The recurrent words in child–child interaction (i.e. words occurring both in one child's utterance and in the other's subsequent utterance) were pooled together for a closer examination of the children's phonological systems.

7.3 Results

7.3.1 The twins' phonological system

The children's phonological systems were identified on the basis of single word speech elicited from picture-naming task and connected speech both in child–child and child–adult interaction.

7.3.1.1 Single word speech

The twins' phonological systems identified in the single word speech (Table 7.1) were compared with the norms which were derived in the same speech mode (Chapter 3). While 90% of the normally developing children would have completed phonetic acquisition by 4;6 and phonemic acquisition by 5;6, there were still four phonemes missing from the twins' phonemic inventories, although both of them had complete phonetic repertoires. Both of them were not able to use /ʂ, tʂ, tʂʰ, ɹ/ contrastively. Compared to the mean PCE of the oldest age group (4;0–4;6) in the normative sample, i.e. 7.8%, DN and EN's PCEs (10.6% and 13.6% respectively) were slightly higher even though they were about two years older than the oldest age group in the normative data. They had very low inconsistency rating (2.3% for both), indicating that they used their phonemes consistently. They did not make any tonal errors.

Table 7.1 The twins' phonological systems identified in the picture-naming task

Measures	*DN*	*EN*
Missing phones	None	None
Missing phonemes	ʂ, tʂ, tʂʰ, ɹ	ʂ, tʂ, tʂʰ, ɹ
PCE	10.6	13.6
Inconsistency rating	2.3	2.3
Delayed error patterns	Fronting /ʂ/ → [s] e.g. /ʂu/ [su] Gliding /ɹ/ → [j] e.g. /ɹoʊ/ [joʊ] Backing /n/ → [ŋ] e.g. /mən/ [məŋ] Stopping /x/ → [k] e.g. /xua/ [kua] Final /n/ deletion e.g. /uan/ [ua]	Fronting /ʂ/ → [s] e.g. /ʂuei/ [suei] Gliding /ɹ/ → [j] e.g. /ɹoʊ/ [joʊ] Backing /n/ → [ŋ] e.g. /mən/ [məŋ] Stopping /tɕ/ → [t] e.g. /tɕiɑo/ [tiɑo] Fronting /k/ → [t] e.g. /kɑŋ/ [tɑŋ] Affrication /ɕ/ → [tɕ] e.g. /ɕi/ [tɕi]
Unusual error patterns	None	/tʂʰ/ → [k/kʰ] e.g. /tʂʰuɑŋ/ [kuɑŋ]

While normally developing children of the same age group would have eliminated almost all the developmental error patterns, some error patterns still persisted in the twins' speech. They shared three delayed error patterns: fronting retroflexes as alveolars, e.g. /ʂoʊ/ [soʊ], gliding, e.g. /ɹoʊ/ [joʊ], and backing /n/ as [ŋ] at syllable-final position, e.g. /ɕin/ [ɕiŋ]. Apart from these, two individual delayed error patterns (replacing /x/ with [k], e.g. /xua/ [kua]; deleting /n/ at syllable-final position, e.g. /uan/ [uae]) were identified in DN's sample. Three delayed error patterns (replacing affricates with stops, e.g. /tɕiɑo/ [tiɑo]; fronting /k/ as [t], e.g. /kɑŋ/ [tɑŋ]; and affricating /ɕ/, e.g. /ɕi/ [tɕi]) were evident in EN's sample. EN also used one unusual error pattern: replacing /tʂʰ/ with [k/kʰ], e.g. /tʂʰɤ/ [kʰɤ].

7.3.1.2 Child–child interaction

In the conversational sample collected in child–child interaction, PCEs for DN and EN were 17% and 24% respectively. Four delayed and one unusual error patterns were found in DN's speech; seven delayed and two unusual error patterns were identified in EN's speech. They shared four delayed error patterns (i.e. fronting, initial consonant deletion, backing /n/ as [ŋ] and vowel reduction (examples are given in Table 7.2).

7.3.1.3 Child–adult interaction

In the conversational sample collected in child–adult interaction, PCEs for DN and EN were 21% and 27% respectively. Six delayed and two unusual error patterns were evident in DN's speech; seven delayed and four unusual error patterns were found in EN's speech. Five delayed error patterns occurred in the speech of both. They were fronting, initial consonant deletion, backing /n/ as [ŋ], vowel reduction and backing /s/ as [ʂ] (examples are given in Table 7.2).

Table 7.2 The twins' PCEs and error patterns identified in the connected speech during child–child and child–adult interaction

	DN	*EN*
Child–child interaction		
PCE	17	24
Delayed error patterns	Fronting /tʂ/→ [ts] e.g. /tʂɑŋ/[tsɑŋ]	Fronting /ʂ/→ [s] e.g. /ʂɑŋ/ [sɑŋ]
	Initial consonant deletion e.g. /xuo/ [uo]	Initial consonant deletion e.g. /kuo/ [uo]
	Backing /n/→ [ŋ] e.g. /san/ [saŋ]	Backing /n/→ [ŋ] e.g. /san/ [saŋ]
	Vowel reduction e.g. /iɑo/ [ɑo]	Vowel reduction e.g. /tɕiou/ [tɕou]
		Stopping /tɕ/→ [t] e.g. /tɕiou/ [tiou]
		Stopping /x/→ [k] e.g. /xuo/ [kuo]
		Backing /s/→ [ʂ] e.g. /san/ [ʂan]
Unusual error patterns	/n/→ [l] e.g. /nA/ [lA]	/ts, tʂʰ/→ [k/kʰ] e.g. /tʂi/ [ki]
		/tʂ/→ [tɕ] e.g. /tʂi/ [tɕi]

Table 7.2 *cont.*

	DN	EN
Child–adult interaction		
PCE	21	27
Delayed error patterns	Fronting /tʂ/→ [ts] e.g. /tʂɑŋ/[tsɑŋ] Initial consonant deletion e.g. /xuo/ [uo] Backing /n/→ [ŋ] e.g. /san/ [saŋ] Vowel reduction e.g. /iɑo/ [ɑo] Backing /s/→ [ʂ] e.g. /si/ [ʂi] Gliding /ɹ/→ [j] e.g. /ɹən/ [jən]	Fronting /ʂ/→ [s] e.g. /ʂɑŋ/ [sɑŋ] Initial consonant deletion e.g. /kuo/ [uo] Backing /n/→ [ŋ] e.g. /san/ [saŋ] Vowel reduction e.g. /tɕiou/ [tɕou] Backing /s/→ [ʂ] e.g. /san/ [ʂan] Stopping /tɕ/→ [t] e.g./tɕiou/ [tiou] Stopping /x/ → [k] e.g. /xuo/ [kuo]
Unusual error patterns	/n/→ [l] e.g. /nA/ [lA] /s/→ [ɹ] e.g. /sɤ/ [ɹɤ]	/tʂ, tʂʰ/→ [k/kʰ] e.g. /tʂi/ [ki] /tʂ/→ [tɕ] e.g. /tʂi/ [tɕi] /ɕ/→ [t] e.g. /ɕiɑŋ/ [tiɑŋ] Final /ŋ/ addition e.g. /xua/ [xuɑŋ]

7.3.2 Recurrent words

The recurrent words were those occurring in two subsequent turns by different children. The recurrent words frequently occurred when one of the children answered a question using one or several words which had appeared in his co-twin's questions. For example, DN said, 'Tell me what *plastic* is made of' and EN answered, '*Plastic* is made of *plastic*'. A close examination of recurrent words can provide information on whether the second child was able to understand and interpret the first speaker's pronunciations – the first child's pronunciation could be the same as or different from that of adults, or the same as or different from that of the second child.

There were 47 recurrent words altogether in child–child interaction (see Table 7.3). The results showed that the two children had the same pronunciations for some words and different pronunciations for some other words. They shared the same pronunciations for 57.4% of the recurrent words (i.e. 27 words). Among the words pronounced the same by the two children, 19 (40.4% of the total recurrent words) were the same as adult forms. The same error patterns occurred to eight words (17.0% of the total recurrent words). Among the words not realised in the same way by the two children (42.6% of the recurrent words), different error patterns were apparent. For example, while DN fronted /tʂ/ as [ts] in the word /tʂi 3/ (meaning *'paper'*), EN substituted [k] for /tʂ/. It was clear from the context that both of them tried to pronounce the target /tʂi/.

Despite the pronunciation differences on some of the words, the twins seemed to have no difficulty in interpreting each other's utterances in the child–child interaction.

Table 7.3 The twins' pronunciation on recurrent words

Target	English	DN first	EN second	Target	English	DN second	EN first
yɛ4·liaŋ0	moon	✓	yɛ·iaŋ	tʂi1·tʰao4	know	tsi·tʰao	tsi·tʰao
ɕiaŋ1·tɕiao1	banana	ɕiaŋ·tɕia	✓	uəŋ1·uəŋ1	onomatopoeia	✓	✓
nA3	which	✓	✓	tʂʰɤ1	car	tsʰɤ	tsʰɤ
niɛn2	year	liɛn	✓	ʂi2·tʰae4	decade	✓	si·tʰae
ʂuei3	water	suei	suei	nA3	which	✓	✓
nA3	which	lA	✓	tɕi3·tɕi3	when	✓	✓
tsʰao3	grass	✓	✓	tʂaŋ3	grow	tsaŋ	tsaŋ
suo4·liao4	plastic	✓	✓	tsʰao3	grass	✓	✓
tsuo4	make	✓	✓	ʂi2·tʰou0	stone	✓	✓
tsuo4	make	✓	kʰɤ	tʂaŋ3	grow	tsaŋ	tsaŋ
ʂan1	mountain	suan	san	tʂi3	paper	✓	tɕi
ʂuei3	water	✓	suei	ʂi4	be	✓	si
tʂi3	paper	✓	tɕi	kʰao1·lou2	building	✓	✓
lou2·faŋ2	building	✓	✓	nan2	south	✓	✓
nA4	that	lA	✓	nA3	which	✓	✓
ʂən2·mo0	what	sən·mo	sən·mo	ɹən4·ʂi0	know	✓	ɹən·si
ʂuo1	say	suo	suo	pʰo1·li0	glass	✓	po·li

Table 7.3 *cont.*

Target	English	DN first	EN second	Target	English	DN second	EN first
fan4	rice	✓	✓	tʂi3	paper	tsi	ki
tʂʰi1	eat	✓	✓	mɑo1	cat	✓	✓
çiɛn4	line	✓	✓	ʂən2·mo0	what	✓	sən·mo
pi2·tʰi4	snivel	✓	✓				
ʂi4	be	✓	si				
tsʰae1	guess	tʂʰae	tae				
suo4·liɑo4	plastic	✓	ʂuo·liɑo				
lu4·in1·tçi1	recorder	✓	✓				
tʂan4·tʂəŋ1	war	tsan·tsəŋ	tsan·tsəŋ				
xuA1	flower	χuɑŋ	✓				

Note: ✓ represents the children's correct realisation of the target. Shaded cells are the recurrent words pronounced in the same way by both children.

7.3.3 Single word comprehension

This task tested the twins' ability to understand adult phonological forms. The two children both achieved 100% accuracy in the discrimination of the adult's productions by picking out all the target pictures according to the naming.

7.4 Discussion

The present case study described the phonological abilities of a set of Putonghua-speaking twins aged 6;2. Speech samples were analysed using a range of qualitative (phonetic and phonemic inventories, and error patterns) and quantitative measures (inconsistency rating and PCE). The children's comprehension of adult forms was assessed by picture recognition and their understanding of each other's speech was examined through the use of recurrent words in child–child interaction. The data were analysed to examine the predictions made at the beginning of the chapter.

7.4.1 Twins' delayed and atypical development

Compared with the baseline data for singletons, the twins' speech evidenced characteristics of delayed and disordered phonological development in the following ways:

- By six years of age, Putonghua-speaking children's phonology is usually free of errors (Chapter 3). However, the twins pronounced 11.6% and 13.6% of consonants incorrectly in the picture-naming task, 21% and 27% of consonants incorrectly in child–adult interaction and 17% and 24% of consonants incorrectly in child–child interaction. Using Shriberg and Kwiatkowski (1982)'s criteria, their speech disorder would be classified as being of mild-moderate severity.
- Although they were able to articulate all the Putonghua sounds, neither of the twins had completed their acquisition of phonemic contrasts. As reported in Chapter 5, eight out of 14 children with phonological disorders had non-age-appropriate phonemic repertoires. Likewise, both of the twins were limited in their use of phonemic contrasts, especially the contrastive use of the retroflex feature.
- Both used some error patterns which were either inappropriate for their chronological age or seldom used by normally developing singletons. Some of the atypical error patterns used by the twins have been observed in the speech of singleton Putonghua-speaking children who have been identified as being phonologically disordered. As reported in Chapter 5, among 14 children diagnosed as having phonological disorders, five were found using the velar stop (e.g. [k]) to replace an alveolar or retroflex affricate (/ts/ or /tʂ/), and two replaced retroflex affricates (e.g. /tʂ/) with an alveolo-palatal affricate (e.g. [tɕ]), apart from other atypical error patterns. Both error patterns have been identified in EN's speech. EN was also found to add [ŋ] at syllable-final position (seven out of 34 opportunities) in the connected speech, showing his preference for CVC syllable structure – the same pattern was reported to be evident in the disordered speech of Putonghua-speaking children.

The existence of such a delayed and disordered phonological system in the Putonghua-speaking twins suggests that twins are at risk for speech difficulties. This is supported by the previous research findings on English-speaking children. For example, Matheny and Bruggemann (1972) reported a high incidence of speech disorders in the twin population. McMahon *et al.*'s (1998) follow-up study of 20 sets of twins with phonological difficulties in the pre-school years found that although most of the children had developed relatively normal speech and language ability, 90% of them performed more poorly than controls on tasks of phonological processing and literacy – similar to singleton children with speech disorders. Johnston *et al.* (1984) also found that twins who had speech or language problems in the pre-school years were likely to have reading difficulties later. This indicates that twins' early patterns of speech difficulties were neither a transient phase nor an alternative route to normal development (cf. Malmstrom & Silva, 1986).

7.4.2 Causaul factor for twins' atypical phonological development

Despite some similarities, the phonological systems of the siblings within the twin set were not identical. Tables 7.1 and 7.2 showed that although the twin set shared some error patterns, both of them used some idiosyncratic error patterns. In the single word speech mode, DN used two error patterns not used by the other twin, and EN used four error patterns, including an unusual one, not evident in his sibling's speech. This finding, similar to those reported for English-speaking twins, provided evidence against the notion of twin language. If the twins shared an autonomous language, they should pronounce words identically. Alternative explanations for their high incidence of phonological delay and disorder should, then, be considered.

While previous research has failed to find reliable associations between biological factors and speech disorder in twins (McEvoy & Dodd, 1992), more and more studies seem to suggest that the nature of twins' language learning situation may play an important causal role (Savic, 1980). Firstly, twins are exposed to qualitatively different language input as the result of the triadic nature of interaction (Tomasello *et al.*, 1986) and have less opportunities for one-to-one interaction than first-born children, single children and children with a larger inter-sibling age (Koch, 1956). In carer–twin interactions, adults are less responsive to individual children, initiate and maintain fewer interactions with individual children and use a more directive style of speech compared to singleton–adult interactions (Tomasello *et al.*, 1986; Stafford, 1987). In addition, twins are each other's primary communicative partner. They were found to engage in preverbal vocal interactions with each other (Keenan & Klein, 1975; Savic, 1980) and to share utterances when playing (McMahon, 1996). These findings suggest that twins' language learning environment is exceptional.

7.4.3 Dual phonological representation

Neither child made errors when asked to identify pictures named by an adult. The analyses of the recurrent words in the child–child interaction showed that the twins had different pronunciations for some of the same words. However, both twins understood all the questions they asked each other. There was no communication breakdown and the children did not ask each other for clarification. English-speaking twins have also been reported to understand their sibling's mispronunciations as well as adult pronunciation (Dodd & McEvoy, 1994). As discussed in Section 1.3.3, one possible explanation for twins' ability to understand both adult and their sibling's forms of pronunciation might be the presence of dual phonological representations for word recognition in twins' lexicon.

The finding that twins and singleton children with phonological disorders used similar atypical error patterns does not imply that singleton children also have dual representations for many lexical items. Rather, the finding emphasises the role of the phonological representations in acquiring the contrasts and constraints of the phonology being learned. Twins' impaired ability to derive those constraints might be due to competing representations of a range of lexical items developed in their exceptional language learning environment. Further research is needed to identify the deficits that might underlie singleton children's impaired ability to derive the phonological contrasts and constraints of the target phonology.

7.5 Summary

Similar to the studies reported in the previous two chapter (Chapters 5 and 6), the single case study of the phonological development of a set of twins is the first of its kind on Putonghua-speaking children. Despite the limited scope of the study, the findings revealed some interesting patterns which contribute to the discussion of a range of theoretical issues regarding the communication profiles of twins. To summarise,

(a)   The co-twins' phonological systems had similarities in that they both evidenced characteristics of delayed or disordered phonological development and shared some error patterns. However, the existence of individual error patterns in each twin's phonological system suggested that their phonological systems were not identical.

(b)   Both twins could understand adult and their sibling's form of pronunciation, indicating that dual phonological representations for some words might exist in their mental lexicon.

It should be emphasised that we do not imply that the twins had an initial deficit in the speech processing chain. What made them different from other children is their developmental circumstances and the possible existence of dual phonological representations for word recognition in their lexicon. Clearly, more research is needed in order to gain a better understanding of the speech and language development of twins.

Chapter 8
Phonological Development of a Putonghua-speaking Child with Prelingual Hearing Impairment: A Longitudinal Case Study

8.1 Introduction

As discussed in 1.1, studies of phonological development in atypical circumstances can reveal 'universals' which operate in the language development of both normally developing children and children growing up in atypical circumstances, irrespective of the languages being acquired. Chapters 5, 6 and 7 have examined the phonological systems of children with functional speech disorders and twins. This chapter examines the development of phonology of a Putonghua-speaking child with prelingual hearing impairment. The general aim of the study is to reveal both cross-linguistic similarities and the influence of the ambient language on the phonological acquisition of children with hearing impairment. In addition, the effect of hearing impairment on phonological acquisition is discussed.

The specific questions this study aims to address are:

(1) What are the longitudinal developmental patterns of the phonological system of the Putonghua-speaking child with severe prelingual hearing loss?
(2) What are the similarities and differences between the phonological acquisition of a Putonghua-speaking child and that of children of other language backgrounds with hearing impairment (for example, Cantonese and English)?

8.2 Method

8.2.1 Participant

The child, referred to as ZL, had a severe bilateral prelingual hearing loss, following ANSI (American National Standards Institute, 1989) classification criterion. Unaided pure tone averages of thresholds at 500, 1K, and 2K Hz were 75 dB in the right ear and 107 dB in the left ear. Aided levels were 54 dB in the right ear and 83 dB in the left ear.

Born in Beijing, ZL was the single child in the family. His mother and father were university clerks and monolingual Putonghua speakers. His parents found out that he could not hear properly when he was eight months old. The possible cause for his hearing impairment was maternal infection during pregnancy. He also had a middle ear infection at the age of six months. He had been wearing binaural hearing aids since he was one year old. The regular check-ups he had showed that his hearing remained stable. ZL was acquiring Putonghua as first language and attended a nursery full time. According to the parental and nursery reports, his cognitive development was within the normal range. There were no abnormalities in his oral structure as assessed by an oromotor examination (Ozanne, 1992), or learning problems as assessed by the Visual-Motor Integration test (Beery, 1989).

8.2.2 Procedure

ZL was assessed in a quiet room at the nursery, using the picture-naming and the picture-description task (the same as the tasks in the cross-sectional study and speech disorder study). The child was first asked to name the objects and actions in 44 pictures three times and then to describe what was happening in five pictures. If the child failed to say the target in the picture-naming task, the examiner would offer semantic or contextual prompts. If the prompts failed, the child would be asked to imitate the examiner. Imitated responses were marked on a record form. The child's speech was audiotaped using a Sony professional micro-recorder. About 20 minutes' free talk before and after assessment was also recorded. Data collection took about 40 minutes. The boy was assessed at the age of 3;5, 3;9, 4;1 and 4;5, following the same procedure.

8.2.3 Data analysis

The speech sample collected in the picture-naming and picture-description tasks was transcribed in IPA by two native Putonghua-speaking linguists. ZL imitated 4.5%, 9%, 9% and 4.5% of the responses in the picture-naming task at the age of 3;5, 3;9, 4;1 and 4;5, respectively. Imitated responses were excluded in the analysis. Inter-transcriber reliability on the child's speech sample collected at the age of 3;5 was 92.1%, 90.1%, 98.4% and 98.2% for syllable-initial word-initial consonants, syllable-initial within-word consonants, syllable-final word-final consonants, and syllable-final within-word consonants respectively.

The following quantitative and qualitative measures were derived to chart the child's phonological ability.

- *Phonetic inventory:* All the sounds produced at least once in the speech sample, irrespective of whether they were the correct targets.
- *Phonemic inventory:* All the sounds produced phonologically correctly on at least two of three opportunities.
- *Percentage of consonants in error (PCE):* PCE for each sample was calculated by the formula: the number of times phonemes are produced in error / the total number of phonemes in the sample × 100%.
- *Z score for PCE:* Z scores were calculated for PCE by the formula: the difference between PCE and mean PCE of the children of the equivalent age band in the normative sample divided by standard deviation. Z scores compared PCE of the child with that of normally developing children of the same age.
- *Error patterns:* Similar to the speech disorder study, each error pattern was classified as either age-appropriate (if used by at least 10% of the children in the same age band in the normative sample), delayed (if used by less than 10% of the children in the same age band in the normative data, but appropriate for younger children) or unusual (if not found among more than 10% of the normally developing children).
- *Inconsistency rating:* Comparison of the three productions of each of the 44 words.

Ten-minute free talk was also transcribed and analysed. The following general measures of language development reflecting language diversity, structure and complexity were derived:

- *Mean length of utterance (MLU):* The sum of the number of morphemes in each intelligible utterance divided by the number of fully intelligible utterances (Miller, 1981). In this study, the syllable was used as the counting unit of MLU in Putonghua. Cheung (1998) found that there was a significant correlation between MLU in word and MLU in syllable during the acquisition by Chinese-speaking children. However, the reliability of MLU in measuring the speech of children with hearing impairment is questionable, since these children often produce partially intelligible utterances or vocalisations. MLVV, devised by Lyon and Gallaway (1990), overcomes this problem (see below).
- *Mean length of vocalisation/verbalisation (MLVV):* The sum of the number of morphemes in each utterance divided by the number of utterances including both intelligible verbalisations and unintelligible vocalisations (Lyon & Gallaway, 1990).

- *Mean maximum length of utterance (MaxLU):* The average number of morphemes in the five longest utterances (Lyon & Gallaway, 1990).
- *Type-token ratio (TTR):* The number of different words used (type) divided by the total number of words used (token) (Miller, 1981).

8.3 Results

8.3.1 General index of language development

Figure 8.1 illustrates that ZL had a steady increase in mean length of utterance, mean length of verbalisation and vocalisation and maximum length of utterance over the observation period. Though no normative data is available to compare the scale of development, the increase in these measures of spontaneous expressive language shows that ZL's syntactic ability was developing, albeit slowly. As predicted, MLVV was much lower than MLU, as the result of the presence of a significant number of unintelligible syllables and vocalisations in ZL's speech.

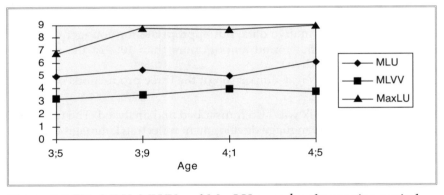

Figure 8.1 ZL's MLU, MLVV and MaxLU over the observation period

ZL's Type-token ratio also increased during the observation period, reflecting the growing diversity of his vocabulary. TTRs were 0.46, 0.50, 0.54, and 0.51 at the age of 3;5, 3;9, 4;1 and 4;5, respectively.

8.3.2 Phonological abilities

The child's phonological ability was described primarily using his single word spontaneous speech sample elicited from the picture-naming task. Generally speaking, the intelligibility of his connected speech collected from the picture-description task was lower than his single word speech. The lack of clear-cut context perhaps made his vocalisations in connected speech less interpretable. There were many glottal stops between syllables and repetitions in his connected speech. The analysis of his single word speech showed that he had complete syllable-final consonant and vowel repertoires. He made no tonal errors. The development of weak stress and rhotacisation was also within normal range. In fact, he could use weak stress correctly over at least 88% of weakly stressed syllables at each assessment. He was also able to use rhotacisation appropriately, for example, /xuaɹ/ '*flower*'. Most errors occurred at syllable-initial position.

8.3.2.1 Phonetic and phonemic inventories

Table 8.1 lists ZL's phonetic and phonemic inventories identified in his single word speech sample at each assessment (for ZL's first attempt to produce the targets in the picture-naming task, see Appendix 8). ZL had an almost complete phonetic inventory by the end of the observation period, though there were some phones in his speech which did not belong to Putonghua phonology. In contrast, his phonemic inventory was very limited. At the age of 4;5, in terms of manner of articulation, all the affricates were missing; and in terms of place of articulation, all the retroflexes and alveolo-palatals were missing. The size of ZL's phonemic inventory did not show any sign of growth over the observation period. In fact, he seemed to have lost some contrasts that he had demonstrated in earlier samples. For example, four phonemes, i.e. /k, kʰ, ɕ, tɕ/, which were evident in his speech at the age of 3;5, disappeared from his phonemic inventory when he was assessed again at the age of 3;9, 4;1 and 4;5. ZL's vowel and syllable-final consonant repertoires were complete throughout the observation period.

Table 8.1 ZL's phonetic and phonemic inventories in the four assessments

Age	*Phonetic inventory*	*Phonemic inventory*
3;5	t, tʰ, m, n, k, kʰ, f, x, l, ɹ, ɕ, tɕ, tɕʰ, s, ts, ʂ, tʂ, tʂʰ, ð*	t, tʰ, m, n, k, kʰ, f, x, ɹ, ɕ, tɕ
3;9	t, m, n, pʰ, k, f, x, l, ɹ, ɕ, tɕ, tɕʰ, s, ts, ʂ, θ*, ð*	t, tʰ, m, n, f, x, ɹ
4;1	t, tʰ, m, n, p, pʰ, k, kʰ, f, x, l, ɹ, ɕ, tɕ, tɕʰ, s, ts, tsʰ, g*	t, m, n, pʰ, x, ɹ, tɕʰ
4;5	t, tʰ, m, n, p, pʰ, k, kʰ, f, x, l, ɹ, ɕ, tɕ, tɕʰ, s, ts, tsʰ, ʂ, tʂʰ	t, tʰ, m, n, pʰ, kʰ, f, x, l, ɹ

Note: Phones marked by * are not Putonghua phones.

8.3.2.2 Error patterns

Table 8.2 shows all the error patterns identified in ZL's speech sample. Some delayed error patterns, i.e. fronting /k/ as [t] (e.g. /kaŋ/ [taŋ]), stopping /s/ as [t] (e.g. /san/ [tan]) and final /ŋ/ deletion (e.g. /pʰiŋ/ [pʰi]), presented in his phonology when assessed at the age of 3;9, 4;1 and 4;5. One error pattern, i.e. syllable-initial deletion (e.g. /tʂuei/ [uei], /ɕiɛ/ [iɛ], /ɕywn/ [ywn]) had a high frequency of occurrence in the child's speech during the observation period. In the single word speech sample collected at the age of 4;5, he deleted 19 syllable-initial consonants, 27.5% of all the syllable-initial consonants in his speech. A closer examination of the errors showed that syllable-initial deletion occurred most frequently before high vowels, /i, y, u/. In fact, only five out of 62 errors involving syllable-initial deletion did not take place before the high vowels. The study on normally developing Putonghua-speaking children in Chapter 3 also reported that syllable-initial consonant deletion tended to occur before these high vowels. Discussions of this error pattern in relation to the flexible function of these vowels in Putonghua phonology can be found in Chapter 3. The frequently deleted consonants were alveolo-palatals (/ɕ, tɕ, tɕʰ/) and retroflexes (/ʂ, tʂ, tʂʰ/). A number of unusual error patterns such as replacing /ts, tʂ/ with [k] (e.g. /tʂuo/ [kuo]) and replacing /ʂ/ with [f] (e.g. /ʂu/ [fu]), which have never been used by more than 10% of normally developing children, also occurred in his production.

Table 8.2 ZL's error patterns identified in the four assessments

Normal error patterns	Age			
	3;5	3;9	4;1	4;5
Syllable initial deletion	*	*	*	*
Fronting: /ʂ/→ [s]		*		*
/k/→ [t]	*		*	*
Stopping: /ts/→ [t]	*	*	*	*
/s/→ [t]		*		
/x/→ [k]	*	*		*
X-velarisation	*	*	*	
Final /n/ deletion	*		*	
Backing: /n/→ [ŋ]	*			
Final /ŋ/ deletion			*	

Table 8.2 *cont.*

		Age		
Unusual error patterns	*3;5*	*3;9*	*4;1*	*4;5*
Nasalisation of some sounds	*	*	*	*
	/ʂ/→ [f, ð]	/ʂ/→ [ð]	/ʂ/→ [f]	/ts, tʂ/→ [k]
	/t/→ [p]	/tɕ, ɕ/→ [l]	/f/→ [t]	/p/→ [t]
			/tɕʰ/→ [pʰ]	/tɕʰ/→ [pʰ]
			/s/→ [ɹ]	SI addition

Note: Shaded cells are delayed error patterns for a particular age. Typical examples are given next to error patterns.

8.3.2.3 PCE and Z score for PCE

Figure 8.2 shows the percentage of consonants produced incorrectly in ZL's single word production. The normally developing hearing children aged 3;1–3;6, 3;7–4;0 and 4;1–4;6 on average produced 13.6%, 10.5% or 7.8% of the consonants in error, respectively (see Chapter 3). In contrast, ZL incorrectly produced 35.8%, 53.0%, 55.0% and 54.0% of the consonants in his single word speech at the age of 3;5, 3;9, 4;1 and 4;5. As a result, the gap between ZL and the normal hearing children, measured by Z score, increased significantly. Z scores for PCE were 3.265, 5.183, 8.138 and 7.793 at the age of 3;5, 3;9, 4;1 and 4;5 respectively.

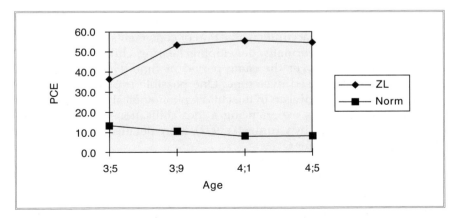

Figure 8.2 ZL's PCE compared to norms over the observation period

8.3.2.4 Inconsistency rating

ZL's inconsistency ratings were 0.194, 0.236, 0.350 and 0.319 at each assessment. The boy's speech seemed to become less consistent over time.

8.4 Discussion

8.4.1 ZL'S phonological systems

ZL, with 75 dB prelingual hearing loss in the better ear, was assessed every four months between the age of 3;5 and 4;5. His syntactic ability, measured by mean length of utterance, mean length of vocalisation/ verbalisation and maximum length of utterance, showed a slow but steady increase. The diversity of his vocabulary also grew over time, as indicated by Type-Token Ratio. The analysis of his single word speech showed that he had complete syllable-final consonant (two in total) and vowel repertoires (22 in total). His acquisition of tones, weak stress and rhotacisation was within the normal range. However, he had difficulties with syllable-initial consonants:

- Distorted articulation. Several illegal phones existed in his speech.
- Restricted phonemic inventory. While his phonetic inventory was relatively age-appropriate, his phonemic inventory was restricted to a small number of phonemes. For example, while 90% of the children aged 3;7–4;0 in the normative data would have mastered 12 phonemes, he had only 7 phonemes in his inventory when assessed at the age of 3;9.
- The phenomenon of 'recidivism' (i.e. loss of contrastiveness which has been established, Smith, 1973). Some phonemes (e.g. /ç, tç/) which the child was able to use accurately at the age of 3;5 'disappeared' in his subsequent three assessments. Accordingly, his PCE, as a measure of inaccurate realisation of consonants, increased over time, while the normally developing hearing children tended to eliminate errors over the same period of time. His inconsistency rating also increased over time. One possible explanation for the occurrence of recidivism in the child's phonological development is that the child was experiencing a 'destabilisation' developmental stage as proposed by Grunwell (1992). More detailed discussion can be found in Chapter 6.
- Highly frequent use of syllable-initial consonant deletion error pattern and the presence of delayed and unusual error patterns.

Compared to his single word spontaneous speech, his connected speech had lower intelligibility, with frequent occurrence of glottal stops between syllables and repetitions.

8.4.2 Error patterns

A number of error patterns were identified in ZL's speech sample. Seven error patterns were 'normal' in the sense that they have been found in more than 10% of normally developing children in the same age band as ZL (see Table 3.9 in Chapter 3). However, three other error patterns, i.e. fronting /k/ as [t], stopping /s/ as [t] and final /ŋ/ deletion persisted when his phonology was assessed at the age of 3;9, 4;1 and 4;5 and were no longer age-appropriate.

The persistence of non-age-appropriate error patterns in the boy's speech may be attributable to the lack of auditory information which is essential for stimulating changes in early developmental stages. The time from birth to five years is regarded as an optimal and critical period for establishing a phonological system and hearing children's exposure to language stimulus begins long before they could produce any speech (Carney & Moeller, 1998). Even if the visual perception of speech movement can complement the auditory modality to certain extent (Dodd, 1987), the deprivation or degradation of speech sound during development might result in the slower rate of phonological acquisition.

Apart from the presence of error patterns typical of younger normally developing hearing children, 10 unusual error patterns were evident in ZL's speech. These error patterns have rarely occurred in the speech of normally developing children with intact hearing. Some of these patterns, e.g. replacing /t/ with [p] and replacing /ts, tʂ/ with [k], have been identified in the phonology of children with consistent phonological disorder. It is argued that phonologically disordered children are restricted in their ability to accurately extract knowledge from the mental lexicon about the nature of the phonological system to be learned (Dodd *et al.*, 1989). The presence of unusual error patterns identical to those in the speech of phonologically disordered children suggests that children with hearing impairment might also have difficulties in generalising accurate information about the regularities of the target phonological system.

Research on phonological awareness (implicit knowledge of the constraints and contrasts of the phonological system to be learned) of children with hearing loss also lends support to the argument that the children with prelingual hearing impairment may have difficulties in processing and analysing phonological information. Miller (1997) compared the phonological awareness of deaf children with excellent skills in sign language and that of orally trained deaf children. He found no group difference in the assessment task, although both groups of deaf children scored less well than hearing controls. This suggested that the children with prelingual hearing impairment might have difficulty in processing phonological information, and this deficit could not be compensated for by intensive exposure to a speaking environment alone. This argument has important clinical implications for children with hearing impairment. Special training programmes should be designed and administered to hearing impaired children, including both children using spoken language as their principle means for communication and children acquiring sign language as their primary language, to develop their phonological awareness.

8.4.3 Cross-linguistic similarities and the influence of the ambient language

Similarities exist in the acquisition of phonological units among the children with hearing impairment irrespective of language background. The Putonghua-speaking boy seemed to have little difficulty in acquiring vowels. A similar finding was also reported for Cantonese-speaking children (Dodd & So, 1994) and English-speaking children (Abberton *et al.*, 1990). The early mastery of vowels by hearing impaired children may be related to perceptual and cognitive factors. Perceptually, the cues for vowels are more easily extracted with residual hearing than consonants, because vowels have 'relatively simpler, low frequency, more slowly changing acoustic patterns' (Abberton *et al.*, 1990: 212), and vowels are more powerful and sonorous than consonants (Gimson, 1989). However, phonological acquisition is far from simply being a perceptual process, for perception itself 'is very much constrained by one's sense of phonological structure and lexical expectation' (Locke, 1980: 207). Cognitively, vowels have higher phonological saliency than consonants, because they are a compulsory syllable component and carry a high information load (for definition of phonological saliency and detailed discussion of saliency value of each syllable component, see 3.6.5).

It has been suggested that hearing impaired children of a tonal language are able to acquire tonal contrasts due to their usable low frequency residual hearing (Fok, 1984). However, the same explanation cannot account for the difficulties that English-speaking children with hearing loss have with pitch. Their speech is often characterised by 'deaf tone' (Cantwell & Baker, 1987). Alternatively, the almost error-free tonal acquisition by Putonghua- and Cantonese-speaking children with hearing impairment may be the result of the high saliency value of tones in these two tonal languages. Carrying lexical information, tones are essential for functional communication in both languages.

ZL had a complete syllable-final consonant repertoire while his syllable-initial consonant inventory was far from complete. Similar findings were reported for Cantonese-speaking children (Dodd & So, 1994). However, the opposite pattern was apparent for English-speaking children whose syllable-final consonants were more likely to be affected by hearing loss (Abraham, 1989). These similarities and differences reflect the influence of the ambient language on language acquisition. The relative ease with which Putonghua- and Cantonese-speaking children acquire final consonants may be related to the fewer number of syllable-final consonants and the absence of syllable-final syntactic markers in Cantonese and Putonghua (Dodd & So, 1994). It is also possible that the lower number of syllable-final consonants in Cantonese and Putonghua provides a relatively smaller range of visual cues that need to be discriminated, allowing the children with hearing impairment to extract important phonological information by lip reading (Dodd, 1987).

8.5 Summary

The phonological ability and development of a Putonghua-speaking child with severe prelingual hearing impairment between the age of 3;5 and 4;5 was described using the measures of MLU, MLVV, MaxLU, TTR, PCE, inconsistency rating, error patterns, and phonetic and phonemic inventory. Comparison of the developmental patterns identified in the child's speech and that of children speaking English and Cantonese revealed both cross-linguistic similarities and the influence of the ambient language on the phonological acquisition of children with hearing impairment. The presence of unusual error patterns in his phonological systems reflected the effect of hearing impairment on phonological acquisition and indicated that hearing impaired children might have difficulty in abstracting knowledge from the mental lexicon about the nature of the phonological system to be learned.

Chapter 9
General Discussion and Conclusion

9.1 Introduction

The last two decades of the 20th century saw a remarkable upsurge of interest in cross-linguistic studies of language acquisition (as exemplified in Slobin, 1985, 1992, 1995, 1997). However, some aspects of language (e.g. syntax) seem to have received much more attention than others. This book aims to fill the gap in the knowledge about phonological acquisition by Putonghua- (Modern Standard Chinese) speaking children.

A satisfactory account of language acquisition should be able to address both normal development and developmental disorders. For this reason, the present book contains a series of case studies of the phonological development of children in atypical circumstances, in addition to the studies of normally developing children.

This concluding chapter summarises the key findings from the studies reported in the book, in relation to the factual and theoretical research questions outlined in 1.4. In addition, the developmental patterns identified in monolingual Putonghua-speaking children, who are acquiring the target language in normal or atypical conditions, are discussed in the framework of 'developmental universals' and 'particulars'. The general professional implications of the research findings are highlighted. Finally, areas which need further investigations are proposed.

9.2 Review of the major research findings

Six studies have been reported in this book. They are:

- A cross-sectional study of 129 normally developing Putonghua-speaking children aged 1;6–4;6. The speech sample was collected through picture-naming and – description tasks (Chapter 3).
- A longitudinal study of four Putonghua-speaking children. The age ranges of the children under study were 1;1.15–2;0.15, 1;0.0–2;0.15, 0;10.15–2;0.15, and 1;2.0–1;8.0. The speech sample was collected through child-parent interaction (Chapter 4).
- Case studies of the phonological systems of 33 Putonghua-speaking children with functional speech disorders aged 2;8–7;6. The speech

172

sample was collected through picture-naming and picture-description tasks (Chapter 5).

- A follow-up study of the development and change in the phonology of seven Putonghua-speaking children with speech disorders, who received no clinical intervention. The speech sample was collected twice over an interval of about 11 months through picture-naming and picture-description tasks. The children were aged between 2;2 and 4;3 at the initial assessment (Chapter 6).

- A case study of a set of Putonghua-speaking twins aged 6;2. The speech sample was collected through picture-naming task, child–child and child–adult interaction. A single word comprehension task was also administered to test their ability to understand adult phonological forms (Chapter 7).

- A longitudinal study of a Putonghua-speaking child with severe prelingual hearing impairment between the age of 3;5 and 4;5. The speech sample was collected through picture-naming and picture-description tasks (Chapter 8).

These studies aimed to address the factual and theoretical questions outlined in 1.4. These questions are reviewed in turn in the following section.

9.2.1 Factual research questions addressed in the book

9.2.1.1 Normally developing children
Order of acquisition of syllable components

Among the four possible syllable components, the acquisition of tones was completed first; followed by syllable-final consonants and vowels; syllable-initial consonants were last.

Age of acquisition of vowels

The acquisition of vowels took place mainly between the age of 1;0 and 2;0. The longitudinal data provided an opportunity to examine the age at which the children were able to produce a vowel phonologically correctly for the first time (for detailed information, see Table 4.2). The specific patterns are:

- Simple vowels seemed to emerge earliest among the three types of vowels (simple vowels, diphthongs and triphthongs). Diphthongs and triphthongs emerged slightly later than simple vowels and were more prone to systematic errors.

- The central low vowel /A/ and back high vowel /u/ occurred earliest in the children's production in the stage of first words. The retroflex vowel /ɚ/ and the back vowel /o/ seemed to be among the last simple vowels to emerge in the children's production.

- Among the diphthongs, /ei/ tended to be acquired first and /yɛ/ last.
- Among the triphthongs, /iou/ tended to be acquired first and /uae/ last.

Age of acquisition of syllable-final consonants

By the age of 1;9, the two syllable-final consonants /n, ŋ/ have become stabilised (i.e. a sound was produced phonologically correctly on at least two of three opportunities) in the speech of all of the four children in the longitudinal study.

Age of acquisition of syllable-initial consonants

Normative data on age of emergence (i.e. a sound was produced at least once by the child, irrespective of whether it was the correct target) of syllable-initial consonants were derived, using the criteria of 90% of the children in an age band in the cross-sectional study (Table 3.3). The longitudinal study provided complementary information on the early sequential development of phonemes (Tables 4.3 and 4.4). The specific patterns are:

- The phonetic acquisition of the syllable-initial consonants (21 in total) was complete by 3;6 for 75% of children.
- Nasals and bilabials tended to emerge earlier than other sounds.
- In terms of features, unaspirated sounds tended to emerge earlier than aspirated sounds.

The norm on age of stabilisation of syllable-initial consonants was presented in Table 3.4. The specific patterns include:

- By 4;6, 90% of the children were able to use all the syllable-initial consonants correctly on two thirds of occasions with the exception of four affricates and a retroflex fricative (i.e. /tʂ, tʂʰ, ts, tsʰ, ʂ/).
- Among the sounds stabilised early were bilabial nasal /m/, alveolar stop /t/ and bilabial stop /p/.
- The last 10 sounds to be stabilised (i.e. /l, s, ɹ, tɕ, tɕʰ, ʂ, tʂ, tʂʰ, ts, tsʰ/) include all the three retroflexes, all the six affricates and both liquids.

Chronology of error patterns

Error patterns affecting syllable-initial consonants can be generalised into three groups: assimilation, deletion and systematic substitution. Fourteen error patterns were present in the speech of more than 10% of the children in the youngest age group (1;6–2;0) in the cross-sectional study and five of these patterns (i.e. fronting alveolar-palatal as alveolar, stopping alveolar fricative as alveolar stop, affrication, aspiration, and gliding) disappeared in more than 90% of the children in the oldest age group (4;6–4;6). The percentage of children using error patterns affecting syllable-initial consonants in each age band was listed in Table 3.8. The chronology of these error patterns (i.e. the age of onset, persistence, and disappearance of error patterns) was given in Appendix 9.

The three syllable-final consonant error patterns used by more than 10% of the children were /n/ deletion, /ŋ/ deletion, and replacing /n/ with [ŋ]. Syllable-final consonant addition and replacing /ŋ/ with [n] were rarely used. The percentage of children using error patterns affecting syllable-final consonants was presented in Table 3.9.

The three systematic vowel error patterns used by more than 10% of the children were triphthong reduction, diphthong reduction and vowel substitution co-occurring with syllable-final consonant deletion. The percentage of children using error patterns affecting vowels can be found in Table 3.5.

Age of tonal acquisition

Age of emergence and stabilisation of tones in the four children in the longitudinal study were summarised in Tables 4.5 and 4.6 respectively. High level and falling tones were present at the beginning of the children's lexical use between the age of 1;2 and 1;4. Falling–rising tones emerged last, between the age of 1;4 and 1;7. In terms of stabilisation, high level tones were first to reach 66.7% accuracy rating in the speech of all the four children, followed by high falling tones. Rising and falling–rising tones were stabilised last.

Patterns of tonal acquisition

Despite individual preferences, most of tonal substitutions were systematic. High level tones were used as unmarked and frequently replaced high falling, rising and falling–rising tones, while high falling tones were preferred as a substitute when errors occurred to high level tones.

Age of acquisition of tone sandhi

Individual differences and the nature of spontaneous data made it difficult to generalise on the age and order of acquisition of various types of tone sandhi rules. Some children were able to use some tone sandhi rules correctly as early as at the age of 1;4. By the age of 1;11.15, all the types of sandhi rules had emerged and stabilised in the children's speech. The morphonologically conditioned tone sandhi rule seemed to emerge and become stabilised earlier than other types of sandhi rules.

Patterns of acquisition of tone sandhi

When an error occurred with tone sandhi, the children usually used citation tones of the syllables involved, where tone sandhi should apply.

Age of acquisition of weak stress

Weak stress, especially weak stress in reduplication, emerged early in the children's speech (a child was able to use weak stress in reduplicated word forms as early as at the age of 1;2). Fluctuation in accuracy rating characterised the children's learning of weak stress. Its stabilisation was not completed until about the age of four.

Patterns of weak stress acquisition

Using a citation tone for a weakly stressed syllable was the most common error pattern among the children. Weakly stressed syllable deletion was frequent, especially with the affix type of weak stress.

Group variations – the effect of gender or second language exposure on phonological development

There was no difference in the rate of phonological acquisition between boys and girls. No interaction was found between gender and age. The children who were learning English did not show any significant difference in the rate of phonological acquisition from the children who were not.

9.2.1.2 Children in exceptional circumstances

Characteristics of the disordered phonology of Putonghua-speaking children

- Putonghua-speaking children were not a heterogeneous group. Among 33 children with speech difficulties randomly selected for the study, 3% children had an articulation disorder, 54.5% had delayed development, 24.2% used unusual error patterns consistently, and 18.2% children's speech was primarily characterised by inconsistency of production.
- The phonology of the children with speech disorders was systematic and sensitive to the structure of the ambient language. The syllable components with higher saliency value (such as tone, syllable-final consonants) were less likely to be subject to disorder than those with a lower saliency value (such as syllable-initial consonants).
- Phonemes that were problematic for children with speech disorders were not necessarily the same phonemes acquired late by normally developing children.
- The children with disordered speech showed one or several of the following characteristics: restricted phonetic or phonemic inventory, persisting delayed error patterns, unusual error patterns, variability, and systematic sound or syllable preference.

Patterns of spontaneous changes in the disordered phonology of children with functional phonological disorders

As a group, the children under study showed a tendency to make statistically fewer errors, use fewer error patterns and perform more consistently over time. While their phonetic inventories expanded over time, there was no significant increase in their phonemic use. There was a significant reduction in the number of normal error patterns. However, there was no significant change in the unusual error patterns.

Children with different underlying deficits follow different paths of development. Delayed phonological development may spontaneously resolve, while consistent and inconsistent disorders are resistant to spontaneous change.

Characteristics of phonology of twins

The co-twins' phonological systems had similarities in that they both evidenced characteristics of delayed or disordered development and shared some error patterns. However, the existence of individual error patterns in each twin's phonological system suggested that their phonological systems were not identical.

Characteristics and developmental patterns in the phonology of a child with hearing impairment

While the child's syntax and vocabulary evidenced steady growth during the observation period, his phonological abilities showed little sign of development. His phonology was characterised by the following patterns: relatively error-free acquisition of vowels and lexical tones compared to consonants; the tendency to simplify syllable structures by deleting syllable-initial and syllable-final consonants, and the presence of both delayed error patterns and unusual substitutions.

9.2.2 Theoretical research questions addressed in the book

9.2.2.1 Existing theories of phonological acquisition

The developmental patterns in terms of age and order of phonemic acquisition and error patterns identified in Putonghua-speaking children have a number of implications for the theoretical interpretation of cross-linguistic similarities and differences that have been reported in the existing literature. Briefly,

- Cross-linguistic differences in the order of phoneme acquisition cannot be accounted for in terms of the frequency of the phonemes across the world languages (cf. 'law of irreversible solidarity', Jakobson, 1941/1968, see further discussion in 3.6.1).

- Nor can they be explained by appealing to the biological constraints or articulatory limitations of young children (cf. biological model proposed by Locke, 1980, 1983; Kent, 1992, see further discussion in 3.6.1).
- Although there is a clear developmental sequence in terms of 'feature', the theoretical concept of universal 'markedness' or 'default features' has a number of explanatory inadequacies (see further discussion in 3.6.2 and 3.6.3).
- There are language-specific influences on the order of phoneme acquisition. However, while the current proposal of 'functional load' (Pye *et al.*, 1987) directly links the order of phoneme acquisition to the role of these phonemes in a language, it fails to investigate the impact of aspects of phonology other than consonants on the order of acquisition; moreover, there are difficulties in the measurement of functional load (see further discussion in 1.2.1.2 and 3.6.3).
- Some cross-linguistic variations in the rate and order of acquisition of vowels, consonants and prosodic features such as tones are better accounted for by the concept of *phonological saliency*. Components with higher phonological saliency would be acquired earlier than components with lower saliency. Phonological saliency of a particular component is a weighted combination of several factors: the status of a component in the syllable structure, the capacity of a component in differentiating lexical meaning of a syllable and carrying communicative intent, and the number of permissible choices within a component of the syllable structure. For example, tones in Putonghua have the highest saliency because they are compulsory for every syllable. Change of tones would vary lexical meaning, and there are only four alternative choices. The effect of the high saliency value of tones on the process of phonological acquisition of Putonghua-speaking children was reported in the studies on normally developing children, children with speech disorders and children with hearing impairment (see further discussion in 3.5.5). Clearly, there is a need for refining the notion of 'phonological saliency' so that it would be able to capture cross-linguistic differences in phonological acquisition and development. This issue will be further discussed below (9.2.3.1).

9.2.2.2 Differential diagnosis of children with speech disorders

Categorisation of children with speech disorders is essential for understanding the nature of phonological impairment and providing clinical intervention. However, the 'etiologic' approach, i.e. classifying subgroups of children with speech disorders according to the causal factors of their phonological impairment (Shriberg & Kwiatkowski, 1994), has difficulties in classifying children whose etiologic causes are not clear or children who have a range of causal factors. The 'linguistic' approach differentiates 'phonetic disorders' from 'phonological disorders' (Winitz, 1969; Ingram, 1989b; Fey, 1992; Bernthal & Bankson, 1998; Gierut, 1998) and 'delay' from 'disorder' (Leonard, 1985; Ingram, 1989b; Fletcher, 1990). Nevertheless, this approach tends to focus on speech sounds rather than error patterns and does not take account of children's inconsistent productions, another important feature evident in the speech of some children with speech disorders.

The 'four subgroup categorisation system' proposed by Dodd (1993) made use of two dimensions, i.e. error patterns and production consistency, in the differential diagnosis. The four subgroups are:

- articulation disorder – consistent distortion of a phone either in isolation or in any phonetic context;
- delayed development – use of error patterns that are inappropriate for the child's chronological age but appropriate for a younger child;
- consistent disorder – use of error patterns which are atypical of normal phonological development (i.e. not used by more than 10% of normally developing children);
- inconsistent disorder – inconsistent or variable productions of the same words or phonological features.

The findings in this book provide further cross-linguistic support for the 'four subgroup categorisation system', along with other cross-linguistic studies (Cantonese, So & Dodd, 1994; Turkish, Tobpas, 1997; German, Fox, 1997; Cantonese–English, Dodd *et al.*, 1997; Punjabi–English, Holm *et al.*, 1999; Italian–English, Holm & Dodd, 1999). In addition, it is argued that

- the differences between the delayed and normally developing groups are more quantitative than qualitative in nature; and
- no continuous relationship exists between severity of speech errors and degree of inconsistency (McCormack & Dodd, 1998).

9.2.2.3 History of phonological disorders (i.e. emergence, persistence or recovery of phonological disorders)

The study of development and change in the phonological systems of Putonghua-speaking children with speech disorders suggests that:

- Children with different surface error patterns follow different paths of development, perhaps as the result of different underlying deficits.

- Delayed development may be caused by external environmental factors (such as the quality and amount of language input). Therefore, it may occur at any stage of children's phonological acquisition and may spontaneously resolve later.
- The surface error patterns of the children with consistent or inconsistent disorders (whose speech is characterised by consistent use of atypical error patterns or inconsistent productions) have been shown to be associated with underlying deficits in the children's internal speech processing mechanism operating at the speech onset (Dodd & McCormack, 1995). There appears to be little spontaneous change in their phonological systems, if these deficits are not specifically targeted in intervention programmes.

9.2.2.4 Causal factors for the impaired phonology in twins

It is often argued that twins share a private language, i.e. 'twin language' between themselves. However, the analysis of the phonological systems of the co-twins in the study showed that their phonological systems were not identical. It is further suggested that phonological difficulties, which have been reported to be the most salient feature of twins' communicative profile, might be attributable to twins' unique language learning situation. Since twins within sets are each other's primary communication partner, each child is consistently exposed to two phonological forms for many lexical items (one is the adult form, and the other the co-twin's developmental form). This would result in the existence of dual phonological representations in twins' mental lexicon, which would make it difficult for twins to derive an awareness of the constraints and contrasts of the ambient phonological system.

9.2.2.5 The nature of phonology of children with hearing impairment

The presence of unusual error patterns in the phonological system of the child with prelingual hearing impairment reported in this book suggested that children with hearing impairment may have difficulties in generalising accurate information about the regularities of the target phonological system, as the result of early deprivation or degradation of auditory input.

9.2.3 Developmental universals

The studies reported in this book centred on the phonological development of different populations of Putonghua-speaking children. Both similarities and differences were found across groups and between Putonghua-speaking children and children from other language backgrounds. These similarities and differences are discussed in the following section in relation to 'developmental universals' and 'particulars'.

9.2.3.1 Similarities and differences across different populations of Putonghua-speaking children

Different populations of Putonghua-speaking children showed similar sensitivity to the structure of the phonological system they were acquiring. It was argued that the phonological acquisition patterns across different populations of Putonghua-speaking children were influenced by the saliency value of syllable components (i.e. the status of a component in the syllable structure, the capacity of a component in differentiating lexical meaning of a syllable and carrying communicative intent, and the number of permissible choices within a component of the syllable structure). The notion of phonological saliency accounts well for the acquisition of tones which have the highest saliency value. The studies reported in this book found that:

- Tonal acquisition was completed earlier than syllable-initial consonants, syllable-final consonants, and vowels in normally developing Putonghua-speaking children.
- Tone was resistant to impairment during the process of phonological acquisition. The study on 33 Putonghua-speaking children with speech disorders did not find any children who had difficulty with tones, even among the most severely disordered children. A boy aged 3;7 with inconsistent speech disorder presented an interesting case. He had preference for three consonant-vowel combinations: /tia/, /tɕia/ and /tɕɐ/. While these three combinations substituted for a number of different syllables (sometimes in reduplicated forms), the original tones of target syllables were maintained in the boy's speech.
- The effect of hearing loss on tonal acquisition was minimal. The longitudinal study on the child with prelingual severe hearing impairment found that although the boy had a low speech intelligibility, his tone was almost error-free.

In comparison, syllable-final consonants have a lower saliency value, because they are an optional component in a Putonghua syllable. However, their saliency value is higher than syllable-initial consonants, because there are only two syllable-final consonants (i.e. /n, ŋ/) in Putonghua. Specific acquisitional patterns associated with syllable-final consonants were: the acquisition of syllable-final consonants was relatively error-free and less likely to be subject to impairment than syllable-initial consonants. For example,

- The phonetic acquisition of syllable-final consonants was completed by the age of two, while that of syllable-initial consonants was not completed until 4;6 for 90% of the children.

- Syllable-final consonants were less likely to be subject to impairment than syllable-initial consonants: only four children (12%) were found to have used delayed error patterns affecting syllable-final consonants.
- The child with hearing impairment had a complete syllable-final consonant repertoire while his syllable-initial inventory was far from complete.

Vowels have a higher saliency value, compared with syllable-initial consonants. Although vowels are a compulsory syllable component, the relatively large number of vowels lowers their saliency. The value of saliency of vowels influenced its acquisitional patterns:

- The vowels emerged early in the children's production, between the age of 1;0 and 2;0. The proportions of vowel errors in the total number of speech errors in each age group were between 9.2% and 20.0% (in contrast, syllable-initial consonant errors took up 65.8%–79.3% of the total speech errors).
- The vowels were more resistant to impairment than syllable-initial consonants. One child (3%) used delayed error patterns affecting vowels and four children (12%) made unusual errors with vowels.
- The child with hearing impairment had little difficulty in acquiring vowels.

Syllable-initial consonants have the lowest saliency among the four syllable components, since their presence in a syllable is optional and there is a range of 21 syllable-initial phonemes that can be used. The low saliency value of the syllable-initial consonants resulted in its late acquisition and vulnerability to impairment. This is supported by the findings that

- syllable-initial consonants were the last syllable component to be acquired by the normally developing children in the cross-sectional study; and
- syllable-initial consonant errors had a remarkably higher proportion than other syllable components both in the speech of normally developing children, that of children with speech difficulties and that of children with hearing impairment.

9.2.3.2 Similarities and differences between Putonghua-speaking children and children speaking other languages

The studies reported in this book also showed similarities and differences between the Putonghua-speaking children and children acquiring the phonology of other languages.

Normally developing children

In terms of error patterns, Putonghua-speaking children showed a tendency for structural and systemic simplifications in their production, which is similar to English-speaking children (Grunwell, 1981). However, there are also some cross-linguistic differences in the error patterns. For example, syllable-initial consonant deletion and backing, which were considered atypical error patterns in English, were evident in the speech of the normally developing children acquiring Putonghua. In addition, substitution patterns and realisation rules of the same error patterns may vary from one language to another.

In terms of phoneme acquisition, the features of aspiration, affrication and retroflex were acquired last. The late acquisition of affrication has been reported in English (Olmsted, 1971; Prather *et al.*, 1975), Cantonese (So & Dodd, 1995), Russian (Timm, 1977, cited in Locke, 1983). However, the opposite pattern has been proposed in Japanese (Yasuda, 1970; Battacchi *et al.*, 1964, both cited in Locke, 1983). The late acquisition of the feature of aspiration is less controversial, and it is supported by Cantonese data (So & Dodd, 1995).

In terms of tonal acquisition, tones were found to be acquired earlier than segments by Putonghua-speaking children. The same pattern was found in Tse's study (1978) on the phonological acquisition of Cantonese. In addition, high level tones were acquired earlier than other tones by Putonghua-speaking children (possibly due to the fact that it only consists of the default feature – level tones). This is consistent with Tse's (1978) finding on Cantonese tonal acquisition, which suggested that all the level tones were acquired earlier than contour tones (cf. A. Tse, 1992).

Children with speech disorders

Subgroups of speech disorders (e.g. delay, consistent and inconsistent disorders) found in speech disordered Putonghua-speaking children were consistent with that of speech disorders identified in children speaking English (Dodd, 1995), Cantonese (So & Dodd, 1994), Turkish (Topbas, 1997) and German (Fox, 1997). Putonghua-speaking children shared the characteristics common to speech disordered children speaking other languages. These characteristics include persisting delayed error patterns, unusual error patterns, variability, restricted phonetic or phonemic inventory, and systematic sound or syllable preference.

Sensitivity to the ambient phonology is another characteristic shared by children with speech disorders, irrespective of the language being learned. Putonghua-speaking children with speech disorders made fewest errors on tones, fewer errors on syllable-final consonants and most errors on syllable-initial consonants – the same pattern was also reported for normally developing Putonghua-speaking children.

Despite these similarities, criteria used in diagnosing speech disorder should be language-specific. In other words, whether a specific error pattern is considered as non-age-appropriate or atypical is relative to the normal patterns associated with the children acquiring that language. For example, a Cantonese-speaking child using a backing error pattern would be considered disordered while a Putonghua-speaking child would not.

Twins

The findings based on the study of Putonghua-speaking twins confirmed the previous findings on English-speaking children (e.g. Dodd & McEvoy, 1994):

- The phonological systems of the co-twins were not identical, though both evidenced characteristics of delayed or disordered phonological development and shared some error patterns;.
- They were able to comprehend both adult and their sibling's phonological forms, suggesting dual phonological representations in their mental lexicon.

Children with hearing impairment

Comparison of the phonological acquisition of the Putonghua-speaking child with prelingual hearing impairment with that of hearing-impaired children speaking English (Oller & Kelly, 1974; Dodd, 1976; Stoel-Gammon, 1983; Abraham, 1989) and Cantonese (Dodd & So, 1994) revealed both cross-linguistic similarities and the influence of the ambient language on the phonological acquisition of children with hearing impairment. Among those characteristics shared by children speaking different languages were: the relatively error-free acquisition of vowels and lexical tones compared to that of consonants; the tendency to simplify syllable structures, the presence of both delayed error patterns and unusual substitutions in the phonology. However, while Putonghua-speaking and Cantonese-speaking children with hearing impairment tended to have intact syllable-final consonant repertoires, syllable-final consonants were more likely to be affected by hearing loss in the phonological development of children speaking English. Whereas English-speaking children with hearing loss tend to have difficulty with pitch, Putonghua and Cantonese-speaking children are able to acquire tonal contrasts (possibly as the result of the nature of lexical tones in these two languages).

9.3 Professional Implications

The studies reported in this book have a number of implications for professional practice.

- The norms on the phonological development of Putonghua-speaking children provide a much-needed diagnostic tool for assessing phonological development of Putonghua-speaking children and identifying speech disorders. The information on the age of phoneme acquisition and chronology of error patterns is essential in designing intervention schemes.

- The plausible existence of different underlying deficits calls for differential diagnosis and treatment of different subgroups of children with speech disorders (i.e. articulation disorder, delayed development, consistent disorder and inconsistent disorder).

- A number of qualitative measures (phonetic and phonemic inventories; and error patterns) and quantitative measures (PCE and inconsistency) in screening speech disordered Putonghua-speaking children were proposed and their effectiveness in diagnoses of speech disorders was evaluated. While quantitative measures are very effective in screening delayed phonological development, qualitative measures, especially error patterns, are more important in diagnosing consistent and inconsistent disorders.

- Whether a child should be considered as 'typical' or 'atypical' in his or her phonological development should be assessed in relation to the normal patterns of the ambient language. The criteria such as age of acquisition and chronology of error patterns vary from one language to another.

- Different spontaneous developmental patterns found in different subgroups of speech disorders again imply the need for differential diagnosis and treatment. The fact that some children with delayed development would resolve spontaneously without intervention and children with consistent or inconsistent disorders would make little progress over time needs to be considered in deciding clients' priority for therapy and treatment targets. Those aspects of the phonological system that appear to be developing non-age-appropriately do not necessarily need to be targeted in therapy. Rather, therapy should centre on those aspects of the system that are developing atypically.

- The fact that dual phonological representations might exist in twins' mental lexicon needs to be taken into consideration in providing intervention for twins, whose speech is more likely to be subject to delayed or atypical development.

- The existence of unusual error patterns in the speech of the child with hearing impairment suggests that children with hearing impairment might have difficulty in generalising accurate information about the regularities of the target phonological form. Specific programmes should be designed to develop the phonological awareness of the children with hearing impairment.

- The findings in this book reiterated an urgent need for providing speech therapy service and raising people's awareness of the existence of speech disorders, along with other specific language impairment, in China. The current situation is far from satisfactory – nearly all the children with phonological disorders are left untreated, and a small number of children with unintelligible speech, who get treated in hospitals, are uniformly treated as having an articulation disorder.

9.4 Pointers for Further Research and Conclusion

This book investigates the influence of universal tendencies and language-specific features on phonological development of Putonghua-speaking children in both normally developing and exceptional circumstance (i.e. children with speech disorders, children with hearing impairment, and twins). It raises many issues for further research. For example,

- What factors affect the patterns of children's systemic simplification of speech? In particular, why do children in different language environments use different substitutes for the same phonemes such as the case with /ɹ/?
- How can the notion of 'phonological saliency' be refined in the context of developmental universals so that it would be able to capture cross-linguistic similarities and differences in phonological acquisition and development?
- What results in the phenomenon of 'recidivism' evident both in the phonological development of normally developing children and in that of children in exceptional circumstances?
- What are the early prognostic indicators of spontaneous recovery from delayed development with regard to children with delayed development, the largest subgroup of children with speech disorders?

Much more research needs to be carried out before these questions can be answered.

I'd like to conclude the discussion by noting the approach adopted in this book. There are two main approaches in child language studies: one starts with a particular theory or hypothesis and sets out to test the plausibility of the hypothesis by looking at some aspects of child data. In such a case, thorough and complete analysis of child data sometimes has to give away to a relatively more focused scrutiny of a particular aspect of child language relevant to the hypothesis being evaluated. The other approach, primarily aimed at describing the whole data and then specifying any patterns, usually embraces several theoretical frameworks. The studies conducted in this approach have the advantage of presenting the whole picture of child development first, rather than offering piecemeal information on a particular aspect of child development. In addition, evaluation of a theory can be carried out *post hoc* with regard to its effectiveness in interpreting developmental patterns. The studies in this book follows the second approach.

While a full discussion of the current phonological theories and their implications for the study of language acquisition and disorder is not the aim of this book, the data described in the studies could be accounted for by a number of phonological theories and models, apart from those mentioned in the book. For example, the late acquisition of affrication, aspiration and retroflex could be explained within the framework of generative phonology, and the early acquisition of suprasegmental features such as tones in both normally developing children and children in exceptional circumstances could be accounted for with reference to the multilayered and hierarchically organised representations postulated in autosegmental phonology.

References

Abberton, E., Hazan, V. and Fourcin, A. (1990) The development of contrastive-ness in profoundly deaf children's speech. *Clinical Linguistics and Phonetics* 4, 209–20.

Abraham, S. (1989) Using a phonological framework to describe speech errors of orally trained hearing impaired school-agers. *Journal of Speech and Hearing Disorders* 54, 600–9.

Acevedo, M. A. (1988) Development of Spanish consonants in three to five year olds. Paper presented at the Annual ASHA Convention, Boston.

Allen, G. D. and Hawkins, S. (1980) Phonological rhythm: Definition and development. In G. H. Yeni-Komshian, J. Kavanagh and C. Ferguson (1980) *Child Phonology, Vol. 1: Production* (pp. 227–56). New York: Academic Press.

Aginsky, B. W. and Aginsky, E. G. (1948) The importance of language universals. *Word* 4, 168–72.

Amayreh, M. M. and Dyson, A. T. (1998) The acquisition of Arabic consonants. *Journal of Speech, Language, Hearing Research* 41, 642–53.

American National Standards Institute (1989) *Specifications for Audiometers (ANSI S3.6-1989)*. New York: Acoustical Society of America.

Anderson, J. L. (1983) The markedness differential hypothesis and syllable struc-ture difficulty. In G. S. Nathan (ed.) *Proceedings of the Conference on the Uses of Phonology*. Carbondale: Southern Illinois University.

Bahr, R. H. (1998) Articulation and phonologic disorders. In C. Seymour and E. Nober (eds) *Introduction to Communication Disorders: A Multicultural Approach* (pp. 111–36). Boston: Butterworth-Heinemann.

Bankson, N. and Bernthal, J. (1998) Factors related to phonologic disorders. In J. Bernthal and N. Bankson (eds) *Articulation and Phonological Disorders* (pp. 172–232). Boston: Allyn and Bacon.

Bao, Zhiming (1990) Fanqie languages and reduplications. *Linguistics Inquiry* 21, 317–50.

Battacchi, M. W., Facchini, G. M., Manfredi, M. M. and Rubatta, C. O. (1964) Presentazione di un reattivo per l'esame dell'articolazione fonetica nei fanciulli in eta prescolare di lingua italiana. *Bollettino della Societa Italiana di Fonetica, Foniatria e Audiologia* 13, 441–86.

Bernthal, J. E. and Bankson, N. W. (eds) (1998) *Articulation and Phonological Dis-orders* (4th edn). Boston: Allyn and Bacon.

Beery, K. (1989) The VMI: *Developmental Test of Visual-motor Integration*. Cleveland: Modern Curriculum Press.

Bortolini, U. and Leonard, L. B. (1991) The Speech of phonologically disordered children acquiring Italian. *Clinical Linguistics and Phonetics* 5, 1–12.

Bradford, A. and Dodd, B. (1994) The motor planning abilities of phonologically disordered children. *European Journal of Disorders of Communication* 29, 349–69.

Bradford, A. and Dodd, B. (1996) Do all speech-disordered children have motor deficits? *Clinical Linguistics and Phonetics* 10, 77–101.

British Society of Audiology (1981) Recommended procedures for pure-tone audiometry using a manually operated instrument. *British Journal of Audiology* 15, 213–16.

Brown, J. (1984) Examination of grammatical morphemes in the language of hard-of-hearing children. *Volta Review* 86, 229–38.

Bruck, M. and Genesee, F. (1995) Phonological awareness in young second language learner. *Journal of Child Language* 22, 307–24.

Buffery, C. (1970) Sex-differences in the development of hand preference, cerebral dominance for speech and cognitive skill. *Bulletin of the British Psychological Society* 23, 233.

Buffery, C. (1971) Sex differences in the development of hemispheric asymmetry of function in the human brain. *Brain Research* 31, 364–5.

Campbell, R. and Sais, E. (1995) Accelerated metalinguistic (phonological) awareness in bilingual children. *British Journal of Developmental Psychology* 13, 61–8.

Cantwell, D. and Baker, L. (1987) *Developmental Speech and Language Disorders.* New York: Guildford Press.

Carney, A. E. and Moeller, M. P. (1998) Treatment efficacy: Hearing loss in children. *Journal of Speech, Language and Hearing Research* 41, S61–84.

Catford, J. C. (1988) Functional load and diachronic phonology. In Y. Tobin (ed.) *The Prague School and its Legacy.* Amsterdam: John Benjamins.

Cermack, S. A., Ward, E. A. and Ward, L. M. (1986) The relationship between articulation disorders and motor coordination in children. *American Journal of Occupational Therapy* 40, 546–50.

Chao, Y. R. (1930) A system of tone letters. *Le Maitre Phonetique troisieme serie* 30, 24–7.

Chao, Y. R. (1951/1973) The Cantian idiolect: An analysis of the Chinese spoken by a twenty-eight-month-old child. In C. A. Ferguson and D. I. Slobin (eds) *Studies of Child Language Development.* New York: Holt, Rinehart and Winston.

Chao, Y. R. (1968) *A Grammar of Spoken Chinese.* Berkeley, CA: University of California Press.

Chen, Ping (1999) *Modern Chinese: History and Sociolinguistics.* Cambridge: Cambridge University Press.

Cheung, H. (1998) Utterance length and the development of Mandarin Chinese. Paper presented in the First Asia Pacific Conference on Speech, Language and Hearing, Hong Kong, October 1998.

Chomsky, N. (1965) *Aspects of the Theory of Syntax.* Cambridge, MA: MIT Press.

Chomsky, N. and Halle, M. (1968) *The Sound Pattern of English.* New York: Harper and Row.

Clumeck, H. (1977) Studies in the acquisition of Mandarin phonology. Unpublished PhD thesis, University of California, Berkeley.

Clumeck, H. (1980) The acquisition of tone. In G. Yeni-Komshian, J. Kavanagh and C. Ferguson (eds) *Child Phonology 1* (pp. 257–76). New York: Academic Press.

Compton, A. (1976) Generative studies of children's phonological disorders: Clinical ramifications. In D. Morehead and A. Morehead (eds) *Normal and Deficient Child Language* (pp. 61–96). Baltimore: University Park Press.

Comrie, B. (1987) *The Major Languages of East and South-east Asia.* London: Routledge.

Conway, D., Lytton, H. and Pysh, F. (1980) Twin-singleton differences. *Canadian Journal of Behavioural Sciences* 12, 264–71.

Croft, W. (1990) *Typology and Universals.* Cambridge: Cambridge University Press.

Curtiss, S., Prutting, C. A. and Lowell, E. L. (1979) Pragmatic and semantic development in young children with impaired hearing. *Journal of Speech and Hearing Research* 22, 534–52.

Davis, J. (1974) Performance of young hearing-impaired children on a test of basic concepts. *Journal of Speech and Hearing Research* 17, 342–57.

Davis, J. (1977) Reliability of hearing-impaired children's response to oral and total presentations of the Test of Auditory Comprehension of Language. *Journal of Speech and Hearing Disorders* 42, 520–7.

Day, E. (1932) The development of language in twins. A comparison of twins and single children. *Child Development* 3, 179–99.

Dean, E., Howell, J., Hill, A. and Waters, D. (1990) *Metaphon Resource Pack.* Windsor: NFER-Nelson.

DeFrancis, J. (1984) *The Chinese Language: Fact and Fantasy.* Honolulu: University of Hawaii Press.

Demuth, K. (1993) Issues in the acquisition of the Sesotho tonal system. *Journal of Child Language* 20, 275–301.

Dinnsen, D. (1992) Variation in developing and fully developed phonetics inventories. In C. A. Ferguson, L. Menn and C. Stoel-Gammon (eds) *Phonological Development: Models, Research, Implications.* Timonium, MD: York Press.

Dinnsen, D. (1997) Nonsegmental phonologies. In M. Ball and R. Kent (eds) *The New Phonologies: Developments in Clinical Linguistics* (pp. 77–126). San Diego: Singular Publishing Group.

Dodd, B. (1976) The phonological systems of deaf children. *Journal of Speech and Hearing Disorders* 41, 185–98.

Dodd, B. (1987) Lip-reading, phonological coding and deafness. In B. Dodd and R. Campbell (eds) *Hearing by Eye.* London: Lawrence Erlbaum.

Dodd, B. (1993) Speech disordered children. In G. Blanken, J. Dittmann, H. Grimm, J. Marshall and C-W. Wallesch (eds) *Linguistic Disorders and Pathologies* (pp. 65–92). Berlin: De Gruyter.

Dodd, B. (1995) *Differential Diagnosis and Treatment of Children with Speech Disorder.* London: Whurr Publishers.

Dodd, B. and Hermelin, A. (1977) Phonological coding by the prelinguistically deaf. *Perception and Psychophysics* 21, 413–17.

Dodd, B., Holm, A. and Li Wei (1997) Speech disorder in preschool children exposed to Cantonese and English. *Clinical Linguistics and Phonetics* 11, 229–43.

Dodd, B. and Iacano, T. (1989) Phonological disorders in children: Changes in phonological process use during treatment. *British Journal of Disorders of Communication* 24, 333–51.

Dodd, B. and Leahy, J. (1989) Phonological disorders and mental handicap. In M. Beveridge, G. Conti-Ramsden and I. Leudar (eds) *Language and Communication in Mentally Handicapped People* (pp. 33–56). London: Chapman & Hall.

Dodd, B., Leahy, J. and Hambly, G. (1989) Phonological disorders in children: Underlying cognitive deficits. *British Journal of Developmental Psychology* 7, 55–71.

Dodd, B. and McCormack, P. (1995) A model of speech processing for differential diagnosis of phonological disorders. In B. Dodd (ed.) *The Differential Diagnosis and Treatment of Children with Speech Disorder* (pp. 65–90). London: Whurr Publishers.

Dodd, B. and McEvoy, S. (1994) Twin language or phonological disorder. *Journal of Child Language* 21, 273–89.

Dodd, B. and So, L. (1994) The phonological abilities of hearing impaired Cantonese speaking children. *Journal of Speech and Hearing Research* 37, 671–79.

Donegan, P. J. and Stampe, D. (1979) The study of natural phonology. In D. A. Dinnsen (ed.) *Current Approaches to Phonological Theory* (pp. 126–73). Bloomington: Indiana University Press.

Dow, F. D. (1972) A discussion on tone sandhi problems in Chinese. *Journal of International Phonetic Association* 2 (19), 13–19.

Duanmu, San (1990) A formal study of syllable, tone, stress and domain in Chinese language. Unpublished PhD thesis, Massachusetts Institute of Technology.

Duanmu, San (2000) *The Phonology of Standard Chinese.* Oxford: Oxford University.

Dunn, C. and Davis, B. (1983) Phonological process occurrence in phonologically disordered children. *Applied Psycholinguistics* 4, 187–207.

Eckman, F. R. (1977) Markedness and the contrastive analysis hypothesis. *Language Learning* 27, 315–30.

Edwards, M. L. (1974) Perception and production in child phonology: The testing of four hypotheses. *Journal of Child Language* 1, 205–19.

Eilers, R. E. and Oller, D. K. (1976) The role of speech discrimination in developmental sound substitutions. *Journal of Child Language* 3, 319–29.

Elbert, M. (1992) Clinical forum: Phonological assessment and treatment. Consideration of error types: A response to Fey. *Language, Speech and Hearing Services in Schools* 23, 241–6.

Elfenbein, J. L., Hardin-Jones, M. A. and Davis, J. M. (1994) Oral communication skills of children who are hard of hearing. *Journal of Speech and Hearing Research* 37, 216–26.

Ellis, R. (1985) *Understanding Second Language Acquisition.* Oxford University Press.

Enderby, P. and Philipp, R. (1986) Speech and language disorders: Towards knowing the size of the problem. *British Journal of Disorders of Communication* 21, 151–65.

Erbaugh, M. S. (1992) The acquisition of Mandarin. In D. Slobin (ed.) *The Cross-linguistic Study of Language Acquisition* (Vol. 3, pp. 373–456). NJ: Erlbaum.

Ferguson, C. (1978) Historical background of universals research. In J. Greenburg (ed.) *Universals of Human Language* (pp. 9–31). Stanford, CA: Stanford University Press.

Ferguson, C. A. and Farwell, C. (1975) Words and sounds in early language acquisition. *Language* 51, 419–39.

Fey, M. (1992) Articulation and phonology: Inextricable constructs in speech pathology. *Language, Speech and Hearing Services in Schools* 23, 225–32.

Fletcher, P. (1990) The breakdown of language: Language pathology and therapy. In N. Collinge (ed.) *An Encyclopaedia of Language* (pp. 422–57). London: Routledge.

Fok, C. Y. Y. (1984) The teaching of tones to children with profound hearing impairment. *British Journal of Disorders of Communication* 19 (3), 225–36.

Fox, A. (1997) Classification of speech disorders in German-speaking children. MSc dissertation, University of Newcastle upon Tyne.

Fromkin, V. and Rodman, R. (1993) *An Introduction to Language* (5th edn). New York: Harcourt Brace Jovanovich.

Gandour, J. (1998) Aphasia in tone languages. In P. Coppens, Y. Lebrun and A. Basso (eds) *Aphasia in Atypical Populations* (pp. 117–42). London: Lawrence Erlbaum Associates.

Geers, A. and Moog, J. (1978) Syntactic maturity of spontaneous speech and elicited imitations of hearing impaired children. *Journal of Speech and Hearing Disorders* 43, 380–91.

Gierut, J. (1998) Treatment efficacy: Functional phonological disorders in children. *Journal of Speech, Language and Hearing Research* 41, S85–100.

Gimson, A. (1989) *An Introduction to the Pronunciation of English* (4th edn). Sevenoaks, UK: Edward Arnold.

Goldsmith, J. A. (1976) *Autosegmental Phonology*. Bloomington: Indiana University Linguistics Club.

Goldstein, B. (1996) Error groups in Spanish-speaking children with phonological disorders. In T. W. Powell (ed.) *Pathologies of Speech and Language: Contributions of Cinical Phonetics and Linguistics* (pp. 171–7). New Orleans, LA: ICPLA.

Grech, H. (1998) Phonological development of normal Maltese speaking children. Unpublished PhD thesis, University of Manchester.

Greenberg, J. H. (1966) *Universals of Language* (2nd edn). Cambridge, MA: MIT press.

Greenberg, J. H. (1978) *Universals of Human Languages* (4 vols). Stanford, CA: Standford University Press.

Grunwell, P. (1981) *The Nature of Phonological Disability in Children*. London: Academic Press.

Grunwell, P. (1982) *Clinical Phonology*. London: Croom Helm.

Grunwell, P. (1987) *Clinical Phonology* (2nd edn). London: Croom Helm.

Grunwell, P. (1991) Developmental phonological disorders from a clinical-linguistic perspective. In M. Yavas (ed.) *Phonological Disorders in Children: Theory, Research and Practice* (pp. 37–64). London: Routledge.

Grunwell, P. (1992) Assessment of child phonology in the clinical context. In C. A. Ferguson, L. Menn and C. Stoel-Gammon (eds) *Phonological Development: Models, Research, Implications* (pp. 457–83). Timonium, MD: York Press.

Grunwell, P. (1992) Process of phonological change in developmental speech disorders. *Clinical Linguistics and Phonetics* 6, 101–22.

Grunwell, P. (1995) Assessment of phonology. In K. Grundy (ed.) *Linguistics in Clinical Practice* (pp. 108–33). London: Whurr Publishers.

Guo Jinfu (1993) *Hanyu shengdiao yudiao chanyao yu tansuo*. Beijing: Beijing Yuyan Xueyuan Press.

Halle, M. and Stevens, K. (1971) A note on laryngeal features. *MIT Quarterly Progress Report* 101, 198–212.

Hay, D., O'Brien, P., Collect, S. and Williams, N. (1984) *Language Development in Young Twins*. Melbourne: La Trobe Twin Study of Behaviour and Biological Development Report.

Hewlett, N. (1985) Phonological versus phonetic disorders: Some suggested modifications to the current use of the distinction. *British Journal of Disorders of Communication* 20, 155–64.

Hodson, B. W. (1980) *The Assessment of Phonological Processes*. Danville, IL: Interstate.

Hoffman, P., Norris, J. and Monjure, J. (1990) Comparison of process targeting and whole word language treatments for phonologically delayed preschool children. *Language, Speech and Hearing Services in Schools* 21, 102–9.

Holm, A. and Dodd, B. (1999) Differential diagnosis of phonological disorder in two bilingual children acquiring Italian and English. *Clinical Linguistics and Phonetics* 13, 113–29.

Holm, A. and Dodd, B. (1999) A longitudinal study of the phonological development of two Cantonese–English bilingual children. *Applied Psycholinguistics* 20, 349–76.

Holm, A., Dodd, B., Stow, C. and Pert, S. (1999) Identification and differential diagnosis of phonological disorder in bilingual children. *Language Testing* 16, 271–92.

Hsu, J. (1987) A study of the various stages of development and acquisition of Mandarin Chinese by children in Taiwan milieu. MA dissertation, College of Foreign languages, Fu Jen Catholic University.

Hudgins, C. and Numbers, F. (1942) An investigation of the intelligibility of the speech of the deaf. *Genetic Psychology Monographs* 25, 289–392.

Ingram, D. (1979) Cross-linguistic evidence on the extent and limit of individual variation in phonological development. *Proceedings of the 9th International Congress of Phonetic Sciences* 2, 150–4.

Ingram, D. (1981) *Procedures for the Phonological Analysis of Children's Language.* Baltimore, MD: University Park Press.

Ingram, D. (1986) Phonological development: Production. In P. Fletcher and M. Garman (eds) *Language Acquisition.* Cambridge: Cambridge University Press.

Ingram, D. (1989a) *First Language Acquisition: Method, Description and Explanation.* Cambridge: Cambridge University Press.

Ingram, D. (1989b) *Phonological Disability in Children* (2nd edn). London: Whurr Publishers.

Irwin, J. V. and Wong, S. P. (eds) (1983) *Phonological Development in Children 18 to 72 months.* Carbondale, IL: Southern Illinois University Press.

Jakobson, R. (1941/1968) *Child Language, Aphasia and Phonological Universals.* The Hague: Mouton.

Jeng, Heng-hsiung (1979) The acquisition of Chinese phonology in relation to Jakobson's laws of irreversible Solidarity. *Proceedings of the 9th International Congress of Phonetic Sciences.* University of Copenhagen.

Jimenez, B. C. (1987) Acquisition of Spanish consonants in children of aged three to five years seven months. *Language Speech and Hearing Services in Schools* 18, 357–61.

Johnston, C., Prior, M. and Hay, D. (1984) Prediction of reading disability in twin boys. *Developmental Medicine and Child Neurology* 26, 588–95.

Kagan, J. (1971) *Change and Continuity in Infancy.* New York: Wiley.

Katamba, F. (1989) *An Introduction to Phonology.* London: Longman.

Katz, J. J. and Postal, P. (1964) *An Integrated Theory of Linguistic Descriptions* (Research Monograph 26). Cambridge, MA: MIT Press.

Keenan, E. and Klein, E. (1975) Coherency in children's discourse. *Journal of Psycholinguistic Research* 4, 365–79.

Kent, R. (1992) The biology of phonological development. In C. A. Ferguson, L. Menn and C. Stoel-Gammon (eds) *Phonological Development: Models, Research, Implications* (pp. 65–90). Timonium, MD: York Press.

Kirkpatrick, E. and Ward, J. (1984) Prevalence of articulation errors in N.S.W. primary schools. *Australian Journal of Human Communication Disorders* 12, 55–62.

Klein, H. (1984) Learning to stress: A case study. *Journal of child Language* 11, 375–90.

Koch, H. (1956) Sibling influence on children's speech. *Journal of Speech and Hearing Disorders* 21, 322–8.

Kubler, C. and Ho, G. T. C. (1984) *Varieties of Spoken Standard Chinese, Vol II: A Speaker from Taipei* 1–13. Dordrechet: Foris Publications.

Ladefoged, P. and Maddieson, I. (1996) *The Sounds of the World's Languages*. Oxford: Blackwell.

Lanham, L. W. (1969) Generative phonology and the analysis of Nguni consonants. *Lingua* 24, 155–62.

Larsen-Freeman, D. and Long, M. (1991) *An Introduction to Second Language Acquisition Research*. London: Longman.

Leahy, J. and Dodd, B. (1987) The development of disordered phonology: A case study. *Language and Cognitive Processes* 2, 115–32.

Leahy, J. and Dodd, B. (1995) The acquisition of disordered phonology: A treatment case study. In B. Dodd (ed.) *The Differential Diagnosis and Treatment of Children with Speech Disorder* (pp. 167–80). London: Whurr Publishers.

Lee, Thomas H.-T. (1996) Theoretical issues in language development and Chinese child language. In C.-T. James Huang and Y.-H. Audrey Li (eds) *New Horizons in Chinese Linguistics* (pp. 293–356). Dordrecht: Kluwer Academic Publishers.

Leitao, S., Hogben, J. and Fletcher, J. (1997) Phonological processing skills in speech and language impaired children. *Journal of Communication Disorders* 50, 4–13.

Leonard, L. (1985) Unusual and subtle phonological behaviour in the speech of phonologically disordered children. *Journal of Speech and Hearing Disorders* 50, 4–13.

Leonard, L. (1995) Phonological impairment. In P. Fletcher and B. MacWhinney (eds) *The Handbook of Child Language* (pp. 573–602). New York: Blackwell.

Leonard, L. B., Newhoff, M. and Mesalam, L. (1980) Individual differences in early child phonology. *Applied Psycholinguistics* 1, 7–30.

Leopold, W. F. (1939–49) *Speech Development of a Bilingual Child: A Linguist's Record* (4 vols). Evanston, IL: Northwestern University Press.

Levitt, H. and Stromberg, H. (1983) Segmental characteristics of the speech of hearing-impaired children: Factors affecting intelligibility. In I. Hochberg, H. Levitt and M. Osberger (eds) *Speech of the Hearing Impaired: Research, Training and Personnel Preparation* (pp. 53–73). Baltimore, MD: University Park Press.

Lewis, B. A. and Freebairn, L. (1997) Subgrouping children with familial phonologic disorders. *Journal of Communication Disorders* 30 (5), 385–401.

Li, C. N. and Thompson, S. A. (1977) The acquisition of tone in Mandarin-speaking children. *Journal of Child Language* 4, 185–99.

Li, C. N. and Thompson, S. A. (1981) *Mandarin Chinese. A Functional Reference Grammar*. Berkeley, CA: University of California Press.

Li, Paul J.-K. (1977) Child language acquisition of Mandarin phonology. In R. Cheng, Y. C. Li and Ting-chi Tang (eds) *Proceedings of the Symposium on Chinese Linguistics: 1977 Linguistic Institute of the Linguistic Society of America* (pp. 295–316). Taipei: Student Books.

Lin, T. and Wang, L. (1992) *Yuyinxue jiaocheng [A course book to phonetics]*. Beijing: Beijing University Press.

Lindblom, B. (1998) Systemic constraints and adaptive change in the formation of sound structure. In J. R. Hurford, M. Studdert-Kennedy and C. Knight (eds) *Approaches to the Evolution of Language: Social and Cognitive Bases*. Cambridge: Cambridge University Press.

Locke, J. (1980) The prediction of child speech errors: implications for a theory of acquisition. In G. H. Yeni-komshian, J. F. Kavanagh and C. A. Ferguson (eds) *Child Phonology, 1: Production* (pp. 193–210). New York: Academic Press.

Locke, J. (1983) *Phonological Acquisition and Change*. New York: Academic Press.

Lu Yunzhong (1995) *Putonghua de qingsheng he erhua [The weak stress and rhotacisation of Putonghua]*. Beijing: Shangwu Press.

Luria, A. and Yudovich, F. (1959) *Speech and the Development of Mental Processes in the Child*. London: Staple Press.

Lyon, M. and Gallaway, C. (1990) Measuring the spontaneous language of hearing-impaired children. *Clinical Linguistics and Phonetics* 4 (2), 183–95.

Macken, M. and Ferguson, C. A. (1983) Cognitive aspects of phonological development. In K. E. Nelson (ed.) *Children's Language* (Vol. 4, pp. 256–82). Hillsdale, NJ: Lawrence Erlbaum Associates.

Magnusson, E. (1983) *The Phonology of Language Disordered Children: Production, Perception and Awareness*. Travaux de 'institut de linguistique de lund. XVII. Lund: CWK Gleerup.

Malmstrom, P. and Silva, M. (1986) Twin talk: Manifestations of twin status in the speech of toddlers. *Journal of Child Language* 13, 293–304.

Mann, D. M. and Hodson, B. (1994) Spanish-speaking children's phonologies: Assessment and remediation of disorders. *Seminars in Speech and Language* 15, 2, 137–48.

Matheny, A. and Bruggemann, C. (1972) Articulation proficiency in twins and singletons from families of twins. *Journal of Speech and Hearing Research* 15, 845–51.

McClelland, J., Rumelhart, D. and the PDP Research Group. (1986) *Parallel Distributed Processing: Explorations in the Microstructures of Cognition, Vol. 2: Psychological and Biological Models*. Cambridge, MA: MIT Press.

McCormack, P. and Dodd, B. (1998) Is inconsistency in word production an artifact of severity in developmental speech disorder? Poster presented at Child Language Seminar 4–6 September 1998, Sheffield.

McEvoy, S. and Dodd, B. (1992) Communication abilities of 2- to 4-year-olds twins. *European Journal of Disorders of Communication* 27, 73–87.

McMahon, S. (1996) Communication skills of twins and higher multiple birth children. Unpublished PhD thesis. University of Queensland.

McMahon, S. and Dodd, B. (1997) A comparison of the expressive communication skills of triplet, twin and singleton children. *European Journal of Disorders of Communication* 32, 328–45.

McMahon, S., Stassi, K. and Dodd, B. (1998) The relationship between multiple birth children's early phonological skills and later literacy. *Language, Speech and Hearing Services in Schools* 29, 11–23.

McNutt, J. and Hamayan, E. (1982) Subgroups of older children with articulation disorder. In R. Daniloff (ed.) *Position Papers in Speech, Hearing and Language* (pp. 51–70). Baltimore: College Hill.

McReynolds, L. V. (1988) Articulation disorders of unknown etiology. In N. Lass, L. V. McReynolds, J. L. Northern and D. Yoder (eds) *Handbook of Speech–Language Pathology and Audiology* (pp. 419–41). Toronto: B.C. Decker Inc.

Meline, T. (1997) Description of phonological patterns for nineteen elementary-age children with hearing losses. *Perceptual Motor Skills* 85 (2), 643–53.

Menn, L. and Stoel-Gammon, C. (1995) Phonological development. In P. Fletcher and B. MacWhinney (eds) *The Handbook of Child Language* (pp. 335–60). Cambridge, MA: Blackwell.

Menyuk, P. (1968) The role of distinctive features in children's acquisition of phonology. *Journal of Speech and Hearing Research* 11, 138–46.

Miller, J. (1981) *Assessing Language Production in Children: Experimental Procedures.* London: Edward Arnold.

Miller, P. (1997) The effect of communication mode on the development of phonemic awareness in prelingually deaf students. *Journal of Speech, Language and Hearing Research* 40, 1151–63.

Mitchell, R. and Myles, F. (1998) *Second Language Learning Theories.* London: Arnold.

Mittler, P. (1970) Biological and social aspects of language development in twins. *Developmental Medicine and Child Neurology* 12, 741–57.

Mohring, H. (1938) *Lautbildungsschwierigkeiten im Deutschen. Zeitschrift fuer Kinderforschung* 47, 185–235.

Morley, M. E. (1972) *The Development and Disorders of Speech in Childhood.* London: Churchill Livingstone.

Mowrer, D. and Burger, S. (1991) A comparative analysis of the phonological acquisition of consonants in the speech of two and a half and six year old Xhosa- and English-speaking children. *Clinical Linguistics and Phonetics* 5, 139–64.

National Institute of Health (1993) Early identification of hearing impairment in infants and young children. *Program and Abstracts from the Consensus Development Conference.* Bethesda, MD: Author.

National Institute on Deafness and Other Communication Disorders (1994) *National Strategic Research Plan.* Bethesda, MD: Department of Health and Human Services.

Nettelbladt, U. (1983) *Developmental Studies of Dysphonology in Children.* Lund: CWK Gleerup.

Norman, J. (1988) *Chinese.* Cambridge: Cambridge University Press.

O'Grady, W. (1987) *Principles of Grammar and Learning.* University of Chicago Press.

Oller, D. and Kelly, C. (1974) Phonological substitution processes of a hard-of-hearing child. *Journal of Speech and Hearing Disorders* 39, 65–74.

Olmsted, D. (1971) *Out of the Mouths of Babes.* The Hague: Mouton.

Ozanne, A. (1992) Normative data for sequenced oral movements and movements in context for children aged three to five years. *Australian Journal of Human Communication Disorders* 20, 47–63.

Packard, J. (1993) *A Linguistic Investigation of Aphasic Chinese Speech.* Dordrecht: Kluwer Academic Publishers.

Packard, J. (2000) *The Morphology of Chinese: A Linguistic and Cognitive Approach.* Cambridge: Cambridge University Press.

Peters, A. (1983) *The Units of Language Acquisition.* Cambridge: Cambridge University Press.

Platt, J. (1988) What can case studies do? *Studies in Qualitative Methodology* 1, 1–23.

Poole, I. (1934) Genetic development of articulation of consonant sounds in speech. *Elementary English Review* 11, 159–61.

Powers, M. (1971) Functional disorders of articulation: Symptomatology and etiology. In L. Travis (ed.) *Handbook of Speech Pathology and Audiology* (pp. 837–76). Englewood Cliff, NJ: Prentice Hall.

Prather, E., Hedrick, D. and Kern, C. (1975) Articulation development between two and four years. *Journal of Speech and Hearing Disorders* 40, 179–91.

Presnell, L. (1973) Hearing-impaired children's comprehension and production in oral language. *Journal of Speech and Hearing Research* 16, 12–21.

Pye, C., Ingram, D. and List, H. (1987) A comparison of initial and final consonant acquisition in English and Quiche. In K. E. Nelson and A. Van Kleek (eds) *Children's Language* (Vol. 6, pp. 174–90). Hillsdale, NJ: Erlbaum.

Quigley, P. and Paul, P. (1984) *Language and Deafness.* San Diego: College-Hill Press.

Ramsey, S. R. (1987) *The Language of China.* NJ: Princeton University Press.

Ritterman, S. I. and Richtner, U. E. M. (1979) An examination of the articulatory acquisition of Swedish phonemes. In H. Hollien and P. Hollien (eds) *Current Issues in Linguistic Theory* (Vol. 9), Part III. Amsterdam: John Benjamins.

Rubin, H. and Turner, A. (1989) Linguistic awareness skills in grade one children in a French immersion setting. *Reading and Writing: An Interdisciplinary Journal* 1, 73–86.

Rutherford, W. (1983) Language typology and language transfer. In S. Gass and L. Selinker (eds) *Language Transfer in Language Learning.* Rowley, MA: Newbury House.

Sachs, J. (1977) The adaptive significance of linguistic input to prelinguistic infants. In C. Snow and C. A. Ferguson (eds) *Talking to Children: Language Input and Language Acquisition.* Cambridge: Cambridge University Press.

Savic, S. (1980) *How Twins Learn to Talk.* London: Academic Press.

Schirmer, B. R. (1985) An analysis of the language of young hearing-impaired children in terms of syntax, semantics and use. *American Annals of the Deaf* 130, 15–19.

Shiu, Huei-shiou (1990) The phonological acquisition by Mandarin-speaking children: A longitudinal case study on children from 9 months through three years old. Unpublished MA thesis, Taiwan Normal University.

Shriberg, L. D. and Kwiatkowski, J. (1980) *Natural Process Analysis: A Procedure for Phonological Analysis of Continuous Speech Samples.* New York: John Wiley & Sons.

Shriberg, L. D. and Kwiatkowski, J. (1982) Phonological disorders III: A procedure for assessing severity of involvement. *Journal of Speech and Hearing Disorders* 47, 256–70.

Shriberg, L. D. and Kwiatkowski, J. (1988) A follow-up study of children with phonological disorders of unknown origin. *Journal of Speech and Hearing Disorders* 53, 144–53.

Shriberg, L. D. and Kwiatkowski, J. (1994) Developmental phonological disorders I: A clinical profile. *Journal of Speech and Hearing Research* 37, 1100–26.

Shriberg, L. D., Kwiatkowski, J., Best, S., Hengst, J. and Terselic-Weber, B. (1986) Characteristics of children with phonological disorders of unknown origin. *Journal of Speech and Hearing Disorders* 51, 140–61.

Shriberg, L. D., Austin, D., Lewis, B. A., McSweeny, J. L. and Wilson, D. L. (1997) The Percentage of Consonants Correct (PPC) Metric: Extensions and reliability data. *Journal of Speech, Language, and Hearing Research* 40, 708–22.

Shucard, D. W., Janet, L. S. and Thomas, D. G. (1987) Sex differences in the patterns of scalp-recorded electrophysiological activity in infancy: Possible implications for language development. In S. U. Philips, S. Steele and T. Christine (eds) *Language, Gender, and Sex in Comparative Perspective* (pp. 278–96). Cambridge: Cambridge University Press.

Skarakis, E. A. and Prutting, C. A. (1977) Early communication: Semantic functions and communicative intentions in the communication of the preschool child with impaired hearing. *American Annals of the Deaf* 122, 382–91.

Skinner, B. F. (1957) *Verbal Behaviour.* Englewood Cliffs, NJ: Prentice-Hall.

Slobin, D. (1979) *Psycholinguistics* (2nd edn). Glenview, IL.: Scott, Foresman.

Slobin, D. (ed.) (1985, 1992, 1995, 1997) *The Crosslinguistic Study of Language Acquisition.* NJ: Erlbaum.

Smith, N. (1973) *The Acquisition of Phonology: A Case Study.* Cambridge: Cambridge University Press.

Snow, C. (1996) Issues in the Study of Input: Finetuning, universality, individual and developmental differences and necessary causes. In P. Fletcher and B. MacWhinney (eds) *The Handbook of Child Language* (pp. 180–93). Oxford: Blackwell.

Snow, C. and Ferguson, C. (eds) (1977) *Talking to Children.* Cambridge: Cambridge University Press.

So, L. K. H. and Dodd, B. (1994) Phonologically disordered Cantonese-speaking children. *Clinical Linguistics and Phonetics* 8 (3), 235–55.

So. L. K. H. and Dodd, B. (1995) The acquisition of phonology by Cantonese-speaking children. *Journal of Child Language* 22, 473–95.

Sommers, R. (1984) Nature and remediation of functional articulation and phonological disorders. In S. Dickson (ed.) *Communication Disorders: Remedial Principles and Practices.* Glenview IL: Scott Foresman.

Sommers, R. (1988) Prediction of fine motor skills of children having language and speech disorders. *Perceptual and Motor Skills* 67, 63–72.

Stafford, L. (1987) Maternal input to twin and singleton children: Implications for language acquisition. *Human Communication Research* 13, 429–62.

Stampe, D. (1969) The acquisition of phonetic representation. *Papers from the Fifth Regional Meeting of the Chicago Linguistic Society* (pp. 433–44). Chicago, IL: Chicago Linguistic Society.

Stampe, D. (1973) A dissertation on natural phonology. PhD thesis, University of Chicago.

Stoel-Gammon, C. (1982) The acquisition of segmental phonology by normally-hearing and hearing-impaired children. In I. Hochberg, H. Levitt and M. Osberger (eds) *Speech of the Hearing Impaired: Research, Training and Personnel Preparation.* Baltimore, MD: University Park Press.

Stoel-Gammon, C. (1991) Theories of phonological development and their implications for phonological disorders. In M. Yavas (ed.) *Phonological Disorders in Children* (pp. 16–36). London: Routledge.

Stoel-Gammon, C. and Dunn, C. (1985) *Normal and Disordered Phonology in Children.* Baltimore: University Park Press.

Su, A.-T. (1985) The acquisition of Mandarin phonology by Taiwanese children. MA thesis, Fu Jen Catholic University.

Templin, M.C. (1957) *Certain Language Skills in Children, their Development and Interrelationships.* Institute of Child Welfare, Monographs Services, No. 26. Minneapolis: University of Minnesota Press.

Timm, L. A. (1977) A child's acquisition of Russian phonology. *Journal of Child Language* 4, 329–39.

Tobin, Y. (ed.) (1988) *The Prague School and its Legacy.* Amsterdam: John Benjamins.

Tomasello, M., Mannle, S. and Kruger, A. C. (1986) Linguistic environment of 1-2-year-old twins. *Developmental Psychology* 22, 169–76.

Topbas, S. (1997) Phonological acquisition of Turkish children: Implications for phonological disorders. *European Journal of Disorders of Communication* 32, 377–96.

Tse, J. (1978) Tone acquisition in Cantonese: A longitudinal case study. *Journal of Child Language* 5, 191–204.

Tse, A. C.-Y. (1992) The acquisition process of Cantonese phonology: A case study. M.Phil. thesis, University of Hong Kong.

Vasanta, D. (1997) Coarticulation in the temporal domain: Evidence from Telugu-speaking prelingually deaf children. *Asia Pacific Journal of Speech Language and Hearing* 2, 139–47.

Vihman, M. M. (1996) *Phonological Development.* Oxford: Blackwell.

Vihman, M. M. (1998) Early phonological development. In John Bernthal and N. W. Bankson (eds) *Articulation and Phonological Disorder* (pp. 63–112). Boston: Allyn & Bacon.

Wan, I-Ping and Jaeger, J. (1998) Speech errors and the representation of tone in Mandarin Chinese. *Phonology* 15, 417–61.

Wang, J. Z. (1989) Mandarin syllable structure and its implications for phonemic analysis. Unpublished PhD thesis, University of Delaware.

Wang, W. (1967) Phonological features of tone. *International Journal of Applied Linguistics* 33, 93–105.

Waterson, N. and Snow, C. (eds) (1978) *The Development of Communication.* New York: John Wiley and Sons.

Weiner, F. (1979) *Phonological Process Analysis (PPA).* Baltimore, MD: University Park Press.

Weiner, F. and Wacker, R. (1982) The development of phonology in unintelligible speakers. In N. Lass (ed.) *Speech and Language: Advances in Basic Research and Practice* (Vol. 8) (pp. 51–126). New York: Academic Press.

Weiss, C., Gordon, M. and Lillywhite, H. (1987) Clinical Management of Articulatory and Phonological Disorders. Baltimore: Williams & Wilkins.

Wellman, B. L., Case, I. M., Mengert, I. G. and Bradbury, D. E. (1931) Speech sounds of young children. *University of Iowa Studies in Child Welfare* 5 (2).

Wells, G. (1985) *Language Development in the Pre-school Years.* Cambridge: Cambridge University Press.

Wells, G. (1986) Variation in child language. In P. Fletcher and M. Garman (eds) *Language Acquisition* (pp. 109–40). Cambridge: Cambridge University Press.

West, J. and Weber, J. (1973) A phonological analysis of the spontaneous language of a four-year-old hard-of-hearing girl. *Journal of Speech and Hearing Disorders* 38, 25–35.

Williams, E. (1976) Underlying tone in Margi and Igbo. *Linguistic Inquiry* 7, 463–84.

Winitz, H. (1969) *Articulatory Acquisition and Behavior.* New York: Appleton-Century-Crofts.

Winitz, H. and Darley, F. L. (1980) Speech production. In F. M. Lassman, R. O. Fisch, D. K. Vetter and E. S. La Benz (eds) *Early Correlates of Speech, Language and Hearing* (pp. 232–65). MA: PSG Publishing.

Woo, N. (1969) Prosody and phonology. PhD thesis, MIT.

Wu Congji (ed.) (1991) *Xiandai hanyu yuyin gaiyao*. Beijing: Huayu Jiaoxue.

Wu Renyi and Yin Binyong (1984) Putonghua shehui diaocha [A survey of Putonghua]. *Wenzi Gaige* 11, 37–8.

Xiandai Hanyu Cidian (1979) *Modern Chinese Dictionary*. Beijing: Shangwu yinshu guan.

Xu Shirong (1980) *Putonghua yuyin zhishi [Basics of Putonghua pronunciation]*. Beijing: Language Reform Publishing House.

Yasuda, A. (1970) Articulatory skills in three-year-old children. *Studia Phonologica* 5, 52–71.

Yavaş, M. (1997) Feature enhancement and phonological acquisition. *Clinical Linguistics and Phonetics* 11 (2), 153–72.

Yavas, M. and Lamprecht, R. (1988) Processes and intelligibility in disordered phonology. *Clinical Linguistics and Phonetics* 2, 329–45.

Yin, Y. M. (1989) Phonological aspects of word formation in Mandarin Chinese. Unpublished PhD thesis. University of Texas at Austin.

Yip, M. (1980) The tonal phonology of Chinese. PhD thesis, MIT.

Zazzo, R. (1960) *Les Jumeaux: le Couple et la Personne II; L'Individuation Psychologique*. Paris: Presses Universitaires de France.

Zazzo, R. (1978) Genesis and peculiarities of the personality of twins. In W. E. Nance, G. Allen and P. Parisi (eds) *Twin Research: Progress in Clinical and Biological Research*. New York: Academic Press.

Appendices

Appendix 1
Items Used in Picture-naming Task

No.	English	Pinyin	IPA
1	nose	bizi	pi2·tsi0
2	ear	erduo	ɚ3·tuo0
3	mouth	zui	tsuei3
4	finger	shouzhi	ʂoʊ3·tʂi3
5	hair	toufa	tʰoʊ2·fA0
6	foot	jiao	tɕiɑo3
7	shoe	xie	ɕiɛ2
8	skirt	qunzi	tɕʰyn2·tsi0
9	apple	pingguo	pʰiŋ2·kuo3
10	watermelon	xigua	ɕi1·kua0
11	banana	xiangjiao	ɕiɑŋ1·tɕiɑo1
12	meat	rou	ɹoʊ4
13	vegetable	cai	tsʰae4
14	bowl	wan	uan(ɹ)3
15	chopsticks	kuaizi	kʰuae4·tsi0
16	knife	dao	tɑo1
17	table	zhuozi	tʂuo1·tsi0
18	water	shui	ʂuei3
19	wash face	xilian	ɕi3·liɛn3
20	brush teeth	shuaya	ʂua1·iA2
21	bed	chuang	tʂʰuɑŋ2
22	gate	men	mən(ɹ)2

Items used in picture-naming task *cont.*

No.	English	Pinyin	IPA
23	light	deng	təŋ1
24	umbrella	yusan	y3·san3
25	sun	taiyang	tʰae4·iaŋ0
26	moon	yueliang	yɛ4·liaŋ0
27	star	xingxing	ɕiŋ1·ɕiŋ (ɹ)0
28	flower	hua	xuA(ɹ)1
29	bird	niao	niɑo(ɹ)3
30	panda	xiongmao	ɕyʊŋ2·mɑo(ɹ)1
31	plane	feiji	fei1·tɕi1
32	car	xiaoqiche	ɕiɑo3·tɕʰi4·tʂʰɤ(ɹ)1
33	ball	qiu	tɕʰioʊ2
34	piano	gangqin	kɑŋ1·t ɕʰin2
35	girl	nühai	ny3· xae(ɹ)2
36	boy	nanhai	nan2· xae(ɹ)2
37	red	hong	xʊŋ2
38	heart	xin	ɕin1
39	thank you	xiexie	ɕiɛ4· ɕiɛ0
40	goodbye	zaijian	tsae4·tɕiɛn4
41	stick	gunzi	kuən(ɹ)4· tsi0
42	book	shu	ʂu1
43	clip	jiazi	tɕia1·tsi0
44	circle	yuanquan	yan2·tɕʰyan(ɹ)1

Note: Pinyin is Chinese romanisation system. The numbers used in IPA transcription are tone indicators, representing high level, rising, falling–rising and high falling tones respectively. Weakly stressed syllable is marked by the number 0. Rhotacised feature is marked by parentheses.

Appendix 2

Frequency Distribution of Phonological Features in Picture-naming Task

Syllable-Initial Consonants (total occurrence in the test = 57)

Phonemes	Frequency	Phonemes	Frequency
p	1	x	4
pʰ	1	s	1
t	3	ts	2
tʰ	2	tsʰ	1
k	4	ç	9
kʰ	1	tç	5
m	2	tçʰ	5
n	3	ş	4
f	2	tş	2
l	2	tşʰ	2
ɹ	1		

Vowels (total occurrence in the test = 67)

Phonemes	Frequency	Phonemes	Frequency
i	12	oʊ	3
u	1	ia	5
y	3	iɛ	5
o	1	ua	5
ɤ	1	uo	3
A	4	yɛ	1
ə	6	iɑo	4
ɚ	1	ioʊ	1
ae	5	uae	1
ei	1	uei	2
ɑo	2		

Syllable-final consonants (total occurrence in the test = 21)

Phonemes	Frequency	Phonemes	Frequency
n	11	ŋ	10

Tones (total occurrence in the test =58)

Tones	Frequency	Tones	Frequency
Tone 1	17	Tone 2	16
Tone 3	15	Tone 4	10

Tone sandhi (total occurrence in the test = 6)

Tone sandhi type	Frequency
Falling–rising tone becomes rising if followed by another falling–rising tone	3
Falling–rising tone retains the falling part in its contour only without rising in the pitch if followed by high level, rising and falling tones	2
High falling tone becomes low falling tone before another high falling tone	1

Weak stress (total occurrence in the test =13)

Weak stress type	Frequency
Noun suffixes are weakly stressed	6
Reduplicated second syllables are weakly stressed	2
Second lexemes in some compounds are weakly stressed	5

Rhotacisation (total occurrence in the test =7)

Rhotacisation type	Frequency
Words which are always rhotacised	4
Words which are optionally rhotacised	3

Appendix 3

Comparison of Putonghua, Cantonese, English and Xhosa Phonology

	Putonghua	*Cantonese*	*English*	*Xhosa*
Tones	4	9	None	9
Vowels	9 monophthongs 9 diphthongs 4 triphthongs	11 monophthongs 11 diphthongs	12 monophthongs 9 diphthongs 5 triphthongs	7 monophthongs
Syllable-final consonants	2	8	21	None
Syllable-initial consonants	21	17	23	41
Clusters	None	2	49	Very Few
Syllable structure	[C]V[C]	[C] [G]V [C/G]	$[C_{0-3}]$ V $[C_{0-4}]$	CV

(Adapted from So & Dodd, 1995)

Appendix 4

Procedures for Pure Tone Audiometry

Recommended procedures for pure-tone audiometry using a manually operated instrument, published by British Society of Audiology in 1981, are adapted in the present study.

(1) *Conditions for audiometry:*
     Quiet, comfortable, and safe.

(2) *Instructions given to the children (originally in Putonghua):*
     'We are now playing a game. You are going to put on the head-phones. You may hear a sound in one of your ears. As soon as you hear a sound, put one ball into the box.'

(3) *Pre-test trial to familiarise the children with the task:*
     Present a tone of about three seconds duration at a level that is expected to be clearly audible to the children, which is usually about 30 dB above the roughly estimated threshold. When giving signal, avoid using any possible auditory, visual and tactile clues and avoid a rhythmic presentation of the tone both in interval between tones and their duration. Check that the children responds correctly, i.e. putting the ball into the box as soon as they hear something in their headphones. Make sure that the children's response must not generate any audible sound and must involve minimal movement. If there is no response, raise the level in 20 dB steps until a response is obtained.

(4) *Order of test:*
     Start with the better-hearing ear (if the tester is informed). Start with 1000 Hz. Next proceed to test 2000, 4000, 8000, 500 and 250 Hz. For the first ear only, retest at 1000Hz. If the retest value is more than 5dB more acute than the original value, retest the next frequency and so on. Where needed and practicable, test also at intermediate frequencies 750, 1500, 3000, 6000 Hz. Then test the opposite ear in the same order without the retest at 1000 Hz.

(5) *Finding auditory threshold:*
     At each level (1000, 2000, 4000, 8000, 500 and 250 Hz), starting with 10 dB, a tone is presented three or four times to the children at variable intervals. If the children give the expected response at least twice, reduce the levels in 10 dB steps until the children no longer respond. Then raise in 5 dB steps until the children respond again.

The threshold is the lowest level at which correct responses occur at least twice. Plot the threshold at each level on audiogram.

(6) *Assessment of hearing loss:*
The average dB at 500, 1000 and 2000 Hz is calculated.
Degree of Hearing Loss:
- Normal hearing: Less than 25 dBHL
- Mild hearing loss: 25 to 40 dBHL
- Moderate hearing loss: 45 to 65 dBHL
- Severe hearing loss: 70 to 90 dBHL
- Profound hearing loss: More than 90 dBHL

Appendix 5

Oromotor Examination

A Chinese version of oromotor examination is adapted from Ozanne (1992).

Procedures:

The children are asked to perform five sequenced oral movements. For each sequenced oral movement, the examination is administered in two steps. First, the examiner gives the children verbal instructions and demonstrates each movement to the children. The children are encouraged to have the first trial of each movement, following demonstration. Second, the examiner asks the children to repeat the movement. A score would be given to the children's second trial. The scoring sheet is used.

The scoring sheet of oromotor examination

	Trial 2	
	Movement 1	*Movement 2*
Blow and put your tongue up		
Lick and roar		
Kiss and cough		
Yawn and lick the side		
Tongue up and to the side		

Scoring system for sequenced oral movements:

Each movement will be rated as 0, 1, 2, or 3. The criteria are given below:

Score	Criteria
3	Accurate performance immediately follows oral command.
2	Accurate performance preceded by protracted pauses during which unsuccessful movements may be present.
1	Overall pattern of gesture acceptable, but defective in terms of amplitude, accuracy, force and/or speed.
0	An important part of the gesture is lacking though the rest is performed correctly; gestures elicited by preceding items are performed; an incorrect oral gesture or speed sound is produced; or no oral movement is produced.

Appendix 6

Visual-Motor Integration Test

The developmental test of Visual-Motor Integration, or VMI, by Beery (1989) is a developmental sequence of 24 geometric forms to be copied with paper and pencil. It assesses the children's visual and motor skills which are correlated significantly with their academic achievement. The VMI can be either group or individually administered in about 10 to 15 minutes and can be used with pre-school children through adults.

In the present study, the short form of VMI (for children aged 3;0–8;0) is administered individually to each child. The procedures recommended by Beery (1989) are:

(1) The child is given a pencil without an eraser.

(2) Place the test booklet (only the first 15 geometric forms which are suitable for children up to 8;0 are included) before the child. Keep both the test booklet and the child's body centred and squared to the desk throughout testing.

(3) Open the booklet to the first page and point to Form 1 and then the blank space below it. Say: Make one like that. Make yours right here.

(4) Encourage the child if necessary. Do not trace the form with a finger or pencil, as such motions provide important cues. Do not let the child trace the form either. Avoid calling the form by its name or by a descriptive term.

(5) If the child does not understand the task or does not copy any one of the first three forms well enough to earn a point, turn to the blank sheet on page 2 and make repetitive vertical pencil marks at the top, left side of the sheet. Invite the child to make marks like the example just blow the example.

(6) Whether or not the child draws vertical lines in imitation of examples – after ample opportunity – make repeated horizontal lines at the top centre of page 2 and invite the child to imitate you in the space below the example. Whether or not the child responds, repeat this procedure with circular lines at the top right of page 2.

(7) If the child responds by imitating the example on any one of the three forms, turn again to the first three printed forms on page 4 and allow the child to try to copy the forms directly.

(8) Prompt by pointing and saying 'Make one like this for as many forms as is necessary'. Allow only one try per form, with no erasing. As soon as the child is responding well, say: Good. Go ahead and do the rest of them. You may turn to the next page when you finish this one.

(9) Record your test observations inconspicuously. The child should not be timed overtly or otherwise pressured.

(10) Testing may be ended after three consecutive forms for which the child earns no points.

(11) Each of the child's drawings is rated according to the criteria given in the manual. The score is recorded onto the Recording and Scoring sheet. The total score is added and compared to the normative data provided in the manual (research indicates that the VMI is virtually culture-neutral).

Five examples of geometric forms used in the test:

Appendix 7

Phoneme Grids: Illustration of Inconsistent Productions*

Child 30

	ø	x	kʰ	k	ç	tɕʰ	tɕ	ʂ	tʂʰ	tʂ	ɹ	l	s	tsʰ	ts	n	tʰ	t	f	m	pʰ	p	
p				■																		■	p
pʰ																	■				■		pʰ
m																				■			m
f																			■				f
t																		■					t
tʰ														■			■						tʰ
n																■		■					n
ts	■						■																ts
tsʰ		■												■	■		■						tsʰ
s	■																						s
l												■											l
ɹ										■													ɹ
tʂ	■																	■					tʂ
tʂʰ	■																	■					tʂʰ
ʂ	■							■					■						■				ʂ
tɕ	■						■			■													tɕ
tɕʰ	■					■											■	■					tɕʰ
ç					■	■												■					ç
k	■					■												■				■	k
kʰ																							kʰ
x			■																				x
ø																	■	■					ø
	ø	x	kʰ	k	ç	tɕʰ	tɕ	ʂ	tʂʰ	tʂ	ɹ	l	s	tsʰ	ts	n	tʰ	t	f	m	pʰ	p	

Production

* The phonemes in both left and right edges are targets. The phonemes in both upper and lower edges should be used as references for children's realisations. The shaded cells on the same horizontal line represent children's realisations of the same phoneme on several trials.

Child 32

	ø	x	kʰ	k	ç	tɕʰ	tɕ	ʂ	tʂʰ	tʂ	ɹ	l	s	tsʰ	ts	n	tʰ	t	f	m	pʰ	p	
p	■																					■	p
pʰ																					■		pʰ
m																				■			m
f																			■				f
t				■																			t
tʰ							■								■								tʰ
n																■							n
ts	■																	■					ts
tsʰ																		■					tsʰ
s	■													■	■								s
l	■																						l
ɹ	■																						ɹ
tʂ	■			■				■							■								tʂ
tʂʰ		■													■								tʂʰ
ʂ	■	■											■		■								ʂ
tɕ							■																tɕ
tɕʰ						■	■																tɕʰ
ç					■																		ç
k	■			■														■				■	k
kʰ	■			■																			kʰ
x	■	■																					x
ø	■																						ø
	ø	x	kʰ	k	ç	tɕʰ	tɕ	ʂ	tʂʰ	tʂ	ɹ	l	s	tsʰ	ts	n	tʰ	t	f	m	pʰ	p	

Production

Appendix 8
ZL's First Attempt in Picture-naming Task at the Age of 3;5, 3;9, 4;1 and 4;5

Targets		ZL's realisations			
Items	IPA	3;5	3;9	4;1	4;5
nose	pi2·tsi0	tĩ2·tsi0	ỹ2·tsĩ1	ỹ2·ŋ0	ĩ2·tʁ0
ear	ɚ3·tuo0	ɚ3·tuo0	ə2·uo0	ɚ3·uo1	ɚ3·uo0
mouth	tsuɛ3	uɛ3	uɛ3	uɛ3	kuɛ3
finger	ʂou3·tʂi3	ðou3·ði3	ðou3·θi3	—	—
hair	tʰou2·fʌ0	tʰou2·fʌ0	tʰou2·fʌ4	xɤ2·ua0	tʰou2·ua4
foot	tɕiɑo3	iɑo3	lɑo3	iɑo3	tɕiɑo3
shoe	ɕiɛ2	iɛ2	liɛ2	iɛ2	iɛ2
skirt	tɕʰyn2·tsi0	in2·tsi0 I	—	pʰyn2·tsʁ0	pʰyn2·tsʁ0
apple	pʰiŋ2·kuo3	iŋ2·kuo3	iŋ2·uo3	pʰi2·guʁ3	piŋ2·uo3
watermelon	ɕi1·kua0	i1·ua1	ɕi1·xua1	ɕi1·ua1	i1·ua0
banana	ɕiɑŋ1·tɕiɑo1	ɕiɑŋ1·tɕiɑo1	iɑŋ1·tiɑo1	ɕiɑŋ1·tiɑo1	ɕiɑŋ1·iɑo1
meat	ɹou4	ɹou4 I	ɹou4 I	ɹou4 I	ɹou4 I
vegetable	tsʰae4	tʰae4	tʰae4 I	tʰae4	tʰae4
bowl	uan(ɹ)3	uaŋ3	uan3	ua3	tʰuan3
chopsticks	kʰuae4·tsi0	kʰuae4·tsi0	kuae4·tsi0	kʰuae4·dʒi0	kʰuae4·tsi0
knife	tɑo1	tɑo1	tɑo1	tɑo1	tɑo1
table	tʂuo1·tsi0	uo1·tsi0	uo1·tsi0	uo1·dʒi0	kuo1·tsi0
water	ʂuɛi3	uɛi3	uɛi3	uɛi3	uɛi3
wash face	ɕi3·liɛn3	_·iɛn3	ɕi3·iɛn3	ɕi3·liɛn3	i3·liɛn3
brush teeth	ʂua1·ia2	ua1·ia2	xua1·ia2	ua1·ia2	ua1·ia2
bed	tʂʰuaŋ2	xuaŋ2	uaŋ2	xuaŋ2	tsʰuaŋ2
gate	mən(ɹ)2	mən2	mən2	mən2	mənɹ2
light	tʌŋ1	ʌŋ1	ʌŋ1	tʌŋ1	tʌŋ1
umbrella	y3·san3	y3·san3	y3·tan3	y3·ɹan3	y3·uan3
sun	tʰae4·iaŋ0	tʰae4·iaŋ0	tʰae4·iaŋ0	tʰae4·iaŋ0	tʰae4·iaŋ0
moon	yɛ4·liaŋ0	yɛ4·iaŋ0	yɛ4·iaŋ0	yɛ4·iaŋ0	yɛ4·liaŋ0
star	ɕiŋ1·ɕiŋ (ɹ)0	ɕiŋ1·ɕiŋɹ0	ɕiŋ1·iŋ0	iŋ1·iŋ0	iŋ1·iŋ0 I

ZL's first attempt in picture-naming task at the age of 3;5, 3;9, 4;1 and 4;5 *cont.*

Targets		ZL's realisations			
Items	**IPA**	**3;5**	**3;9**	**4;1**	**4;5**
flower	xua(ɹ)1	kuaɹ1	kuaɹ1	uaɹ1	kuaŋ1
bird	niao(ɹ)3	niao3	niao3	niaŋ3	niao3
panda	çyωŋ2·mao(ɹ)1	yωŋ2·maoɹ1	yωŋ2·maoɹ1	çyωŋ2·maoɹ1	ɹən2·mao1
plane	fei1·tçi1	fei1·tçi1	fei1·tçi1	tei1·tçi1	fei1·tçi1
car	çiao3·tçʰi4·tʂʰɤ(ɹ)1	_·tçʰi4·tʂʰɤ1	_·_·tsɤ1	çiao3·_·xɤ1	_·tçʰi4·tʂʰɤ1
ball	tçʰiou2	tçʰiou2	tʰiou2	tçʰiou2	tçʰiou2
piano	kaŋ1·tçʰin2	taŋ1·in2	_·in2	taŋ1·tçʰi2 I	taŋ1·tçin2
girl	ny3·xae(ɹ)2	ny3·xaeɹ2	ny3·xae2	—	—
boy	nan2·xae(ɹ)2	nan2·xaeɹ2	nan2·xae2	—	—
red	xωŋ2	xωŋ2	xωŋ2	xωŋ2	ωŋ2
heart	çin1	çin1	in1	in1 I	in1
thank you	çiɛ4·çiɛ0	çiɛ4·çiɛ0	iɛ4·iɛ0	—	—
goodbye	tsae4·tçiɛn4	tsae4·tçiɛn4	tae4·tiɛn4	tae4·tiɛn4	tsae4·iɛn4
stick	kuan(ɹ)4·tsi0	kuən4·tsi0	kuən4·tsi0 I	kuaɹ4·_	kuən4· tsi0
book	ʂu1	fu1	ʂu1	fu1	u1
clip	tçia1·tsi0	tçia1·tsi0	ia1·tsi0	tçia1·tsi 0	ia1·tsi0
circle	yan2·tçʰyan(ɹ)1	yan2·xuaɹ1	yan2·tçʰian 1 I	yan2·tçʰyaɹ1 I	yan2·pʰyaɹ1

Note: The numbers (1, 2, 3, and 4) used in IPA transcription are tonal markers, representing high level, rising, falling–rising and high falling tones respectively. The tones of weakly stressed syllables are marked by the number 0. The rhotacised feature, which is optional, is marked by parentheses. In the child's realisations, 'I' stands for imitation; '—' marks those occasions in which the child did not produce the target words.

Appendix 9
Chronology of Error Patterns

Error patterns	Age (years)					
	1;6–2;0	*2;1–2;6*	*2;7–3;0*	*3;1–3;6*	*3;7–4;0*	*4;1–4;6*
Consonant assimilation	────	────	────	────	────	- - - -
Syllable initial deletion	────	────	────	────	- - - -	- - - -
Syllable-initial*						
Fronting: /ʂ/→ [s]	────	────	────	────	────	────
/ɕ/→ [ʃ/ʂ]	────	────	────	────	────	
/k/→ [t]	────	────	- - - -	- - - -	- - - -	- - - -
Backing: /s/→ [ʂ]	────	────	────	────	────	────
Stopping: /ts/→ [t]	────	────	────	────	────	- - - -
/s/→ [t]	────	────	- - - -			
/x/→ [k]	- - - -	- - - -	- - - -	- - - -	- - - -	- - - -
Affrication: /ɕ/→ [tɕ]	────	────	────			
Deaspiration: /tʰ/→ [t]	────	────	────	────		
Aspiration: /t/→ [tʰ]	────	────	────	────	────	- - - -
X-velarisation	────	────	────	────		
Gliding	────	────	────	────	────	- - - -
Syllable-final						
Final /n/ deletion	────	────	────	────	────	────
Backing: /n/→ [ŋ]	────	────	────	────	────	────
Final /ŋ/ deletion	────	────	- - - -	- - - -		
Vowels						
Triphthong reduction	────	────	────	────	────	────
Diphthong reduction	────	────	────	- - - -	- - - -	

- - - - - - indicates that 10–20% of the children of an age group used an error pattern;

──────── indicates that more than 20% of the children of an age group used an error pattern;

* Typical examples are given next to error patterns.

Index

45-49, 86-88, 116-122, 134-135, 165,
174, 181-182
– description, 33-34
– error pattern, 6-13, 63, 66-74, 96-97,
175
Syllable-initial consonant
– age and order of acquisition, 6-13,
45-49, 55-56, 86-88, 116-122, 134-135,
165, 174, 182
– description, 33-34
– error pattern, 6-13, 59-62, 66-74,
96-97, 135-137, 175
Syllable-initial consonant deletion,
definition of, 62

Taiwan Mandarin, *see* Guoyu
Tone sandhi
– age of acquisition, 80, 91-92, 96, 175
– error patterns, 93, 96, 175
– order of acquisition, 80, 91-92, 96, 175
– rules, 37
Tone
– age of acquisition, 79, 89-90, 95, 175
– description system, 36-37
– error patterns, 90-91, 95-96, 175
– factors, 98-102, 181, *see also*
Phonological saliency,
– hearing loss, 181
– order of acquisition, 79, 89-90, 95, 175
Tone-bearing units, 40-41
Triphthong reduction, definition of, 57
Turkish, 12, 21
Twin language, 23-24, 158, 180
Twins
– dual phonological representation,
23-25, 158-159

– multiple birth set, 25
– phonological difficulties, 23, 147-148,
156-160, 184
Type-token ratio (TTR), 164

Unit of analysis, 5-6
Universals
– developmental universals, 4-6,
180-184
– typological universals, 1-2
– universal grammar, 2-4

Variable
– age, 64
– exposure to English, 65, 75
– gender, 65, 74
Variations, *see* Individual differences,
Inconsistency, Variables
Vihman, Marilyn, 71, 83-84, 148
Visual-motor integration test, 209
Voicing, definition of, 8
Vowel
– acquisition, 45-49, 56-57, 84-86, 96-97,
173-174, 182
– description, 34-36

Weak stress
– acquisition, 58, 66, 81, 93-94, 176
– description, 37-38
– error patterns, 94-96, 176
Weak stress deletion, definition of, 7

Xhosa, 73
X-velarisation, definition of, 62

Z score, 109-114